清华语言学

第一辑

Tsinghua Linguistics

张 赪 主编

商务印书馆
创于1897 The Commercial Press

图书在版编目(CIP)数据

清华语言学.第1辑/张赪主编.—北京:商务印书馆,2022

ISBN 978-7-100-20763-8

Ⅰ.①清… Ⅱ.①张… Ⅲ.①语言学—丛刊
Ⅳ.①H0-55

中国版本图书馆CIP数据核字(2022)第031529号

清华语言学(第一辑)

张赪 主编

商务印书馆出版
(北京王府井大街36号 邮政编码100710)
商务印书馆发行
北京虎彩文化传播有限公司印刷
ISBN 978-7-100-20763-8

2022年7月第1版　开本710×1000 1/16
2022年7月北京第1次印刷　印张12

定价:80.00元

《清华语言学》编委会信息

《清华语言学》实行双向匿名审稿制度

目　　录

The theory of something

Stephen Crain, Takuya Goro, Peng Zhou

Abstract: Sentences with two logical expressions often exhibit semantic ambiguities. In certain cases, however, one interpretation holds a monopoly on meaning. The English existential expressions *something* and *anything* are cases in point. From both a syntactic and a semantic perspective, *something* and *anything* are polar opposites in sentences with negation. Yet there is no semantic enmity between *something* and *anything* in certain linguistic contexts; both expressions make sentences true in the same circumstances. We investigate four linguistic contexts that cancel the meaning differences between *something* and *anything* in order to evaluate the proposal that disjunction words are polarity sensitive in some languages but not in others. If a disjunction word is polarity sensitive in a language, then the linguistic environments that cancel the polarity sensitivity of English *something* should also cancel the polarity sensitivity of the disjunction word. We discuss four such linguistic environments as part of a cross-linguistic comparison between English and two languages, Japanese and Mandarin Chinese, in which disjunction words are argued to be polarity sensitive.

Key words: polarity, negation, disjunction, ellipsis, focus adverbs, downward entailment

1. Introduction

Sentences with two logical expressions often exhibit semantic ambiguities. For example, the sentence *All airplanes do not carry pets* has two interpretations. These interpretations turn on the scope relations between the quantificational NP, *all airplanes*, and the negation word, *not*. If *all airplanes* takes priority over negation, then the sentence conveys the meaning that no airplanes carry pets (ALL >

NOT). If negation takes priority, then the sentence means that not all airplanes carry pets (NOT > ALL). This second interpretation invites the inference that some airplanes do carry pets. Semantic ambiguities such as this are called scope ambiguities. Another example of scope ambiguity is *Someone loves everyone*. On one interpretation, the existential quantificational NP *someone* takes scope over universal quantificational NP *everyone*. On this interpretation, some person has a big heart. On the other interpretation, every person is lucky enough to be paired with someone who loves them.

In certain sentences with two logical expressions, one interpretation holds a monopoly on meaning. The English polarity expressions *some* and *any* are cases in point. This can be witnessed in the negative sentences (1) and (2).

(1) Tony did not enjoy some of the desserts.

(2) Tony did not enjoy any of the desserts.

These sentences clearly convey different messages. Sentence (1) asserts that there are some desserts that Tony did not enjoy. Sentence (2) asserts that there are no desserts that Tony enjoyed. The difference in meaning between (1) and (2) can be formulated as a difference in scope assignment, yet the two scope bearing expressions appear to be locked in place in these sentences. [1] The English existential expression *some* must take scope over negation in (1), and the English existential expression *any* must be licensed by negation in (2).

From a semantic perspective then *some* and *any* are polar opposites. This opposition is reinforced by the fact that *some* but not *any* is acceptable in simple affirmative sentences, as illustrated in (3) and (4).

(3) Tony enjoyed some of the desserts.

(4) Tony enjoyed *any of the desserts.

In some linguistic environments, there is no semantic enmity between *some* and *any*. In these contexts, it is possible to replace one of these expressions with the other with no effect on truth – in Latin *salva veritate*. Sentences with either expression are true in the same circumstances.

Sentences (5) and (6) illustrate one linguistic context in which *some* and *any* are substitutable *salva veritate*. Because the negative adverb *never* resides outside the clause that contains *some* in (5), *some* cannot take scope over negation. By contrast, the negative adverb *never* in sentence (6) continues to license *any*, despite being outside the clause that contains *any*. In this configuration, *some* is interpreted *in situ*, so sentences (5) and (6) are true in the same circumstances.

(5) You' ll never convince me that Tony enjoyed some of the desserts.

(6) You' ll never convince me that Tony enjoyed any of the desserts.

We will refer to sentences in (5) and (6) as cases of EXTERNAL NEGATION. External negation is the first example of a linguistic environment that cancels the semantic opposition between *some* and *any*. Under external negation, if it is *not something*, then it is *not anything*.

The present paper focuses on a variant of this linguistic environment and on three other environments that cancel the polarity sensitivity of English *some*, such that *some* and *any* are substitutable in sentences, without altering their truth. We use these linguistic environments to evaluate a recent proposal about some observed differences in the interpretation of disjunction words across languages. The proposal under consideration is that disjunction words are polarity sensitive in some languages but not in others. If disjunction words are polarity sensitive, they are expected to pattern like English *some* in negative sentences, taking scope over local negation. In other languages, where disjunction words are not polarity sensitive, they are interpreted *in situ*.

However, if the differences in interpretation across languages are due to polarity sensitivity, then the linguistic environments that cancel the polarity sensitivity of English *some* should also cancel the polarity sensitivity of disjunction words. If the polarity sensitivity account is correct, then disjunction will be interpreted *in situ* in these linguistic environments in all languages. These linguistic environments, then, may reveal linguistic universals. We will describe four linguistic environments and we will examine two languages, Japanese and Mandarin Chinese, where disjunction has been argued to be polarity sensitive.

2. The interpretation of disjunction in negative sentences

The English existential expression *some* takes scope over local negation. In English, the disjunction word *or* does not take scope over local negation. The disjunction word *or* is interpreted *in situ*. In sentence (7), for example, the negation word *not* takes scope over the disjunction phrase, ***Spanish or French*** in the surface syntax, and negation takes scope over disjunction in the semantic interpretation. As a consequence of negation taking wide scope, sentence (7) makes two entailments, (7a) and (7b). Each of these entailments is a negative statement about one of the two disjuncts in the original sentence. These entailments are lawfully conjoined in (8). In English, then, a negated disjunction is logically equivalent to a conjunction of two negative statements. We will refer to this as the CONJUNCTIVE INTERPRETATION of disjunction in negative sentences.

(7) Ali does **not** speak Spanish **or** French.

a) Ali does not speak Spanish.

b) Ali does not speak French.

(8) Ali does **not** speak Spanish **and** Ali does **not** speak French.

The conjunctive interpretation of disjunction conforms to one of the laws of propositional logic, where disjunction is inclusive-*or*. This law of propositional logic asserts an equivalence between negative statements with disjunction, NOT [A or B], and a conjunction of negative statements, [NOT A] and [NOT B]; in symbolic notation $\sim (A \vee B) \leftrightarrow \sim A \wedge \sim B$.

It has been proposed that, in contrast to English, disjunction words in Japanese and in Mandarin Chinese pattern like English *some* (e.g., Goro & Akiba 2004a, b; Goro 2007; Crain & Zhou 2017, 2019). The proposal is that, in these languages, disjunction words take scope over local negation. [2] The Japanese disjunction word is *ka* and the Mandarin disjunction word is *huozhe*. A series of experimental studies reported that adult speakers of these languages judge negative sentences with disjunction words to be true if at least one of the disjuncts is false (e.g., Crain 2012; Crain & Zhou 2017; Goro & Akiba 2004a, b; Grüter et al. 2010; Notley et al. 2012). Examples from Japanese are given in (9), and examples from Mandarin are given in (10). Mandarin has two forms of negation, *bu* and *mei*. The sentences in (10) show that disjunction takes scope over both forms of negation. The sentences in (9) and (10) illustrate, in addition, that linear order is completely orthogonal to scope assignment across languages. Disjunction takes scope over negation in Japanese and in Mandarin, although disjunction generally precedes negation in Japanese and follows it in Mandarin. [3]

(9) **Japanese**

a) *Ali-wa supeingo* ***ka*** *furansugo-o hanasa-**na**-i.*

Ali-TOP Spanish or French-ACC speak-NEG-PRES

'Ali does not speak Spanish ***or*** Ali does not speak French. '

b) *Ali-wa sushi* ***ka*** *pasuta-o tabe-**nakat**-ta.*

Ali-TOP sushi or pasta-ACC eat-NEG-PAST

'Ali didn' t eat sushi ***or*** Ali didn' t eat pasta. '

(10) **Mandarin**

a) *Ali* ***bu*** *shuo xibanyayu* ***huozhe*** *fayu.*

Ali not speak Spanish or French

'Ali does not speak Spanish ***or*** Ali does not speak French. '

b) *Ali* ***mei*** *chi shousi* ***huozhe*** *yidalimian.*

Ali not eat sushi or pasta

'Ali didn' t eat sushi ***or*** Ali didn' t eat pasta. '

Sentences (9a) and (10a) are true in three circumstances: (i) if Ali doesn' t speak French, but speaks Spanish, (ii) if Ali doesn' t speak Spanish, but speaks French, and (iii) if Ali doesn' t speak French and doesn' t speak Spanish. [4] This interpretation can be paraphrased using the English cleft sentences in (11), where disjunction is positioned outside the scope of negation in the surface syntax.

(11) a) It is Spanish **or** French that Ali doesn' t speak.

b) It is sushi **or** pasta that Ali doesn' t eat.

It has been proposed that the interpretation of negative sentences with disjunction in Mandarin and in Japanese is a consequence of the fact that disjunction words are polarity sensitive in these languages. Like English *some*, disjunction words must take scope over local negation. It follows from this proposal that disjunction words in these languages do not license a conjunctive interpretation.

The cross-linguistic difference in the interpretation of disjunction words is restricted to sentences in which local negation takes scope over disjunction in the surface syntax. If disjunction takes wide scope in the surface syntax, then it takes wide scope in the semantic interpretation. That is, the polarity sensitivity of disjunction is obviated if disjunction is the dominant logical expression, as illustrated in (12)–(15). These sentences are all true in the same circumstances, where either a cat or a dog (or possibly both) didn' t win the race.

(12) A cat or a dog didn' t win the race.

(13) It was a cat or a dog that didn' t win the race.

(14) **Japanese**

Neko	***ka***	*inu-ga*	*reesu-ni*	*kata-**nakat**-ta.*
cat	or	dog-NOM	race-DAT	win-NEG-PAST

'A cat or a dog didn' t win the race. '

(15) **Mandarin**

Mao	***huozhe***	*gou*	***mei****(you)*	*ying*	*bisai.*
cat	or	dog	not	win	race

'A cat or a dog didn' t win the race. '

3. Linguistic environments that cancel polarity sensitivity

We will now discuss four linguistic environments that cancel the polarity differences in the interpretation of English *some* and *any*. The aim is to determine whether or not cross-linguistic differences in the interpretation of disjunction are cancelled in these environments.

3.1 Pseudo negatives

When English *some* takes scope over negation in the surface syntax of a sentence, it also takes scope over negation in the semantic interpretation that speakers assign to that sentence. This was the source of the semantic opposition between *some* and *any* in sentences (1) and (2), *Tony did not enjoy some of the desserts* versus *Tony did not enjoy any of the desserts*. Additional examples are (16) and (17). These examples are from Baker (1970).

(16) Some goblin didn' t blow out the candles.

(17) Not any goblin blew out the candles.

Sentence (16) asserts that at least one goblin didn' t blow out the candles. The sentence is true even if three goblins succeeded in blowing out candles, as long as one goblin failed. Different circumstances verify sentence (17), with *any*. Sentence (17) is false if even one of the goblins blew out the candles. The difference in interpretation between sentences (16) and (17) can be expressed as a difference in scope. On one analysis, which we endorse, both English *some* and English *any* are variants of the existential quantifier, ∃ (see section 3. 4). In (16), *some* takes scope over negation (∃ > NOT). In (17), negation takes scope over *any* (NOT > ∃).

The asymmetry in meaning between *some* and *any* in negative sentences vanishes when these expressions are embedded under a certain class of verbs and adjectives. This class is called PSEUDO NEGATIVES. Pseudo negative verbs include *surprise*, *disappoint*, *regret*, and pseudo negative adjectives include *damn glad*, *odd*, and *sorry*. Consider sentences (18) and (19). In these sentences, the pseudo negative verb *surprise* takes scope over the examples from the previous section, sentences (16) and (17).

(18) I was surprised that $_{16}$[some goblin didn' t blow out the candles].

(19) I was surprised that $_{17}$[not any goblin blew out the candles].

When sentences (16) and (17) are embedded under the verb *surprise*, the expression *some ... not* in (16) has the same meaning as the expression *not ... any* in (17). Sentences (18) and (19) are both assigned a 'neither' interpretation, with negation taking scope over *some* (NEG > ∃). This scope assignment is expected for sentence (19), because *any* must be licensed by negation. However, the 'neither' interpretation is quite unexpected for sentence (18), because *some* takes scope over negation in the surface syntax. When sentence (16) is embedded under the pseudo negative verb *surprise*, negation somehow comes to take scope over *some*, yielding the 'neither' interpretation.

The 'neither' interpretation of (18) can be derived by 'reconstructing' *some* to a position beneath negation. Following reconstruction, the sequence of words *some* ... *not* is logically equivalent to the sequence *not* ... *any*.

Why does *some* undergo reconstruction in sentence (18)? We adopt a proposal advanced by Baker (1970). The proposal has two parts. First, a speaker uses the pseudo negative verb *surprise* only if, at some time prior to the utterance, the speaker expected the events expressed in the embedded proposition to take place. That is, a speaker who utters sentence (18) expected some goblin to blow out the candles. Second, a speaker who uses the pseudo negative verb *surprise* conveys the message that events did not turn out as the speaker expected. A speaker who utters sentence (18) conveys the message that, as it turned out, none of the goblins blew out the candles. Sentence (18), therefore, entails (20) and (21).

(20) The speaker expected some goblin to blow out the candles.

(21) It did not turn out that some goblin blew out the candles.

In (21), *some* appears in the scope of external negation. Under external negation, *some* and *any* are substitutable, *salva veritate.* [5] It follows that sentence (21), with *not* ... *some*, is true in the same circumstances as sentence (22), with *not any*.

(22) Not any goblin blew out the candles.

Once their entailments are taken into consideration, the sentence with *some* ... *not* embedded under the verb *surprise*, as in (18), turns out to be true in the same circumstances as the corresponding sentence with *not any*, as in (22). This is a consequence of the meaning of the verb *surprise*. The same analysis applies to the entire class of pseudo negative verbs and adjectives.

The analysis we have offered for *surprise* makes critical use of external negation. In sentences with internal negation, *some* takes scope over local negation (∃ > NOT). This scope assignment is reversed with external negation; negation takes scope over *some* (NOT > ∃). This is why sentence (21), *It did not turn out that some goblin blew out the candles*, has the same truth conditions as sentence (22), *Not any goblin blew out the candles*. The difference in meaning in sentences in which internal negation combines with *some* or *any* is cancelled in sentences with external negation. This reinforces the proposal that *some* and *any* are variants (allomorphs) of the existential quantifier, ∃.

Sentences with external negation (including pseudo negatives) are examples of a linguistic environment that cancels the polarity sensitivity of English *some*, yielding sentences where *some* and *any* are interchangeable without affecting truth. If the observed differences in the interpretation of disjunction across languages are due to differences in scope, then these differences should also be cancelled in sentences with external negation. More specifically, when both disjunction and negation are embedded under a pseudo negative verb (*surprise*, *disappoint*, *regret*), then negation is expected to take scope over disjunction, even if disjunction takes scope over negation in the surface syntax. We anticipate a cross-linguistic convergence in the interpretation of sentences with disjunction.

To test this prediction, consider (23). Sentence (23) has both disjunction and negation embedded under the pseudo negative verb, *surprise*. The Japanese analogue to (23) is sentence (24) and the Mandarin analogue is sentence (25). The sentences in (24) and (25) contain the previous sentences (14) and (15) as constituents. In sentences (14) and (15), disjunction takes scope over local negation (OR > NOT). As predicted by the scope account, when these sentences are embedded beneath a pseudo negative verb, negation takes scope over disjunction instead (NOT > OR). The pseudo negative verb *surprise* initiates a complete reversal in the surface scope relations between disjunction and negation.

(23) I was surprised that a cat **or** a dog did not win the race.

(24) **Japanese**

Boku-wa $_{14}$*[neko* ***ka*** *inu-ga reesu-ni kata-**nakat**-ta] no ni* ***odoroi-ta.***

I-TOP cat or dog-NOM race-DAT win-NEG-PAST COMP at surprise-PAST

'I was surprised that a cat or a dog didn' t win the race. '

(25) **Mandarin**

wo hen ***chijing*** $_{15}$*[mao* ***huozhe*** *gou* ***mei(you)*** *ying bisai].*

I very surprise cat or dog not win race

'I was surprised that a cat or a dog didn' t win the race. '

These sentences all express the proposition that the speaker is surprised that neither a cat nor a dog won the race. That is, the sequence of words *or ... not* is assigned the INVERSE SCOPE interpretation (NOT > OR) in sentences with *surprise* and its analogues in Japanese and in Mandarin. This mirrors the finding that the sequence of words *some ... not* was assigned the inverse scope interpretation when it was embedded under *surprise* in (18). [6] The polarity sensitivity of disjunction is cancelled in sentences with pseudo negative verbs, just as the polarity sensitivity of *some* is cancelled in this linguistic environment.

This concludes the first test of the polarity sensitivity account of the interpretation of disjunction across languages. In a linguistic context that cancels the polarity sensitivity of English *some*, the polarity sensitivity of disjunction was also cancelled in both Japanese and Mandarin. We turn now to a second linguistic environment that cancels the polarity sensitivity of English *some*. First, we will show that the meaning difference between English *some* and *any* is vitiated in this linguistic environment. Then we will show that cross-linguistic differences in the interpretation of disjunction are also vitiated in this linguistic environment in Japanese and in Mandarin.

3.2 Downward entailment

The second linguistic context that unifies English *some* and *any* is the antecedent of a conditional statement. [7] First, recall the contrast in the interpretation of *some* versus *any* in (26). English *some* takes scope over local negation in (26a), whereas negation takes scope over *any* in (26b). The example sentences in (27) and (28) reveal parallel effects in Japanese and in Mandarin.

(26) a) John didn' t eat something.

b) John didn' t eat anything.

(27) **Japanese**

a) *Jon-wa nanika tabe-nakat-ta.*

John-TOP something eat-NEG-PAST

'John didn' t eat something. '

b) *Jon-wa nanimo tabe-nakat-ta.*

John-TOP anything eat-NEG-PAST

'John didn' t eat anything. '

(28) **Mandarin**

a) *Yuehan mei chi yixie dongxi.*

John not eat some thing

'John didn' t eat something. '

b) *Yuehan mei chi renhe dongxi.*

John not eat any thing

'John didn' t eat anything. '

The contrast in interpretation that is exhibited in (26) is vitiated, however, when a similar sequence of words is embedded in the antecedent of a conditional, as in (29). The existential expressions *something* and *anything* are substitutable *salva veritate* in (29). In both sentences, negation takes scope over the existential expression.

(29) a) If John doesn' t eat *something*, he will starve to death.

b) If John doesn' t eat *anything*, he will starve to death.

In Japanese and in Mandarin, the existential expressions corresponding to *something* and *anything* are also substitutable, *salva veritate*, in the antecedent of a conditional. This is shown in (30) and (31). The Japanese sentences in (30) and the Mandarin sentences in (31) are true in the same circumstances as the English sentences in (29).

(30) **Japanese**

a) *Moshi Jon-ga nanika tabe-nai-to kare-wa uejinisu-ru.*
if John-NOM something eat-NEG-COMP he-TOP starve-PRES
'If John doesn' t eat something, he will starve. '

b) *Mosh Jon-ga nanimo tabe-nai-to kare-wa uejinisu-ru.*
if John-NOM anything eat-NEG-COMP he-TOP starve-PRES
'If John doesn' t eat anything, he will starve to death. '

(31) **Mandarin**

a) *Ruguo Yuehan bu chi yixie dongxi, ta hui e si.*
if John not eat something he will starve die
'If John doesn' t eat something, he will starve to death. '

b) *Ruguo Yuehan bu chi renhe dongxi, ta hui e si.*
if John not eat anything he will starve die
'If John doesn' t eat anything, he will starve to death. '

This leads us to ask about the interpretation of disjunction in the antecedent of a conditional. The polarity sensitivity account predicts, first, that English disjunction should license a conjunctive entailment in this linguistic context. Consider sentence (32). As expected, example (32) has two entailments. These entailments are listed in (33a, b). When these are combined, the result is the conjunctive interpretation of disjunction.

(32) If there are cookies or crackers in the pantry, Tony will find them.

(33) a) If there are cookies in the pantry, Tony will find them.

b) If there are crackers in the pantry, Tony will find them.

When negation is added, as in (34), English speakers assign the same 'neither' interpretation, with negation taking scope over disjunction. The truth conditions assigned to (34) are indicated in (35).

(34) If there are no cookies or crackers in the pantry, Tony will feel sad.

(35) a) If there are no cookies in the pantry, Tony will feel sad.

b) If there are no crackers in the pantry, Tony will feel sad.

If disjunction is polarity sensitive in Japanese and in Mandarin, then the polarity sensitivity of disjunction words in these languages should be canceled in the antecedent of a conditional. If so, then disjunction should license a conjunctive interpretation in the Japanese and Mandarin counterparts to the English example (32). That is, disjunction should license the same entailments in Japanese and Mandarin that (32) licenses, namely the entailments stated in (33). Moreover, when negation is added, as in the English example (34), the counterparts to this sentence in Japanese and in Mandarin are expected to assign the same 'neither' interpretation, with negation taking scope over disjunction (see Goro 2007). Both of these predictions are born out. The Japanese examples are given in (36) and the Mandarin examples are given in (37).

(36) **Japanese**

a) ***Moshi*** *todana-ni kukki* ***ka*** *kurakka-ga are-ba, Toni-ga mitsuke-ru.*
if pantry-LOC cookie or cracker-NOM exist-COMP Tony-NOM find-PRES
'If there are cookies or crackers in the pantry, Tony will find them. '

b) ***Moshi*** *todana-ni kukki* ***ka*** *kurakka-ga* ***nakere****-ba, Toni-ga kanashim-u.*
if pantry-LOC cookie or cracker-NOM no-exist-COMP Tony-NOM sad-PRES
'If there are no cookies or crackers in the pantry, Tony will feel sad. '

(37) **Mandarin**

a) ***Ruguo*** *chugui-li you quqi* ***huozhe*** *xiaobinggan,*
if pantry-inside exist cookie or cracker
Tuoni jiu hui zhaodao tamen.
Tony then will find them
'If there are cookies or crackers in the pantry, Tony will find them. '

b) ***Ruguo*** *chugui-li* ***meiyou*** *quqi* ***huozhe*** *xiaobinggan,*
if pantry-inside not cookie or cracker
Tuoni jiu hui hen shangxin.
Tony then will very sad
'If there are no cookies or crackers in the pantry, Tony will feel sad. '

In all three languages, sentences with disjunction license the same interpretation in the antecedent of a conditional. More specifically, the polarity sensitivity of disjunction is cancelled in Japanese and in Mandarin, exactly where the polarity sensitivity of English *some* was cancelled, and where variants of the existential expressions *some* and *any* were found to be substitutable across languages (examples (26)–(31)). This is further evidence supporting the polarity account of the cross-linguistic difference in the interpretation of disjunction in simple negative sentences. The difference in the interpretation of disjunction in simple negative sentences is canceled in the same linguistic environment that cancels the meaning difference between English *some* and *any*. It appears that both differences in meaning derive from the same source.

Why does the antecedent of a conditional cancel polarity sensitivity? It appears that in human languages, as in classical logic, a conditional statement IF A, THEN B is equivalent to a disjunctive statement that negates the antecedent and affirms the consequent, [NOT A] OR B. That is, the English conditional statement (32) can be recast as a disjunction, as in (38). The proposition expressed in the antecedent contains the disjunction phrase, *there are cookies or crackers in the pantry*, so negation takes scope over disjunction in (38).

(38) Either there are no cookies or crackers in the pantry, or Tony will find them.

3.3 The predicate phrase of the focus adverb ONLY

The third linguistic context that unifies English *some* and *any* is in the predicate phrase of a sequence of words beginning with the focus adverb ONLY. This is illustrated by examples (39) and (40). Both *some* and *any* are acceptable in the predicate phrase of the focus adverb ONLY. [8]

(39) Only Tony ate some of the cookies in the pantry.

(40) Only Tony ate any of the cookies in the pantry.

There is no difference in the interpretation assigned to these sentences. Both sentences are true if and only if two events transpire. One event involves Tony. It must turn out that Tony ate some of the cookies in the pantry. This meaning component is often referred to as the presupposition. The presupposition pertains to the element in focus, in this case, Tony. The second event involves a set of people who are being contrasted with Tony. It must turn out that no member of this contrast set ate any of the cookies in the pantry. This second meaning component is often called the assertion (see e.g., Horn 1969).

To specify the truth conditions associated with the first meaning component, the presupposition, we can momentarily disregard the focus adverb ONLY. What remains is referred to as the PREJACENT. The prejacent of sentences (39) and (40) is given in (41a). Notice that *any* is not acceptable in the prejacent of sentence (40). This is indicated by the unacceptability of sentence (41b). The unacceptability of *any* in the PREJACENT (without ONLY) shows that the addition of the focus adverb ONLY contributes covert negation to sentences, since *any* is acceptable in sentence (40).

(41) a) Tony ate *some* of the cookies in the pantry.
b) Tony ate **any* of the cookies in the pantry.

Whereas negation is covert in the original example sentences (39) and (40), negation is an essential element of the second meaning component of ONLY, the assertion. We have offered a semantic analysis of the assertion of (39) and (40) in example (42). Both *some* and *any* are acceptable in this meaning component, the assertion.

(42) Assertion: It did not turn out that anyone else ate *some* of the cookies in the pantry.
Cf. It did not turn out that anyone else ate *any* of the cookies in the pantry.

As we have formulated it in (42), the assertion contains external negation. If the assertion were to be formulated using internal negation, this would make sentences (39) and (40) true in the wrong circumstances. This can be seen by comparing the truth conditions that follow from the assertion, using external negation (42), with the truth conditions that would follow if the assertion were stated using internal negation, as in (43).

(43) Assertion: Everybody else did **not** eat ***some*** of the cookies in the pantry.
Cf. Everybody else did **not** eat ***any*** of the cookies in the pantry.

The problem in using internal negation in the assertion is that *some* is polarity sensitive, so *some* would take scope over the local (internal) negation in (43). Consequently, the original sentences with the focus adverb ONLY (39) and (40) would be true if, say, everybody being contrasted with Tony ate the cookies, as long as they did not eat the crackers. This is contrary to the fact. Sentences (39) and (40) are not true in such a circumstance.

We now investigate sentences with ONLY and disjunction across languages. We begin with the English sentence (44).

(44) Only Tony ate the cookies or crackers in the pantry.

The first step is to partition the meaning of (44) into the presupposition and the assertion.

This reveals a striking parallel to the previous case, with *some*. It turns out that disjunction has one interpretation in the presupposition, and a different interpretation in the assertion.

The presupposition of (44) is the prejacent, in (45). Disjunction in the prejacent makes sentence (40) true if either (or possibly both) of its disjuncts are true. More specifically, sentence (44) is true, for example, if Tony ate just the cookies in the pantry, but not the crackers.

(45) Presupposition: Tony ate the cookies or crackers in the pantry.

Turning to the assertion, the truth conditions of disjunction make sentence (44) true in a narrow range of circumstances. Disjunction is assigned a conjunctive 'neither' interpretation in the assertion made by (44). Sentence (44) is true only if none of the members of the contrast set ate the cookies in the pantry and none of them ate the crackers in the pantry. The assertion meaning component is stated in (46).

(46) Assertion: It did **not** turn out that anyone else ate the cookies **or** crackers in the pantry.

Cf. Everybody else did not eat the cookies **and** everybody else did not eat the crackers.

We are now ready to see how disjunction is interpreted in sentences with the focus adverb ONLY in Japanese and in Mandarin. We expect the polarity sensitivity of disjunction to be vanquished in the assertion of the relevant sentences in these languages, just as it is in English sentences with *only*. The prediction is that the analogues of the English sentence (44), repeated in (47), will be assigned the same interpretation in Japanese and in Mandarin. In the Japanese example (48), the disjunction phrase *kukki ka kurakka* 'cookie or cracker' appears in the predicate phrase of the Japanese focus adverb *dake* 'only. ' In the Mandarin example (49), the disjunction phrase *quqi huozhe xiaobinggan* 'cookie or cracker' appears in the predicate phrase of the Mandarin focus adverb *zhiyou* 'only' .

(47) Only Tony ate the cookies or the crackers in the pantry.

(48) **Japanese**

*Toni-**dake**-ga*	*todana-ni*	*kukki*	***ka***	*kurakka-o*	*tabe-ta.*
Tony-only-NOM	pantry-LOC	cookie	or	cracker-ACC	eat-PAST

'Only Tony ate the cookies or crackers in the pantry. '

(49) **Mandarin**

Zhiyou	*Tuoni*	*chi-le*	*chugui-li*	*de*	*quqi*	***huozhe***	*xiaobinggan.*
only	Tony	eat-ASP	pantry-inside	DE	cookie	or	cracker

'Only Tony ate the cookies or crackers in the pantry. '

As predicted by the polarity account, sentences (49) and (50) are assigned the same interpretation as the English sentence (48). Across languages, then, sentences with ONLY are assigned the same two meaning components, including the 'neither' interpretation of the assertion. Once again, the findings are consistent with the polarity account of the cross-linguistic differences in the interpretation of disjunction. It appears that, in some languages, disjunction is polarity sensitive in simple (one clause) negative sentences. Like English *some*, however, disjunction is not polarity sensitive in sentences with the focus adverb ONLY, due to the covert external negation that is contributed by the meaning of ONLY.

There is another feature of sentences with focus adverb ONLY and *some* which carries over to sentences with ONLY and disjunction. In both cases the assertion must be represented using external negation. The problem with internal negation can be seen in languages where disjunction takes scope over local negation. In these languages, if the assertion was represented using internal negation, it would make sentences true in the wrong circumstances.

To see this, let us suppose that English disjunction takes scope over local negation. Then sentence (44) *Only Tony ate the cookies or crackers in the pantry* would be true if one of the individuals in the contrast set, say Drew, ate some of the cookies in the pantry, as long as Drew did not eat any of the crackers. If disjunction takes scope over local negation, then the assertion could generate the entailment stated in the cleft sentence (50), where disjunction is the primary connective. This is not an entailment of the assertion made by sentence (44). Rather, the assertion entails that no member of the contrast set ate either the cookies or the crackers in the pantry. These truth conditions are expressed by (46), with external negation, but not by (50), with internal negation.

(50) It was the cookies or the crackers that Drew did not eat.
Cf. Drew did **not** eat the cookies **or** Drew did **not** eat the crackers.

Across languages, the assertion of sentences with ONLY and disjunction makes these sentences true in a more restricted set of circumstances. These truth conditions can be expressed using external negation, as in (46), which rules out the possibility that anyone in the contrast set ate cookies and the possibility that anyone ate crackers.

3.4 Verb phrase ellipsis

The fourth linguistic environment that we will discuss is Verb Phrase Ellipsis (VP ellipsis). First, we will draw a descriptive generalization about the syntax of VP ellipsis. Then we will describe a challenge to this generalization which is posed by sentences with the polarity sensitive expression *some*. Attempting to solve this challenge entails a review of linguistic arguments that date back to the 1960s.

The majority of cases of VP ellipsis conform to a simple pattern. Consider the sentences in (51)–(52). In each example, the (a) version contains a second conjunct with a full VP. The (b) version contains an elided VP, indicated by the material in brackets.

(51) a) Peng ordered a spicy dish, but Aijun didn' t order a spicy dish.

b) Peng ordered a spicy dish, but Aijun didn' t < ~~order a spicy dish~~ >.

(52) a) Esther is taller than Rozz, but Yiching isn' t taller than Rozz.

b) Esther is taller than Rozz, but Yiching isn' t < ~~taller than Rozz~~ >.

(53) a) Esther was talking to Thomas, but Yiching wasn' t talking to Thomas.

b) Esther was talking to Thomas, but Yiching wasn' t < ~~talking to Thomas~~ >.

There is a simple principle that produces the right interpretation of the elided VP in these cases. The principle is to generate a copy of the verb phrase from the first conjunct (minus tense or the auxiliary verb), and then delete the copy. Although this principle successfully generates the right elided VP in these cases, the 'copy and delete' account of VP ellipsis confronts a problem in cases where the first conjunct is affirmative, and contains the polarity sensitive expression *some*. The problem can be seen in example (54). If the 'copy and delete' analysis is applied to (54), the result is (55). (The example is from Sag 1976, pp. 157f. ; also see Klima 1964; Ladusaw 1996; Johnson 2001, and Merchant 2011).

(54) John saw someone, but Mary didn' t.

(55) John saw someone, but Mary didn' t < ~~see someone~~ >.

Notice that the elided verb phrase contains *someone*. Since *someone* is polarity sensitive, it must take scope over local negation, so the interpretation assigned to (55) can be paraphrased as *John saw someone, but there is someone that Mary didn't see*. These are not the truth conditions that English speakers attribute to sentence (54). Rather, the truth conditions of the elided VP in (54) are accurately represented using *anyone* in place of *someone*, as in (56).

(56) John saw someone, but Mary didn' t < ~~see anyone~~ >.

Does this mean that the 'copy and delete' analysis of VP ellipsis must be abandoned, or can it be salvaged? Several proposals have been advanced to salvage this analysis of VP ellipsis. There are two common features to these accounts. One feature is that existential expressions vary in how they are morphologically realized, depending on the syntactic environment. A second feature is that the insertion of the appropriate lexical variant of the existential expression follows VP ellipsis.

Here is a more detailed account of this approach. We suggested earlier that the lexical items *some* and *any* are variants (allomorphs) of the existential quantifier, ∃. The proposal to salvage the 'copy and delete' analysis of VP ellipsis incorporates this suggestion. There are three steps to VP ellipsis. At the first step, the abstract expression ∃ appears in the VP of the first conjunct. It is copied from there into the VP of the second conjunct, preserving identity. The second step is to elide the VP in the second conjunct. At the third step, one of the allomorphs of ∃ (*some, any*) is inserted into the first conjunct. Which allomorph is inserted depends on the polarity of the first conjunct. If the first conjunct is positive (POS), then *some* replaces ∃. If the first conjunct is negative (NEG), then *any* replaces ∃. The three-step analysis of sentence (54), *John saw someone, but Mary didn't*, is schematically depicted in (57).

(57) Step 1: the VP from the 1st conjunct is copied in the 2nd conjunct

1st: [POS [John saw ∃x person(x)]]

2nd: [NEG [Mary didn' t see ∃x person(x)]]

Step 2: the VP is elided in the 2nd conjunct

1st: [POS [John saw ∃x person(x)]]

2nd: [NEG [Mary didn' t <~~see ∃x person(x)~~>]]

Step 3: Lexical insertion in the 1st conjunct

John saw someone, but Mary didn' t.

Now we turn our attention to the disjunction phrase in the second conjunct of sentences that undergo VP ellipsis. The logical forms we will use to represent the logical forms of these sentences invoke two logical devices. First, we use the possibility operator, ◊, to represent the meaning of the epistemic modal verb, *can*.

The possibility operator, ◊, expresses the ability sense of *can*. The second logical device relies on the equivalence between existentials and disjunctions (Chierchia 2013: 88; Jayaseelan 2001: 79). In a finite domain, a disjunction is equivalent to an existentially quantified option set consisting of the individuals mentioned in the disjunction. This equivalence is indicated in (58). Example (59) is an instantiation of the equivalence that will be used in many of the sentences that follow.

(58) P(a) or P(b) $\leftrightarrow$ $\exists x\,[x \in \{a, b\}]\,P(x)$

(59) *bees or snakes* $\leftrightarrow$ $\exists x\,[x \in \{\text{bee, snake}\}]$

Let us first consider the interpretation that is assigned to sentences with an overt VP in the second conjunct, as in the English example (60).

(60) Papa Rabbit can catch bees or snakes, but Baby Rabbit can' t catch bees or snakes.

In the first conjunct, disjunction is in the scope of the epistemic modal verb *can*. In this configuration, disjunction licenses a FREE CHOICE INFERENCE, so the first conjunct implies that Papa Rabbit can catch bees and Papa Rabbit can catch snakes (Tieu et al. 2016). Recall that we are rendering the epistemic verb using the possibility operator, ◊. According to the free choice inference, ◊[A or B] implies [◊A & ◊B].

The logical form of the second conjunct is different in Japanese and in Mandarin, as compared to English. In English, the disjunction phrase, *bees or snakes*, is interpreted in the scope of negation, so the second conjunct of (61) has the 'neither' interpretation. However, Japanese-speaking adults and Mandarin-speaking adults analyze overt disjunction as taking scope over negation, so the logical form of the second conjunct in these languages would be as follows:

(61) $\exists\, x\, [x \in \{\text{bee, snake}\}\ \&\ \neg\Diamond[\text{catch (x, Baby Rabbit)}]]$.

This yields the interpretation in (62).

(62) ... but it is bees or snakes that Baby Rabbit can' t catch.

Here are examples with overt VPs in the second conjunct, in Japanese and in

Mandarin.

(63) **Japanese**

Otousan-usagi-wa hachi ka hebi-o tsukamae-rare-ta kedo, ...

papa-rabbit-TOP bee or snake-ACC catch-can-PAST but

'Papa Rabbit can catch bees or snakes, but ...

... *akachan-usagi-wa hachi ka hebi-o tsukamae-rare-nakat-ta.*

baby-rabbit-TOP bee or snake-ACC catch-can-NEG-PAST

... Baby Rabbit can' t catch bees or snakes. '

(64) **Mandarin**

Tubaba neng zhuadao mifeng huozhe xiaoshe, danshi ...

papa rabbit can catch bee or snake but

'Papa Rabbit can catch bees or snakes, but ...

... *tubaobao* ***bu*** *neng zhuadao mifeng* ***huozhe*** *xiaoshe.*

baby rabbit not can catch bee or snake

... Baby Rabbit can' t catch bees or snakes. '

Because overt disjunction takes scope over negation in Japanese and in Mandarin, in contrast to English, the second conjunct in (62) and in (63) express the negation of a free choice inference. The second conjunct is true if Baby Rabbit is not able to catch bees, or if Baby Rabbit is not able to catch snakes, or possibly neither.

Let us now consider the interpretation that is assigned across languages if the disjunction phrase is elided from the second conjunct. In this case, speakers of English, Japanese and Mandarin are all expected to interpret the disjunction phrase *in situ*. This prediction is based on the finding with English *some*, namely that negation takes scope over the existential expression that is positioned in the elided VP. If, as predicted, disjunction is interpreted in the scope of negation in an elided VP, the sentence should generate a conjunctive 'neither' interpretation to the second conjunct of (65) (see Gao et al. 2019).

(65) Papa Rabbit can catch bees or snakes, but Baby Rabbit can' t.

The interpretation assigned to sentences with an elided disjunction phrase is essentially the same as for English *some*, in all three languages. The process is schematically depicted in (66). At the first step, an existential expression denoting an option set is copied from the first conjunct into the second conjunct, under identity. The existential is interpreted *in situ* in the second conjunct, under the scope of negation (NOT > ∃). At the second step, the existential expression is elided from the second conjunct. At the third step (externalization), a disjunction phrase, *bees or snakes*, replaces the existential statement, ∃x [x ∈ {bee, snake}].

(66) Step 1: the VP from 1st conjunct is copied in the 2nd conjunct

1st: [Papa Rabbit ◊[catch ∃x [x ∈ {bee, snake}]]]

2nd: [Baby Rabbit ¬◊[catch ∃x [x ∈ {bee, snake}]]]

Step 2: the VP is elided in the 2nd conjunct

1st: [Papa Rabbit ◊[catch ∃x [x ∈ {bee, snake}]]]

2nd: [Baby Rabbit ¬◊[~~catch ∃x [x ∈ {bee, snake~~}]]]

Step 3: Lexical insertion in the 1st conjunct

Papa Rabbit can catch bees or snakes, but Baby Rabbit can' t.

Let us repeat the context we considered earlier: Papa Rabbit was able to catch both bees and snakes, and Baby Rabbit was only able to catch snakes, not bees. Japanese speakers judge (67) to be false as a description of this context, and Mandarin speakers judge (68) to be false as a description of this context. Like English *some*, when disjunction is elided under negation in VP ellipsis, disjunction is interpreted *in situ* in examples (67) and (68). This is a fourth linguistic environment in which disjunction is interpreted *in situ* across languages.

(67) **Japanese**

Otousan-usagi-wa hachi ka hebi-o tsukamae-rare-ta kedo, ...

papa-rabbit-TOP bee or snake-ACC catch-can-PAST but

'Papa Rabbit can catch bees or snakes, but ...

... *akachan-usagi-wa [e] tsukamae-rare-nakat-ta*[9].

baby-rabbit-TOP catch-can-NEG-PAST

... Baby Rabbit can' t. '

(68) **Mandarin**

Tubaba neng zhuadao mifeng huozhe xiaoshe, danshi ...

papa rabbit can catch bee or snake but

'Papa Rabbit can catch bees or snakes, but ...

... *tubaobao* ***bu*** *neng [e].*

baby rabbit not can

... Baby Rabbit can' t.'

To end the discussion of VP ellipsis, we note that Jackendoff (1972) and Jayaseelan (2001) proposed that the meaning of *any* is disjunctive (*this or this or this or ...*). This explains why a disjunction phrase, e.g., *bee or snake*, is assigned a 'neither' interpretation when it resides in the scope of negation. Consider sentences (68) and (69).

(69) Mama Rabbit doesn' t like apples, bananas or oranges.

(70) Mama Rabbit doesn' t like any fruit.

Sentences (69) entails that Mama Rabbit doesn' t like apples and Mama Rabbit doesn' t like bananas, and Mama Rabbit doesn' t like oranges. The same conversion from a single *not ... or* statement to a conjunction of several *not ... and* statements extends to English *any*. When *any* appears in the scope of negation, as in (70), it is interpreted as an infinite disjunction, ***not*** [*apples* ***or*** *bananas* ***or*** *oranges* ***or*** *kiwi fruit* ***or*** ...]. A negated infinite disjunction, in turn, is logically equivalent to an infinite conjunction of negative statements – ***not*** *apples* ***and not*** *bananas* ***and not*** *oranges* ***and not*** *kiwi fruit* ***and not*** ... .

4. Conclusion

There are implications of the findings of the present study for language acquisition. One of the implications has been the focus of intense study in the literature on child language. We have seen that the different interpretations that are assigned to simple (one clause) negative sentences with disjunction across languages stand in a particular semantic relationship. In languages where disjunction is interpreted as taking scope over negation, negative sentences with disjunction are true in three different circumstances. For example, the Mandarin sentence (71) is true if Ali only speaks Spanish, or only speaks French, or doesn' t speak either language. In the other class of languages, where negation takes scope over disjunction, simple negative sentences are true in only one of these circumstances. For example, the English sentence (72) is true only if Ali does not speak Spanish and does not speak French. Therefore, the English sentence (72) is true in a subset of the circumstances that make the Mandarin sentence (71) true.

(71) **Mandarin**

Ali	***bu***	*shuo*	*Xibanyayu*	***huozhe***	*Fayu.*
Ali	not	speak	Spanish	or	French

'Ali does not speak Spanish ***or*** Ali does not speak French. '

(72) *Ali does **not** speak Spanish **or** French.*

'Ali does not speak Spanish **and** Ali does not speak French. '

In the absence of negative evidence, this subset/superset relation between sentence meanings poses a potential problem of language learnability, which can be called the Subset Problem. To solve the Subset Problem, it has been proposed that children initially hypothesize that disjunction is interpreted *in situ*, across languages, with negation taking scope over disjunction in simple negative sentences. If children begin with this restriction on scope assignment, then they will encounter positive evidence if the local language interprets disjunction as taking scope over negation, as in Japanese and Mandarin. To date, the findings of experimental studies investigating children' s initial interpretation of negative sentences with disjunction are consistent with this solution to the Subset Problem (Crain & Zhou 2017; Gao et al. 2019; Goro & Akiba 2004a, b; Grüter et al. 2010; Notley et al. 2012).

The linguistic phenomena we have investigated in the present study pose another potential problem for language learnability in the absence of negative evidence. The issue concerns the acquisition of knowledge about the different scope patterns that characterize the kinds of complex sentences we have examined in the present study. The vast majority of children's experience is limited to simple (one clause) sentences. Most of the simple sentences children encounter are affirmative, but a lesser number of them negative. In determining the scope relations that are assigned to negative sentences, the grammars of language learners must (at some point) distinguish internal and external negation. We saw that sentences with existential expressions in general, and ones with disjunction in particular, are assigned different scope relations with internal versus external negation. If language learners do not come to the task of language acquisition already armed with a distinction between these types of negation, then they are likely to extend the scope assignments that they generate for sentences with internal negation to sentences with external negation. This would lead to a number of non-adult interpretations, which could (theoretically) prove difficult to recover from. In the absence of carefully sequenced input and formal instructions, the acquisition of asymmetrical linguistic phenomena, such as the reversal in scope assignments that are generated by internal and external negation, poses potential learnability problems, referred to as problems of the poverty-of-the-stimulus.

Notes

1. One of the main points of this paper is to show that certain linguistic contexts unlock these logical expressions, such that they participate in scope interactions with negation.

2. The proposal was inspired by Szabolcsi (2002), which demonstrated that Hungarian disjunction *vagy* 'or' takes scope over negation.

3. It has been suggested that the meaning of disjunction words differs across languages. One proposal is that disjunction words are interpreted as exclusive-*or* in some languages, but as inclusive-*or* in other languages (cf. Jennings 1994; Crain & Khlentzos 2010). This is not the source of the difference between the interpretation of disjunction in English on the one hand, and in Japanese and Mandarin on the other. If disjunction were exclusive-*or* in Mandarin and Japanese, then negative sentences with disjunction such as (9) and (10) would be **false** if just one disjunct is true, since exclusive-*or* makes positive sentences **true** only if just one disjunct is true. However, speakers of Japanese and speakers of Mandarin judge negative sentences with disjunction to be **true**

when just one disjunct is true. Hence, disjunction cannot be exclusive-*or* in these languages.

4. As we saw, the interpretation assigned by English speakers to sentence (7) makes it true only in one circumstance, where Ali speaks neither Spanish nor French. This is one of three circumstances that make sentences (9a) and (10a) true for speakers of Japanese and for speakers of Mandarin. So, the interpretation assigned to (7) makes it true in a subset of the circumstances that make sentences (9a) and (10a) true for native speakers. This has important implications for language learnability (we discuss this in section 4).

5. We offered evidence of this earlier in examples (5) and (6), where external negation takes scope over *some* and *any*.

(5) You' ll never convince me that Tony enjoyed some of the desserts.

(6) You' ll never convince me that Tony enjoyed any of the desserts.

6. Other sentences exhibit the same pattern of inverse scope effects in all three languages. These are sentences that combine a pseudo negative verb, in a higher clause, with disjunction and negation in an embedded clause. In these sentences, the inverse scope phenomena illustrated using sentences with *surprise* extend to the pseudo negative verbs *disappoint* (Mandarin *shiwang* 'disappoint' and Japanese *gakkari-suru* 'disappoint-do') and *regret* (Mandarin *yihan 'regret'* and Japanese *zan'nen-da* 'regret-DECL').

7. This is a single but representative case taken from the class of downward entailing expressions. The facts about the interpretation of disjunction in the antecedent of a conditional are predicted to extend to other downward entailing linguistic environments. See Szabolcsi (2004) and Crain (2012) for explication and for further examples.

8. We use upper case ONLY to designate the class of focus adverbs that includes English *only* and its counterparts in Mandarin (*zhiyou*) and in Japanese (*dake*).

9. In this example, the verb *tsukamae-* 'catch' is not elided in the second conjunct. We nonetheless assume that this construction involves VP-ellipsis, adopting the V-stranding analysis of VP-ellipsis proposed, for example, by Otani & Whitman (1991) and Funakoshi (2017). In this analysis, the verb overtly moves out of VP, and then the remnant VP is deleted, stranding the V head.

References

Baker, L. 1970. Double negatives. *Linguistic Inquiry*, 1: 169–186.

Chierchia, G. 2004. Scalar implicatures, polarity phenomena, and the syntax/pragmatics interface.

In A. Belleti & L. Rizzi (Eds.), *Structures and beyond: The cartography of syntactic structures, volume 3*. Oxford: Oxford University Press. 39–103.

Chierchia, G. 2013. *Logic in grammar: Polarity, free choice, and intervention*. Oxford: Oxford University Press.

Crain, S. 2012. *The emergence of meaning*. Cambridge: Cambridge University Press.

Crain, S. & Khlentzos, D. 2010. The logic instinct. *Mind & Language*, 25(1): 30–65.

Crain, S. & Zhou, P. 2017. Acquisition of logical connectives and focus, L1. In Sybesma, R., W. Behr, Y. Gu, Z. Handel, Huang, C. -T. J. & Myers, J. (Eds.), *Encyclopedia of Chinese language and linguistics*. Leiden, The Netherlands: Brill. 34–40.

Crain, S. & Zhou, P. 2019. Semantics and pragmatics: Acquisition of logical connectives and focus. In Huang, C. -T. J. & Sybesma, R. (Eds.), *Encyclopedia of Chinese language and linguistics*. Leiden, The Netherlands: Brill.

Funakoshi, K. 2017. Disjunction and object drop in Japanese. *Tampa Papers in Linguistics*, 4.

Gao, N., Thornton, R., Zhou, P. & Crain, S. 2019. The interpretation of disjunction in VP ellipsis. In Ionin, T. & Rispoli, M. (Eds.), *Three streams of generative language acquisition research. Selected papers from the 7th meeting of generative approaches to language acquisition – North America*. University of Illinois at Urbana-Champaign.

Goro, T. 2007. *Language-specific constraints on scope interpretation in first language acquisition*. Ph. D. dissertation, University of Maryland.

Goro, T. & Akiba, S. 2004a. The acquisition of disjunction and positive polarity in Japanese. In Chand, V., Kelleher, V., Rodriguez, A. J. & Schmeiser, B. (Eds.), *WCCFL 23 proceedings*. Somerville, MA: Cascadilla Press. 251–264.

Goro, T. & Akiba, S. 2004b. Japanese disjunction and the acquisition of positive polarity. In Y. Otsu (Ed.), *Proceedings of the 5th Tokyo conference on psycholinguistics*. Tokyo: Hituzi Shobo Publishing Company. 137–162.

Grüter, T., Moti, L. & Andrea, G. 2010. Acquiring the scope of disjunction and negation in L2: A bidirectional study of learners of Japanese and English. *Language Acquisition*, 17: 127–154.

Horn, L. 1969. A presuppositional approach to *Only* and *Even*. *Proceedings of the Chicago Linguistic Society*, 5: 98–107.

Jackendoff, R. 1972. *Semantic interpretation in generative grammar*. Cambridge Mass: MIT Press.

Jayaseelan, A. 2001. IP-internal topic and focus phrase. *Studia Linguistica*, 55: 39–75.

Jennings, R. 1994. *The genealogy of disjunction*. Oxford: Oxford University Press.

Johnson, K. 2001. What VP ellipsis can do, and what it can' t, but not why. In Balin, M. & Collins, C.

(Eds.), *The handbook of contemporary syntactic theory*. Oxford: Blackwell Publishers.

Kato, Y. 1997. Negation, focus, and interface economy. *Sophia Linguistica*, 41: 29–36.

Klima, S. 1964. Negation in English. In Fodor, J. & Katz, T. (Eds.), *The structure of language: Readings in the philosophy of language*. Englewood Cliffs, New Jersey: Prentice-Hall. 246–323.

Ladusaw, W. 1996. Negation and polarity items. In Lappin, S. (Ed.), *The handbook of contemporary syntactic theory*. Oxford: Blackwell Publishers.

Merchant, J. 2011. Polarity under ellipsis. In Cheng, L. -S. L. & Corver, N. (Eds.), *Diagnosing Syntax*. Oxford: OUP.

Notley, A., Zhou, P., Jensen, B. & Crain, S. 2012. Children' s interpretation of disjunction in the scope of 'before' : A comparison of English and Mandarin. *Journal of Child Language*, 39: 482–522.

Otani, K. & Whitman, J. 1991. V-raising and VP-ellipsis. *Linguistic Inquiry*, 22: 345–358.

Sag, I. 1976. Deletion and logical form. Ph. D. dissertation, Massachusetts Institute of Technology.

Szabolcsi, A. 2002. Hungarian disjunctions and positive polarity. In Kenesei, I. & Siptár, P. (Eds.), *Approaches to Hungarian* 8. Akademiai Kiado, Budapest. 217–241.

Szabolcsi, A. 2004 Positive polarity – negative polarity. *Natural Language and Linguistic Theory*, 22(2): 409–452.

Tieu, L., Romoli, J., Zhou, P. & Crain, S. 2016 Children' s knowledge of free choice inferences and scalar implicatures. *Journal of Semantics*, 33(2): 269–298.

Author work unit: Department of Linguistics, Macquarie University

Author email: Stephen Crain: stephen.crain@mq.edu.au

关于 something 的理论

Stephen Crain, Takuya Goro, Peng Zhou

摘要：内部包含两个逻辑表达的句子经常会有歧义，但是在有些情况下，一种语义阐释会占据主导。英语表存在量化的 something 和 anything 就是这类情况。不管是从句法还是语义来看，something 和 anything 在含否定的句子里都是极性上的两端。但是在有些语境里，两者没有语义上的对立，给定相同的真值条件，两者都可以使句子为真。我们调查了四种可以取消 something 和 anything 语义差异的语境，以此来评价析取表达在有些语言里是极性敏感的而在另一些语言里不是这一论断。如果析取表达在一种语言里是极性敏感的，那么该语言里取消英语 something 极性敏感的语境也应该取消析取表达的极性敏感。日语和现代汉语的析取表达一般被认为是极性敏感的，为对英语和这两种语言进行跨语言比较，我们对四类相关语境进行了探讨分析。

关键词：极性，否定，析取，省略，焦点副词，向下蕴含

作者单位：麦考瑞大学语言学系

作者邮箱：Stephen Crain: stephen.crain@mq.edu.au

中古汉语"床"兼作坐具名的原因

——兼论汉译佛经的作用

朱庆之

摘要：在上古汉语里，"床"是睡觉用的家具名，与今天的用法一样；但是在中古时代，"床"也可以指称某种坐具。本文讨论为什么会有这种变化，是什么原因造成了这个变化。我们的初步结论是，东汉翻译佛经的外来僧人最先用"床"来翻译佛经中指称坐具的词语，这种用法又随着佛经的流传影响到当时的汉语。

关键词：床（睡觉用的家具，SJ），坐具，坐具中的家具（ZJ），佛经翻译，梵汉对勘

1. 引言

"床"（牀），在近现代汉语里的主要用法是做睡觉用的家具（以下简称 SJ）的通名。它与椅子板凳之类的坐具（以下简称 ZJ）分属"家具"中不同的类别，不能混用。[1] 然而，古代的情况有所不同。如果查看代表当今汉语历史辞书最高水平的《汉语大字典》（徐中舒主编，四川辞书出版社 / 湖北辞书出版社，1986—1990；修订本，四川出版集团 · 四川辞书出版社 / 湖北长江出版集团 · 崇文书局，2010。以下简称《大字典》）和《汉语大词典》（罗竹风主编，上海汉语大词典出版社，1986—1994。以下简称《大词典》），你会看到两家都认为在古代"床"既可以指称 SJ，也可以指称 ZJ。[2] 但是，它们又同中有别——前者主张"一床说"，后者主张"两床说"。

《大字典》认为"床"从一开始指称的就是"坐卧之具"，也就是既包括 SJ，也包括 ZJ，二者不分。它把"床"在古代的用法分为 6 个义项：（1）供人坐卧的器具；（2）放置器物的坐架；（3）井栏；（4）形状像床的器具；（5）底

部；（6）量词。其中的义项（1）的书证是：

> 《释名·释床帐》："人所坐卧曰床。床，装也，所以自装载也。"《说文·木部》："床，安身之坐者。"《诗·小雅·斯干》："乃生男子，载寝之床。"《水经注·湘水》："［井］傍有一脚石床，才容一人坐……相承云，［贾］谊宿所坐床。"清全祖望《墨云董丈墓志铭》："太恭人患足疾，卧床数载。"（后略）

《诗经》例中的"床"指称的是 SJ，《水经注》例中的"床"指称的是 ZJ。需要先说明的是，郦道元《水经注》中的"一脚石床"中的"床"的确指称的是 ZJ；不过，这个用例的时代为北魏，不能证明"床"在上古时代也有同样的用法。那么，用来支持《大字典》"一床说"的真正依据其实是《释名》和《说文》这两部没有书证的字书。

《大词典》的"床"有 11 个义项，除去动词用法，名词或名词性用法有（1）供人睡卧的家具；（2）古代坐具；（3）安放器物的支架、几案等；（4）井上的围栏；（5）物之底部；（6）量词。虽然数量同样是 6 个，但内容却有异，它没有《大字典》的义项（4），而是将《大字典》的义项（1）一分为二，即将指称 SJ 和指称 ZJ 的用法分成两个一前一后的义项：

> （1）供人睡卧的家具。《诗·小雅·斯干》："乃生男子，载寝之床。"郑玄笺："男子生而卧于床，尊之也。"汉牟融《理惑论》："年十七，王为纳妃，邻国女也。太子坐则迁座，寝则异床。"唐杜甫《新婚别》诗："结发为妻子，席不暖君床。"（后略）
>
> （2）古代坐具。《礼记·内则》："父母舅姑将坐，奉席请何乡；将衽，长者奉席请何趾，少者执床与坐。"陈澔集说："床，《说文》云：'安身之几坐。'非今之卧床也。"《汉武帝内传》："［西王母］下车登床。帝拜跪问寒温毕，立如也。因呼帝共坐。"唐颜真卿《张长史十二意笔法记》："张公乃当堂踞床而坐，命仆居于小榻。"宋王谠《唐语林·补遗四》："宰相别施一床，连上事官床，南，坐于西隅，谓之压角。"明马愈《马氏日抄·特迦香》："琳坐右侧胡床上。"

从书证看，义项（1）的最早用例是先秦的《诗经》，而义项（2）的最早用例是成书于汉代的《礼记》。类似的义项分合不同，在《大字典》和《大词典》中比比皆是，一点儿都不显眼。但对"床"的释义而言，这个不同则有非同小可的意义。为了将其突显出来，我们把《大字典》的处理称为"一床说"，把《大词典》的处理称为"两床说"。

《大字典》的“一床说”来源于《释名》和《说文》，但这只是它的远源；考察一下近现代的汉语辞书史不难发现，《大字典》之前的汉语历史辞书基本上众口一词，这是它的近源。例如1915年出版的《辞源》巳集爿部“牀”条：

> 俗作床。（1）坐卧之具也。古人亦谓坐榻曰床。（2）器物之架也。如笔床琴床。（3）井榦也。古乐府：后园凿井银作床。谓设架井上，以支桔槔者也。（《辞源（正续编合订本）》，长沙：商务印书馆，1940年，巳集页131）

后来的重要辞书，如《辞海》（舒新城等主编，上海：中华书局，1936—1937）、《大汉和辞典》（诸桥辙次主编，东京：大修馆书店，1955—1960）和《中文大辞典》（高明、林尹主纂，台北：“中国文化大学”研究所出版部，1962—1968）等都持此说。因此，可以说“一床说”是地道的“传统”意见。与之相反，《大词典》的“两床说”暂时还没有找到其他来源，或是编者的新说。二者之中，我们赞同《大词典》的意见，因为它与近代以来学术界不同领域对相关问题研究的新成果更为接近。

首先，基于传统词源学著作《释名》和字源学著作《说文》的“一床说”，从词源和字源的角度主张“床”从一开始就兼指SJ和ZJ；但实际上，这个说法既缺乏古代文献用例的证据，也缺乏其他学科，尤其是考古学的证据。一方面，就像《大字典》，几乎所有主张“一床说”的辞书，举出的“床”的先秦用例，都是指称SJ的，并没有指称ZJ的；[3]而真正指称ZJ的，全部晚至中古时代。慎重起见，我们利用电子资料库重新调查了上古文献里所有含“床（牀）”的用例，同样找不到可以证明“床”指称ZJ的任何用例。[4]另一方面，20世纪以来，考古活动蓬勃发展，大量先秦乃至汉代的遗址被挖掘。在众多的出土文物中，不乏SJ的报道，却没有见到任何ZJ的报道。这说明，在上古时代，除了睡觉用的床外，并无作为坐具的“床”。这个推断还可以从文字学的材料来加以证明。[5]

在上古时代，“坐”这个动作的基本特征是席地而“跪”。《大字典》“坐”条第一个义项说：

> 人的止息方式之一。古人席地而坐，坐时两膝着地，臀部压在脚跟上。椅、凳出现后，凡将臀部着于椅、凳，以支持身体的重量者皆为坐。《左传·昭公二十七年》：“执羞者坐行而入，执铍者夹承之。”杜预注：“坐行，膝行。”《礼记·玉藻》：“退则坐取屦。”孔颖达疏：“坐，跪也。”……清·顾炎武《日知录·杂事·坐》：“古人席地而坐，西汉尚然。”“古人席地之坐，皆以两膝着席。有所敬，引身而起，则为长跪矣。”

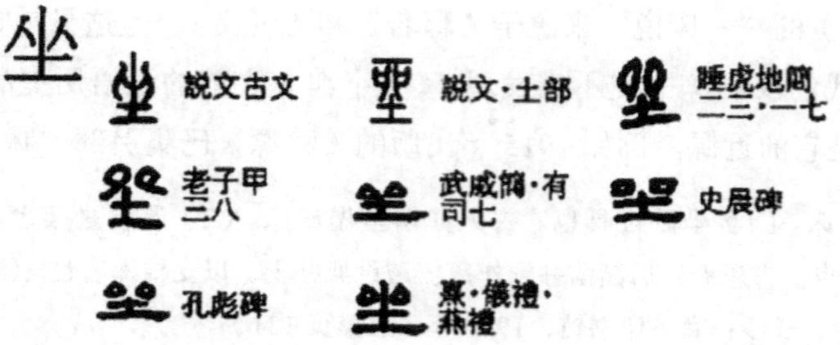

《大字典》对“坐”的解说简明扼要。与“床”有两种一样，“坐”也有两种：一种是中国传统的“坐”；另一种是椅凳这类坐具出现后，坐在其上的“坐”。这绝不是巧合。因为坐具的“床”指称的就是椅凳。

上古中国人的传统坐姿，可以从“坐”这个字的字形看出大概。今本《说文解字》给出的小篆字形作“坐”，解释说：“坐，止也。从土，从留省。土，所止也。此与留同意。坐，古文坐。”林义光《文源》根据这个古文做了如下的解释：“象二人对坐土上形。”

“坐”字在甲骨文和金文中尚未见到，但战国出土文献有多个用例。楚系字形作“坐”，秦系作“坐”。《战国古文字典》（何琳仪著，北京：中华书局，1998）说：“坐，从卩，从土，会人跽坐于地之意。秦系文字以卯易卩，应属繁化。或讹作‘坐’，参银雀山《孙膑》三六坐。小篆作坐，上又讹作卯（按，‘卯’当为‘丣’）形。”（第 881 页）[6]这个解释要比《文源》好得多。

古人之“坐”需要双膝“跪”在地上，通常会有垫子垫在膝盖下面，起到防硌和防潮的作用。这类垫子根据材料的不同，或称为“席”，或称为“荐”，就是与跪坐相配合的坐具。有没有可能古人将这类坐具称为“床”呢？答案是否定的。因为这些坐具都有自己的专名，其形制和作用与睡觉用的床完全不同，没有理由要与睡觉用的家具共享同一个名字。

ZJ“床”的出现与发生在中古时代的坐式和坐具的巨大变化有直接的关系。现代学术界对这个变化及其原因等有许多研究（参看朱大渭，1994；陈振，2000；高建华、刘文金，2007）。简而言之，坐式的变化就是从席地跽坐到垂脚高坐，或者盘腿高坐；坐具的变化就是从铺在地上的席荐，变为有腿的椅凳。这些都不是本土传统坐式坐具的自然发展，而是地道的舶来品。坐式坐具的系统性改变也并非早期零星的中外人员交流能够达成，而是外来民族大规模地入主中原，使得本地居民生活外族化的结果；变化发生的时间，则主要是在所谓的“五胡乱华”的两晋南北朝时期。因此，一方面，说“床”从一开始就同时指称SJ和ZJ，是“坐卧具”的通名，意味着先秦就已经有ZJ床的存在，缺乏根据，殊不可信；另一方面，说汉代或者汉代之前的文献已经有指称ZJ的“床”，同样不可信。

从以上的分析可以看出，“床”这个词在古代的确既可以指称SJ，又可以指称ZJ，但两种用法并不是同时出现的。“床”这个词语在先秦时代产生的时候，“中国”只有用来睡觉的“床”，还没有专门用来坐的“床”，“床”就是一个指称睡觉用的家具的专用名词；后来，当专门用来坐的ZJ出现时，人们用“床”来指称它，“床”才同时有了指称坐具的用法。因此，《大词典》大胆打破传统的“一床说”，创立新的“两床说”，良有以也。[7]

不过，《大词典》并非无懈可击。我们都知道，历史语言辞书每个义项之下的书证有两个基本作用：第一个作用是证明该义项的存在并展示其在具体文献中的使用情况；第二个作用是说明该义项存在的时间，何时出现，何时消亡。义项（2）“古代坐具”下的第一个书证是《礼记·内则》：“父母舅姑将坐，奉席请何乡；将衽，长者奉席请何趾，少者执床与坐。”编者还引用陈澔集说：“床，《说文》云：‘安身之几坐。’非今之卧床也。”将“床”读为坐具。如果这个书证中的“床”确如编者所言，则说明意义是“坐具”的“床”，虽然晚于先秦已经出现的指称SJ的“床”，可是最晚在《礼记》的时代，也就是西汉就已经出现在汉语文献语言当中。可惜的是，《大词典》的编者可能误读了这条材料。

《大词典》的编者没有引全，加上后半段，《礼记》相关文字的全文是：

> 父母舅姑将坐，奉席请何乡（向）；将衽，长者奉席请何趾，少者执床与坐。御者举几敛席与簟，县（悬）衾、箧枕、敛簟而襡之。

这句话并不容易读，要看看孔颖达《正义》是如何解释的：

> 此一节论父母舅姑将坐、将卧奉席之礼。及未卧之前，且敛枕簟衾箧举藏，须卧乃铺。“御者举几”者，谓早旦亲起之后，侍御之人则奉举其几以进尊者，使冯（凭）之；“敛席与簟”者，敛此所卧在下大席，与上衬身之簟，又县（悬）其所卧之衾，以箧贮所卧之枕也。敛簟襡之者，簟既衬身，恐其秽污，故敛此细簟以襡韬之，言簟则韬藏，

席则否。（《英武殿本十三经注疏》）

根据孔疏，这段文字规定了当父母长辈早上离床去“坐”和晚上离座去“卧”时，子辈（包括年长和年少）和用人们应该做的事情。其中“父母舅姑将坐，奉席请何乡；将衽，长者奉席请何趾，少者执床与坐”讲的是子辈的工作。假如在传抄的过程中没有出现文字讹误或错简的话，这段文字的行文应当使用了常见的“互文”笔法。在字词方面，第一个“坐”是动词，第二个“坐”是名词，后来写作“座”。“与坐（座）”的“与”，可以讲成动词，给予，与“持”义近；也可以讲成连词“和”，连接两个名词“床”和“坐（座）”。按前一个理解，正确的读法是：

父母舅姑将坐，[子辈中之]长者奉席请何向，[少者与座]；[父母舅姑]将衽，[子辈中之]长者奉席请何趾，少者执床。

《大词典》的编者似乎并没有把握住文意，以为第二个“坐”仍然是动词，少者执持的“床”就是这个动作的逻辑宾语。

如果《礼记》用例不成立，即便不致影响义项（2）的确立，作为首证，也会影响对义项（2）产生时代的说明。再来看第二条书证：

《汉武帝内传》：“[西王母]下车登床。帝拜跪问寒温毕，立如也。因呼帝共坐。”

首先，从汉语史语料学的角度看，《汉武帝内传》的作者和成书年代均不确定。《四库全书总目提要》卷142“汉武帝内传”条说：“旧本题汉班固撰，《隋志》著录二卷，不注撰人；《宋志》亦注曰不知作者。此本旧题曰班固，不知何据。殆后人因《汉武故事》伪题班固，遂并此书归之欤？”一般相信这部小说为晋以后人所作。《大词典》的编者应该知道这一点，因此并没有提供作者和年代。但是，如果书证没有明确的年代，就不能满足书证所具有的说明该义项使用时间的功能，也就不是一条合格的书证。

其次，读者还会问，编者选取这条材料做书证，是如何知道西王母“登”的“床”一定就是ZJ而非SJ？是不是因为后面的“呼帝共坐”的“坐”？其实，我们考察那些被前人认为是ZJ的“床”的用例，有许多的依据似乎都是如此。如果这个猜测不误，就值得做一点儿说明。在现代汉语里，毫无疑问，“床”就是SJ的通名。床的主要功能是睡卧，与ZJ分属两个不同的范畴。这大概没有人会有异议。但请注意，在日常生活中，床也常常用来当ZJ用。比如我们常常听到“坐在床上”这样的说法。然而，每个人都同意，床虽然也能坐，并不表示它同时也是ZJ，“床”这个词更不是坐卧具的通名。因此，我们将SJ和ZJ放在一起做个对比，如果不考虑特殊情况，二者区别非常明显：能卧又能坐（或基本功能为睡卧同时也可以坐）的只能是SJ，能坐并不能改变其作为SJ的本质特性；能坐不能卧的只能是ZJ，不能卧是确保其作为ZJ的本质特性。如果能坐又能卧，它的性质就改变了，只能是SJ而非ZJ（现代家具有跨界现象，如“沙发”是ZJ，但所谓的长沙发或三人沙发，也可以临时作为SJ。这属于特殊情况，可以不论）。也就是说，一般情形下，既没有只能睡卧不能坐的SJ，也没有能坐又能睡卧的ZJ。因此，不能因为文献里的“床”被人坐了，就认为这个床是ZJ。可见《汉武帝内传》在履行书证的第一个功能方面同样不合格。

根据我们目力所及，现代辞书举出的所指为ZJ的“床”的最早且无歧义的用例是裴松之《三国志注》魏书武帝纪“贼乱取牛马，公乃得渡”句下引的《曹瞒传》：“公将过河，前队适渡，超等奄至，公犹坐胡床不起。”（见于《大词典》“胡床”条）其中的“胡床”，作为一种坐具，其形制、来源和在中国的使用情况，是中西交通史研究的一个热点，从20世纪初日本著名学者藤田丰八的《胡床考》开始，相关的研究至今不绝。[8]“胡床”最初指的就是可以折叠的马扎，它的发明者是西北的游牧民族，传入后风靡一时。“胡床”是带腿的ZJ而非SJ，其中的“床”指称ZJ已成定论。

《曹瞒传》原书早已亡佚，今天知道此书完全仰赖裴《注》。裴《注》中有“吴人作《曹瞒传》”之语，后人据此认为它是三国时期吴国人所作的一部记载曹操生平事迹的书。如果我们放宽语料学标准，认可裴《注》中的“胡床”一语的确来自《曹瞒传》原文，那么，这条材料不仅是传世文献中“胡床”的最早用例，也是指称ZJ的“床”的最早用例。[9]

以上，我们以《大字典》和《大词典》的释义比较为切入点，梳理了两部辞书对“床”在早期文献中的意义和用法的不同看法，并对书证做了力所能及的考辨。初步的结论是，“床”在上古时代的文献语言里指称的只是SJ，但在中古时代，它除了指称SJ外，还有了指称ZJ的新用法。这一用法出现在文献中的时间，就目前掌握的资料来看，大概在魏晋之间。

上述工作的目的何在？

其实，当辨明了是非，厘清了事实之后，我们更为关心的问题就呼之欲出了——为什么原本指称 SJ 的汉语固有词“床”，中古时在保留原来用法的同时，又会拿来指称作用和形制完全不同的 ZJ？这个新用法说明“床”在中古发生了词义变化，导致这个变化的原因是什么？“始作俑者”是谁？这似乎是过去还没有引起太多关注的汉语历史词汇学问题。作为一个汉语历史语言学的研究者，这就是笔者打算在本文讨论并且试图给出一种答案的问题。

2. 提出问题——马扎为什么叫“（胡）床”？

前面已经提到，中古文献出现的“胡床”指称的就是今天人们熟悉的马扎一类的 ZJ，也是“床”这个词可以指称 ZJ 的第一个重要证据。因此我们就以马扎为什么可以称为“床”作为正式讨论的新切入点。

“胡床”一词的文献使用史相当长，这从《大词典》“胡床”条的书证可见一斑：

> 《三国志·魏志·武帝纪》“贼乱取牛马，公乃得渡”裴松之注引《曹瞒传》：“公将过河，前队适渡，超等奄至，公犹坐胡床不起。”南朝宋刘义庆《世说新语·自新》：“渊在岸上，据胡床指麾左右，皆得其宜。”唐杜甫《树间》诗：“几回沾叶露，乘月坐胡床。”宋程大昌《演繁露·交床》：“今之交床，本自虏来，始名胡床，桓伊下马据胡床取笛三弄是也。隋高祖意在忌胡，器物涉胡言者，咸令改之，乃改交床。”宋陶谷《清异录·逍遥座》：“胡床施转关以交足，穿便绦以容坐，转缩须臾，重不数斤。”清赵翼《饭馀》诗：“携得胡床临水坐，柳荫深处看荷花。”姚华《曲海一勺·骈史下》：“先生杖履留春，老子胡床玩月。”

从最早的魏晋时代的《曹瞒传》一直到近代的《曲海一勺》，用例延续一千七八百年。

如前所述，学者们公认，胡床在形制和功能上就像今天的“马扎”。它原本是一种可以折叠的“凳子”，方便马背上的民族迁徙时携带。马扎只能坐，不能卧，却也可以称为“床”，这是为什么？在回答这个问题之前，或许有必要对“胡床”这个词的语义结构特点做些分析。

古代中国，主要居住在黄河流域和长江流域的核心地带的汉族，与周边甚至距离遥远的其他民族的交往的历史可以追溯到史前。当然，西汉开始，这种交往变得越来越方便和频繁。在这个过程中，最直接也最重要的是物质文化物的互通有无。这导致大量异域物品来到中国。这些外来物品有一些是中国没有的，自然地，在汉语中也就没有对它们的称呼；有一些则是中国已有的，但形制等与中国已有者有一些差异。中国人，或者是将这些外来物品带入中国的外族人是如何用汉语来称呼它们的呢？根据此前的研究，除了用音译的方法直接借用之外，比较常见的就是用一个汉语固有词N，前面加上一个来源限定成分——唐代之前用“胡”，唐代以后用“番”，近代用“西”或“洋”等——构成一个偏正式的合成词。“胡床”就是一个例子。

但是“胡N”式合成词中的N在语义上有什么特点？或者说造词者在选取N的时候有什么规律？这对于了解“胡床”这个词有重要的作用。为此，我们调查了《大词典》所收以“胡”作为修饰成分的定中关系合成词，共得到41个。包括（A）植物名11个，有“胡瓜”[10]“胡豆”[11]“胡臬”[12]“胡荽”[13]“胡桐”[14]“胡桃”[15]“胡麻”[16]“胡椒”[17]“胡蒜”[18]“胡蔓草”[19]和“胡萝卜”[20]；（B）乐器名5个，有“胡角”[21]“胡琴”[22]“胡笛”[23]“胡鼓”[24]“胡笳”[25]；（C）日常器物用品名9个，除了“胡床”，还有“胡子”[26]“胡瓶”[27]“胡簏”[28]“胡帽”[29]“胡服”[30]“胡饼”[31]“胡基”[32]和“胡粉”[33]；（D）动作名3个，有“胡坐”[34]“胡跪”[35]“胡拜”[36]；（E）人和动物名8个，有“胡儿/胡人”“胡客”（均指外族人）、“胡姬/胡妲”（胡族的歌姬或舞姬）、“胡奴”（为奴的胡人）、“胡天”（对拜火教神祇的称呼）、“胡羊”（胡地的羊，特殊品种的羊）、“胡马”（胡地的马，特殊品种的马）、“胡雁”（从胡地飞来的大雁）；（F）其他5个，有“胡沙”（胡地的风沙）、“胡食”（胡人的食物）、“胡书”（胡人的文字）、“胡本”（外文原书）、“胡语/胡言”（胡人的语言）。

以上的“胡N”偏正式合成词中做中心成分的N，都是汉语固有词。如果看其原本所指与外来事物之间的关系，上面这些词大概可以分为两个大类，姑且用“疏远”和“接近”来概括。下面先以植物名为例来说明何谓“疏远”和“接近”。

（一）“疏远”类。汉语固有词N的原本所指的与外来的并不是同一植物，将二者联系在一起的充其量只是外形和/或者功能相同。如：

胡桃，俗称核桃。核桃为双子叶植物纲、原始花被亚纲、胡桃目、胡桃科、胡桃属植物，拉丁学名 *Juglans regia*；而汉语的“桃”为双子叶植物纲、原始花被亚纲、蔷薇目、蔷薇亚目、蔷薇科、李属植物，拉丁学名 *Prunus persica*。二者在“目”的层次上“分道扬镳”，可见“胡桃”并不是“桃”，它们大概只是成熟前的外形相似。[37]

胡椒，为双子叶植物纲、原始花被亚纲、胡椒目、胡椒科、胡椒属植物，拉丁学名 *Piper nigrum*；而汉语的“椒”，一般认为就是花椒，为双子叶植物纲、原始花被亚纲、芸香目、芸香亚目、芸香科、花椒属植物，拉丁学名为 *Zanthoxylum bungeanum*。二者同样分属不同的“目”，古人用中文的“椒”来命名，可能因花椒与胡椒外形相似，又均为香料。

胡麻，即芝麻。根据恩格勒植物分类系统，芝麻为双子叶植物纲、合瓣花亚纲、管花目、茄亚目、胡麻科、胡麻属植物，拉丁学名 *Sesamum indicum*；而汉语的“麻”，早期指大麻，拉丁学名 *Cannabis sativa*，为双子叶植物纲、原始花被亚纲、荨麻目、桑科、大麻属植物，其茎皮纤维长而坚韧，古人主要用来织麻布或纺线，制绳索，编织渔网和造纸等，因此“麻”后来成为具有同样用途的植物的总称。其种子可榨油，可做油漆、涂料等。“胡麻”与“大麻”分属于不同的亚纲，不是同一物种，或因它们的外形相似，又同为油料作物。

胡萝卜，为双子叶植物纲、原始花被亚纲、伞形目、伞形科、胡萝卜属，拉丁学名为 *Daucus carota var. sativa*；而用作中心成分的“萝卜”则是双子叶植物纲、原始花被亚纲、罂粟目、白花菜亚目、十字花科、萝卜属，拉丁学名 *Raphanus sativus*。二者在“目”的层次上“分道扬镳”，其相似之处可能在于根茎的形状以及叶子和根茎均可食用这一点上。[38]

（二）“接近”类。汉语词 N 原本所指与外来者虽然不是完全相同，但属于常识上的“同一类”的植物，直观上二者仅有较小的区别。也就是说，在中国已有它们的同科或同属的植物。如：

胡瓜，即黄瓜。是双子叶植物纲、原始花被亚纲、葫芦目、葫芦科、黄瓜属植物，拉丁学名 *Cucumis sativus*。用作中心成分的汉语固有词“瓜”，是一个总称，属上位词；它的下位词都属于植物学上的“葫芦科”，不同的“瓜”，只是“属”或者“种”的不同。它们自然属性十分相近。

胡豆，即蚕豆。是双子叶植物纲、原始花被亚纲、蔷薇目、豆亚目、豆科、野豌豆属植物，拉丁学名 *Vicia faba*。用作中心成分的“豆”，在汉语里指称植物时，也是一个通名，代表上位概念，可统指所有或者大部分“豆科”的植物。

胡蒜，即大蒜。为单子叶植物纲、百合目、百合亚目、百合科、葱属植物的地下鳞茎，拉丁学名 *Allium sativum*。中国本土的“蒜”，中文学名为薤白头，别名小根蒜、紫根蒜，拉丁学名 *Allium macrostemon*，与大蒜同纲同目同科同属，只是不同“种”。

植物名的“疏远”和“接近”的分类同样适用于其他类别的词。不同的是，其他类别的词，大都是“接近”者而几乎没有“疏远”者。如（B）5个乐器名，汉语固有的中心成分“角”“琴”“笛”“鼓”和“笳”，当与来自胡地的被命名为“胡角”“胡琴”“胡笛”“胡鼓”和“胡笳”的乐器大同小异，充其量在材质、形制或者音色上略有差异。（C）9个日常器物用品名，“胡瓶”只不过是在胡地产制的有异域风格的“瓶”，“胡簏”只不过是在胡地产制的有异域风格的“簏”（箭袋），“胡帽”也只不过是胡人所戴的帽子……作为中心成分的“瓶”、“簏”、“帽”、“服”、“饼”、“墼”（土块，胡墼指胡人用来盖房砌墙的土坯）、“孑”（戟属，胡孑是一种刃旁有曲支的戈戟）和“粉”等均是可以表达上位概念的汉语固有词。同样，（D）3个动作名“胡坐”“胡跪”和“胡拜”中的“坐”“跪”“拜”也都是上位概念词，尽管胡人的“坐”“跪”和“拜”的具体形式可能与汉地同样的动作有很明显的不同。如此等等，不一而足。由此可见，除了少数中国原先没有的事物（汉语中没有任何合适的词语可以用来表示，只能采用“格义”的办法），大部分的词语，因为其所指在中国已经有同类存在，汉语也有相应的词语表示，可以用来作为新造词的中心成分。

据此，我们再来看属于（C）类的“胡床”。如果汉语固有的“床”只是SJ的专名，“胡床”既不可能是“疏远”类，也不可能是“接近”类，因为大小至少可以睡卧一个人的“床”与马扎一类的单人坐具不但性质不同，形制也相距甚远。那么为什么可以将马扎称为“床”呢？

显然，这种情形的出现，首先有一个必要的条件，即在将马扎命名为“胡床”时，命名者嘴巴里的“床”应该除了指称SJ外，已经可以同时指称ZJ了。也就是说，“胡床”的发明者并不是“床”指称ZJ这个新用法的“始作俑者”，只是使用者。可是前面已经讨论过，“胡床”又是迄今为止在文献里能够找到的

“床”指称ZJ的最早用例。在这种情况下，另外一种文献就进入了我们考虑的范围，这就是从东汉开始出现的汉译佛经。在东汉的翻译佛经里，与“坐”有关的“床”已经常见；而到了三国时代的译经中，已能见到确定指称ZJ而非SJ的“床”的用例。那我们就有理由怀疑，在“胡床”之前，汉语“床”获得的指称ZJ的用法，极有可能是汉译佛经的又一“杰作”。

3. 汉译佛经中指称坐具的“床”

随着西汉时期中国与域外其他重要国家或者文明的交通通道的正式建立，印度佛教在两汉之交慢慢传入中原地区。最初，外来的传教僧侣用汉语将佛教的经典口头宣讲给当地的民众。到了东汉中期，为了跨越时空的障碍，信众中有人充当“笔受”，将他们宣讲的内容记录下来，从此拉开了延续长达千年的佛经汉译事业的序幕。

汉译佛经有大量的“床”，准确地说有大量与“坐”有关的“床”的记载。这些用例的大部分也与本土文献一样，不容易从上下文来判断出它们指称的究竟是什么。不过，用例多了，总可以找到一些对我们这项研究有重要意义的材料。例如：

（3.1）三国吴康僧会译《六度集经》卷6：“妇人喜悦，令儿驰归，取独坐床欲以坐之，商人乃熟视妇人而笑。妇执高操，意怪商人住笑非宜。儿取床迟，还即搏之，商人又住笑。”（CBETA, T03, no. 152, p. 37, c2-3）

《六度集经》是译者和年代没有什么疑问的三国译经。其中的“独坐床”指称的当是一个具体的印度ZJ。但“独坐床”具体是什么？仅一个用例不容易看明白。

我们利用CBETA（《CBETA电子佛典集成》，中华电子佛典协会，2016年版）查找，“独坐床”一词在东晋南北朝翻译的律藏经典中有多达51个用例，可据此对这个印度家具有更多的了解。如：

（3.2）后秦弗若多罗共罗什译《十诵律》卷34：“佛言：从今听比丘三岁中间得共一床坐，听三比丘共一粗梐床上坐，听细梐床二人共坐，独坐床上一人坐。”[39]（CBETA, T23, no. 1435, p. 243, a19-21）

（3.3）又《十诵律》卷39：“佛言：从今三比丘中间隔三岁，得共大床坐。二人得共一绳床坐，不得三人。独坐床上应一人坐，不应二人。”（CBETA, T23, no. 1435, p. 281, c5-7）

以上两个用例清楚说明“独坐床”只能坐一个人，可知“独”的确切含义就是一个人单独，“独坐床”就是单人“床”。[40]与“独坐床”并举的有可坐三人的“粗梐床”和“大床”，可坐两人的“细梐床”和“绳床”。一方面说明在可用来坐的家具里，还有另外的种类，而“独坐床”只是其中的一种；但是另一方面，可容两个人或者三个人坐的那些“床”，是否就是坐具，也同样不容易确定。

在内容极其丰富的律藏中，还可以看到一些与独坐床形制有关的文字。如：

（3.4）又《十诵律》卷 25：“僧自恣饱满已，持独坐床是中坐欲闻说法。”（CBETA, T23, no. 1435, p. 183, c19-20）

（3.5）姚秦佛陀耶舍共竺佛念译《四分律》卷 55：“时有乞食比丘，晨朝着衣持钵往白衣家，见有独坐床，看左右不见人，自念：‘此于我有益。’即便持去。疑，佛问言：‘汝以何心取？’答言：‘以盗心。’佛言：‘波罗夷。’”（CBETA, T22, no. 1428, p. 976, a8-12）

这两个用例说明，独坐床不大不重，可临时设置，易于搬动甚至“偷”走。

（3.6）又《十诵律》卷 23：“云何‘腹行虫难’？若诸比丘在龙处作僧坊，是中诸小比丘不知宜法，非处大小便、浣弊衣晒之，是中诸龙瞋放毒蛇蜈蚣，入诸比丘床下、床上，榻下、榻上，独坐床下，户耳窗，……经行道头，树下。”（CBETA, T23, no. 1435, p. 172, a22-26）

“腹行虫难”是佛教所谓人间“八难”之一。腹行虫，主要指印度常见的蛇虫之类，在比丘日常生活之所到处横行，造成灾难。例子中“独坐床”与“床”“榻”并举，均为僧房中的家具。一方面，说明“独坐床”不属于供睡卧之用的“床”“榻”之属；另一方面，所谓“独坐床下”，提示这个床有腿，床下是空的，故有蛇虫出没。

（3.7）又《四分律》卷 39：“尔时六群比丘，作皮床、皮独坐床，诸比丘白佛，佛言：‘不应畜。’”（CBETA, T22, no. 1428, p. 848, c18-21）

（3.8）又《十诵律》卷 61：“给孤独居士作五百独座漆画床并褥施僧，僧不受言：‘佛未听我等畜如是上好独坐床。’是事白佛，佛言：‘听受如是净上好独坐床。’”（CBETA, T23, no. 1435, p. 468, b18-20）

“皮独坐床”言“床”的某些部分是用动物皮革制作的，因为涉及杀生，不被佛陀所允许。而孤独居士布施的“独座（坐）漆画床”则是一种高级的独坐床；

同时布施有“褥”，表明独坐床上还配有褥垫。

独坐床的“坐”式是什么样的，律藏也有记载，虽然不够全面。

（3. 9）又《十诵律》卷10：“开一房门，见僧卧具在露地雨湿烂坏，即取捩晒卷叠、举着覆处，便闭房门下撢，还自房舍，独坐床上结加趺坐。”（CBETA, T23, no. 1435, p. 77, a4-7）

“结加趺坐”是印度人修行的一种坐姿，两脚交叠盘坐，脚心朝上。

（3. 10）又《十诵律》卷11：“诣长老般特房前立，謦欬作声扣户言：‘大德般特出来！’长老般特即从禅起出房，至独坐床上端身大坐。”（CBETA, T23, no. 1435, p. 80, b23-26）

例中的“大坐”应该就是禅宗文献里常见的“打坐”。

译经里除了“独坐床”以外，还有一种“小床”，出现的语境与“独坐床”有时非常相似，可能是“独坐床”的更通俗的叫法。例如：

（3. 11）旧题三国吴支谦译《撰集百缘经》卷3：“尔时世尊，着衣持钵，将诸比丘，往诣其家，受其供已，心怀欢喜，取一小床，在佛前坐，渴仰闻法。佛即为其种种说法。”（CBETA, T04, no. 200, p. 215, a4-6）[41]

（3. 12）西晋竺法护译《文殊师利佛土严净经》：“王睹坐定寂靖无声，与后、太子手自斟酌百种供膳；食皆饱讫，行澡水毕，兼施琦宝好衣贡佛，别取小床在佛前坐，专心叉手听受道教，欲化中宫及来会者。”（CBETA, T11, no. 318, p. 892, c3-6）

（3. 13）西晋竺法护译《密迹金刚力士会》（载《大宝积经》卷13）：“于是密迹金刚力士与其宫人婇女、一切诸子及诸眷属，手自斟酌百种肴膳不可计味，……佛及菩萨诸声闻众皆悉充满。饮食毕讫，行澡水竟，密迹金刚力士更取小床于佛前坐，白世尊曰：‘唯加弘慈应时演法宣入法门，使众生类了于道心行所从生。’”（CBETA, T11, no. 310, p. 71, c1-11）

（3. 14）西晋法炬译《频毘娑罗王诣佛供养经》：“尔时，世尊知时已到，便着衣持钵，比丘僧前后围绕，入罗阅城往诣摩竭国王频毘娑罗宫。到已，诸比丘僧各次第坐。尔时，摩竭国王频毘娑罗，见佛比丘僧坐已定，自手执若干种甘馔饮食，饭佛及比丘僧，见世尊饭已摄钵，更敷小床在如来前坐。尔时，世尊为摩竭国王频毘娑罗，说微妙法渐渐共议。”（CBETA, T02, no. 133, p. 856, c7-13）

（3.15）姚秦竺佛念译《出曜经》卷4：“时世尊明清旦着衣持钵，比丘僧前后围绕，至彼长者家，各次第坐。长者躬自行水清净饭食，供养饮食已讫，行清净水，取一小床，在如来前坐，欲得闻法。”（CBETA, T04, no. 212, p. 631, b14-18）

在经藏中，“小床”一般都出现在听佛陀说法时的场合。

在律藏译品里，“小床”出现的场合比较多样。如：

（3.16）又《十诵律》卷17：“尔时居士以多美饮食，自恣与佛及僧竟，自行水知佛洗手摄钵，取小床，坐佛前听说法。”（CBETA, T23, no. 1435, p. 124, a20-22）

这是听佛说法时，也可以听其他人说法。如：

（3.17）又《四分律》卷13：“尔时居士白舍利弗、目连坐，即就座而坐。时居士出种种甘美饮食供养，食已除去食器，头面礼足已，更取小床在一面坐，白言：‘我欲得闻法。’”（CBETA, T22, no. 1428, p. 653, b17-20）

（3.18）南朝宋佛陀什共竺道生译《五分律》卷4：“明日食时，以所得食为长老优波斯那及跋难陀设供。时至皆往，下种种食，食讫行水，取小床于众前坐，请说妙法。优波斯那为说法已，从坐而去。”（CBETA, T22, no. 1421, p. 25, c24-27）

“小床”偶尔会出现在不“严肃”的场合。如：

（3.19）又《五分律》卷2：“佛在舍卫城。尔时长老优陀夷为欲火所烧，作是念：‘故出不净，世尊已制，今当方便与女人相触，取细滑乐。’便扫洒房内，敷好床座，取一小床于露地坐。有诸女人同来游观，语优陀夷言：‘我等故来欲看房舍。’答言：‘姊妹！随意看之。’”（CBETA, T22, no. 1421, p. 10, c25-p. 11, a1）

优陀夷长老为了勾引异性，搬了一张“小床”坐在院子里。

“小床”是不是就是“独坐床”？或者说类似的“小床”是否只能是ZJ而非SJ？上面的用例并不够清楚。

律藏里“小床”常常与“大床”共现。一般情况下，“大床”指SJ，“小床”指ZJ。下面的例子将这种区别讲得十分明白：

（3.20）又《四分律》卷27：“尔时婆伽婆在舍卫国祇树给孤独园。时偷罗难陀比丘尼，到时着衣持钵诣一居士家敷座而坐。时彼居士妇，脱身璎珞衣服入后园洗浴。时偷罗难陀比丘尼，辄着他璎珞衣服，在居士床上卧。……'时诸比丘尼闻，其中有少欲知足、行头陀、乐学戒、知惭愧者，嫌责偷罗难陀言：'汝云何着他妇璎珞衣服在床上卧？'即往白诸比丘，诸比丘往白世尊。世尊以此因缘集比丘僧，呵责偷罗难陀言：'汝所为非，非威仪、非沙门法、非净行、非随顺行，所不应为。云何入居士家，着他妇璎珞衣服在床上卧，使居士嫌怪耶？'以无数方便呵责已，告诸比丘：'此比丘尼多种有漏处，最初犯戒。自今已去与比丘尼结戒，集十句义乃至正法久住，欲说戒者当如是说：若比丘尼入白衣舍内，在小床、大床上，若坐、若卧，波逸提。''比丘尼'义如上。'白衣舍'者，村。'小床'者，坐床。'大床'者，卧床。彼比丘尼，入白衣舍内，在小床、大床上若坐若卧，随胁着床，一转一一波逸提。"（CBETA, T22, no. 1428, p. 753, b8-c5）

印度佛教僧团内部的法律制度，是典型的普通法。通常由释迦牟尼根据"案情"来判定犯案人是否犯法以及犯了什么法，或者对某种法的适用性根据不同的情况做进一步的解释。上述案例中，比丘尼偷罗难陀做了"坏事"被其他比丘尼告发。释迦牟尼根据案情判决，从今以后，如果比丘尼进到白衣舍内，在人家的小床上坐或大床上卧，就犯了"波逸提"罪。然后律文又为"比丘尼""白衣舍""小床""大床"等关键词语进行定义。其中明确地说，"小床"是"坐床"，"大床"是"卧床"。

在僧团内部，释迦牟尼不但制定"法律"，还制定"法度"。下面的例子中佛陀同样根据一个具体的事件，规定了"大床"和"小床"的形制，同时也对两种不同的床的所指做了解释。

（3.21）唐义净译《根本说一切有部毘奈耶》卷 49："……时六众苾刍闻是制已，遂作高床，脚长七肘，缘梯上下。诸婆罗门居士等见生嫌贱，时诸苾刍以缘白佛。佛言：'我今以此为缘，为诸苾刍广说，乃至制其学处，应如是说：若复苾刍作大小床，足应高佛八指。若过作者应截去。波逸底迦。'如是世尊为诸苾刍制学处已。时具寿邬陀夷身形长大，坐彼床时颏拄着膝。苾刍白佛，佛言：'前是创制，此更随开，应如是说：若复苾刍作大小床，足应高佛八指，除入梐木。若过者应截去，波逸底迦。''若复苾刍'者，谓六众也。'作大小床'者，谓自作、使人造此大床及小座时。"（CBETA, T23, no. 1442, p. 895, b6-19）

律文将佛陀的“法度解释”中的“大小床”解释为“大床及小座”。

在译经里，还有“小床座（坐）”的说法，所指与以上的“小床”同。如：

（3.22）又《十诵律》卷40：“时忧楼伽贤者即请阿难将入自舍，敷座令坐，自手与水，多美饮食自恣饱满。饱满已洗手摄钵，贤者取小床座，欲听法故。”（CBETA, T23, no. 1435, p. 290, a28-b2）

（3.23）东晋佛陀跋陀罗共法显译《摩诃僧祇律》卷11：“我从聚落还时，汝当敷小床座，与我水并授树叶食时，以扇扇食已洗钵令干，举着常处。”（CBETA, T22, no. 1425, p. 318, c15-17）

（3.24）又《摩诃僧祇律》卷18：“佛住舍卫城，广说如上。时阿利咤比丘不舍恶见，众僧作举羯磨已，往尊者难陀、优波难陀所，见已赞言：‘善来！’即起迎，与小床坐、洗足水，与涂足油、非时浆，与房舍、床褥卧具，共法食味食。”（CBETA, T22, no. 1425, p. 367, c13-17）

在最后这个用例中，“小床坐”与“床褥卧具”共现，说明它不属于后者的范围。

“小床座”是形容词“小”修饰“床座”。作为词的“床座”多指ZJ，用例很多。时间较早的如：

（3.25）东汉支谶译《阿阇世王经》下：“于众会中复有菩萨，名曰法来，则得敕令而具床座。应时受教，捭指顷有二万三千床座。其绕綖若干种色，名珠好绣绮异色物悉布在上。文殊师利及诸菩萨声闻一切皆悉就坐。”（CBETA, T15, no. 626, p. 400, a3-7）[42]

（3.26）三国吴支谦译《维摩诘经》卷1：“佛复告文殊师利：‘汝诣维摩诘问疾。’……长者维摩诘心念：‘今文殊师利与大众俱来，吾将立空室合座为一座，以疾而卧。’文殊师利既入其舍，见其室空，除去所有，更寝一床。维摩诘言：‘劳乎，文殊师利！不面在昔，辱来相见。’……贤者舍利弗心念：‘无床座，是菩萨大弟子当于何坐？’维摩诘知其意，即谓言：‘云何贤者，为法来耶？求床座也？’舍利弗言：‘居士！我为法来，非利所安。’维摩诘言：‘唯，贤者！其利法者，不贪躯命，何况床座。’”（CBETA, T14, no. 474, p. 525, b18-c25）

（3.27）西晋竺法护译《德光太子经》：“其城中央，为德光太子作七宝宫殿、八重交露；彼一讲堂，上有四亿床座，以给太子。”（CBETA, T03, no. 170, p. 414, b23-24）

（3.28）译同上《文殊师利普超三昧经》中：“复有菩萨名曰法超。濡首告曰：‘卿，族姓子！严办众座。’应时受教举手弹指，于彼殿馆二万三千床座自然具足，若干种饰微妙庄严，无数座具而敷其上，濡首童真诸菩萨众悉俱就座，声闻次之。”（CBETA, T15, no. 627, p. 420, b6-11）

（3.29）又《四分律》卷 19：“尔时佛在舍卫国祇树给孤独园。时尊者迦留陀夷预知世尊必从此道来，即于道中敷高好床座，迦留陀夷遥见世尊来，白佛言：‘世尊看我床座！善逝看我床座！’”（CBETA, T22, no. 1428, p. 693, a17-28）

（3.30）又《四分律》卷 25：“尔时婆伽婆在罗阅祇耆阇崛山中。时罗阅城中有一不信乐大臣，有一独坐床，无人敢坐上者。偷罗难陀比丘尼，常入出其家以为檀越。偷罗难陀到时着衣持钵往诣其家，不语便坐大臣床座上。大臣见已问言：‘谁令此比丘尼坐我床上？’”（CBETA, T22, no. 1428, p. 742, a9-14）

上面例子中“独坐床”“床座”和“床”三个词异称同指。

除了“床座（坐）”，还有“坐床”。如：

（3.31）西晋法炬共法立译《大楼炭经》卷 3：“忉利天上宫中……有四坐床，金床银床水精床琉璃床，以天坐其上，念万姓善，亦念诸天善。”（CBETA, T01, no. 23, p. 293, a3-5）

（3.32）又《十诵律》卷 41：“若先到食处，应敷座床，取揩脚物、拭脚物、安水瓨、水瓶，应扫洒食处涂地。”（CBETA, T23, no. 1435, p. 298, c28-p. 299, a1）

（3.33）南朝宋求那跋陀罗译《杂阿含经》卷 49：“是时，屈摩夜叉鬼知世尊默然受请已，化作五百重阁房舍，卧床、坐床、踞床，俱褞褥枕，各五百具，悉皆化成。”（CBETA, T02, no. 99, p. 362, a10-12）

译经中能够证明“床”可以确定指称 ZJ 的用例还有一些，为了节省时间和篇幅，不再赘举。

这些用例表明，翻译佛经中指称 ZJ 的“床”比起本土文献，不仅用例多，而且时间早。我们有理由推测，将 ZJ 称为“床”的“始作俑者”，可能正是那些东汉来华传教的僧人。但是问题还没有完。

我们知道，翻译佛经的底本是印度佛经原典，讲的是印度的故事，记录的也是印度人的生活。因此，其中的“床”一定也有平行的源头语词语，指称的也是印度人使用的家具。进一步的问题是，为什么这些译经的人在其译文中不分SJ和ZJ，都用汉语的“床”来翻译？难道在源头语里，也是SJ和ZJ不分，抑或是另有原因？要回答这个问题，只能借助梵汉对勘。

4. 从梵汉对勘资料看译经中的“床”

在翻译佛经里，“床”既指称SJ，也指称ZJ。这一状况在最早的东汉译经中就已经如此。

根据Nattier（2008），今存较为可靠的东汉译经有39部，其中含有“床”的15部，[43]共45个用例。但是，这些“床”（包括含“床”的合成词或词组），除了前举例（3.25）支谶译《阿阇世王经》出现在“床座”一个用例应该指坐具外，其余的用例都难以断定其中的“床”究竟指的是SJ还是ZJ，虽然有不少在语义上做动词“坐”的地点宾语。例如：

（4.1）支谶译《阿阇世王经》卷下：“佛坐其床上，应时佛笑，无央数色光明而从口出遍于十方，还绕身三匝从顶上而入。”（CBETA, T15, no. 626, p. 404, c16-18）

（4.2）译同上《伅真陀罗所问如来三昧经》卷3：“及伅真陀罗八万四千夫人，各各持天珠而奉上佛，则时散佛头上，便化作八万四千交露帐。其中悉有床，具足皆珍宝，皆布天缯以为绨綖。诸交露帐中悉有坐佛，其佛皆三十二相、诸种好悉具。”（CBETA, T15, no. 624, p. 360, c21-26）

（4.3）昙果共康孟详译《中本起经》卷上：“迦叶白佛：‘愿大道人留止，欲相供养。’明旦作饭，自行请佛。佛言：‘便去，今随后到。’迦叶适还，佛如人屈伸臂顷，东适弗于逮数千亿里，取树果名阎逼，满钵而还。迦叶未到，已坐其床。”（T04/150c4-8）

（4.4）又上：“王问优陀：‘悉达在家，吾为作床，精宝四种；于今所坐，何物用作？’”（CBETA, T04, no. 196, p. 154, c9-10）

这是为什么？难道汉语的“床”真的如《辞源》和《大字典》的编者主张的那样，本来就兼指二者？当然不是。前面已经讨论过，在上古时代的汉语和汉文化中，家具这个范畴里并没有今天我们所具有的，与SJ对立，像椅凳一类的ZJ的概念。我们通常听到这样的说法：与今天不一样，古代中国人席地而坐。人们有时还将“席地而坐”简化为“坐在地上”。其实精确地说，当坐的时候，中国人是将臀部“坐”在自己的一双足跟上的。当外族坐具中的ZJ类，包括马扎传入后，中国的家具中才有了与SJ对立的ZJ。

根据以往的相关研究取得的经验，最先能够想到的一个原因是汉语是第二语言或者第三语言的外来译者误用了汉语的“床”。然而，又是什么原因导致其误用？如果佛经原典，也就是源头语中，有SJ和ZJ的严格对立，各用不同的词语来指称，这种误用的可能性不大。对于此种情形，译者更为常见的办法是，如果汉语没有，或者有而他们个人言语系统中没有，就会创造一种形式，哪怕这个形式不符合汉语的规则。因此，稳妥也是必要的办法是对源头语的情形做一番调查。

我们的工作先分为两个步骤：首先，利用英梵词典尽可能找出其中所收的所有表示SJ和ZJ的梵文词语；[44] 然后，利用译经的梵汉对勘资料，看看这些梵文词语在具体翻译时译者是如何翻译的。

（一）梵文中表示SJ和ZJ的词语（详参附录“梵语中表示床和坐具的词语一览表”）。调查发现，梵语中的这类词语，其实可以分为三类。第一类是SJ专用词。第二类是ZJ专用词。第三类是SJ兼指ZJ词，或者ZJ兼指SJ词；抑或是SJ转指ZJ，或ZJ转指SJ类词。

第一类：SJ专用词。共26个。大部分是从几个意义是“睡”或者“铺展”“躺下”的动词词根派生而来的派生词。如：

> **√śī (to lie, to sleep)**: śaya, śayana, śayanāsana, śayanīya, śayanīyaka, keli-śayana, mahā-śayana, śayyā, śira;
>
> **√mand (to sleep)**: mañca, mandurā;
>
> **√stṛ (to spread, to cover)**: stariman, āstara, āstaraṇa, pra-stara, pra-stāra, vi-stara;
>
> **√lī (to lie)**: pra-layana。

也有一些来源暂时不明。如：jāhaka；khaṭvā，khaṭvāṅga；palyaṅka，paryaṅkika；paryastikā；pecaka；talpa-viddha。

第二类：ZJ专用词。共36个。大部分是几个意义是“坐”或者“放置”的动词词根派生而来的派生词。如：

> **√ās (to sit)**: āsa, āsadana, āsana, āsandī, āsandikā, āsanopaviṣṭa, āsita, adhy-āsana, dīrghāsana (dīrghā-asana), upāsana; āspada.

√sad (to sit down): sadas, sadana, sadman; niṣaṇṇaka; pīṭha, pīṭhaka, pīṭhika.

√viś (to sit down upon): vedi, vedikā, upa-veśana, saṃ-niveśa, sam-upaveśa, sam-upaveśana.

√dhā (to put, place, set): dhāna, dhāsi, dhiṣaṇa.

来源暂时不明的有：sthāman，dhi-ṣṭhāna；upa-talpa；āyatana；kṣaya，kṣetratā；malli；nikhaṭvā；paṭṭa。

第三类：“床”“座”兼类或者由 A 变 B 或由 B 变 A 类。共 16 个。

（A）SJ 兼类或变为 ZJ：

āśaya, āśraya, auśīra, laghu-khaṭvikā, mañcaka, mañcikā, niṣadyā, pary-aṅka, pra-staraṇa, praty-āstaraṇa, saṃ-stara, saṃstāra, talpa, viṣṭara

（B）ZJ 兼类或变为 SJ：

saṃ-veśa, saṃ-veśana

可以看到，在梵文里，表示 SJ 和表示 ZJ 的词基本上是分开的。这说明在梵文里，SJ 和 ZJ 是两个不同的概念范畴。不过，也有一些词是兼类的，其中以 SJ 兼 ZJ 为主，可能是在实际的使用中以床为座而导致了词义的变化。

（二）荻原云来《汉译对照梵和大辞典》（1970）中的汉译词。荻原的这部辞典从性质上说是梵和词典，但由于编者是佛教学者，且编纂的目的主要是佛教研究，文献收入当时日本学者所作的十数部佛经的梵汉对勘词汇集中的资料，可以帮助读者了解在这些译经中，译者是如何翻译平行梵文中的相关词语的。经过比对，以上的梵语词只有 37 个在荻原辞典中有对应的汉译词；也就是说，在荻原统计的作过梵汉对勘的梵文佛经里，上述 78 个词，只用过其中的差不多一半。其中译成 SJ 或 ZJ 类词语的更少，只有 18 个，具体的分布和表现如下。

（A）在第一类专指 SJ 的梵语词中，汉译只译成“床”或相关字眼的有：

śayana：卧，卧具，床卧具，床；床，床榻，茵蓐

mahā-śayana：大床

śayanāsana：卧具，床卧，床卧具，床褥

śayyā：卧；卧具；铺，卧处

但其中也有个别的词语，除了译成“床”，同时还译成“座”：

mañca：床，床座，卧床，座，座子，床褥卧具

该词这样的用法在梵文词典中未收，也有可能是在具体的上下文中以床为座，是译者意译的结果。

（B）在第二类专指坐具的梵语词中，汉译只译为“座”或者相关字眼的有：

adhi-ṣṭhāna：座，处，依……

āsana-upaviṣṭa：坐座，处座

āsandī：交椅

niṣaṇṇaka：安坐，安住

pīṭhika：机，机子，椅子，梯

saṃ-śrita：座，依止，依处……

但也有一些译词中含有“床”一类的字眼：

āsana：住处；座，踞座；坐处，床座，坐具

ni-ṣīdana：坐，坐具，卧敷具……

pīṭha：座，坐床，小床，交床，床座，坐具，榻席，辇舆

这是坐具译为“床”的证据。

（C）在第三类梵语词中，汉译词含“床”或“座”的字眼有：

mañcaka：床座

pary-aṅka：床，大床，座，高座，端座，结跏[45]，跏趺坐，结跏趺坐

praty-āstaraṇa：草垫，坐垫，坐具

saṃ-stara：座，敷，蓐，铺，布，散，坐具，敷具，卧具，坐卧具

这些词语从语源上看都属于SJ兼类，即本义应该是SJ，但是可以同时或者单独指称坐具。一方面有可能是因以床为座而意译的结果；另一方面，也必须了解的是，这些词语大都出现在中晚期译经的平行梵本中，或许也是译者“床”“座”不分的表现。

我们要特别注意第一类专指SJ中的śayana和第二类专指ZJ中的āsana这两个词。因为在以下将要看到的梵文佛经里，它们使用最频繁，最具代表性。

（三）译经的梵汉对勘。我们选取的是梵文《般若经》的东汉支谶译本《道行般若经》，《维摩经》的三国支谦译本《维摩诘经》（这部经还有姚秦鸠摩罗

什的异译本《维摩诘所说经》和唐玄奘的异译本《说无垢称经》可供比较）和《法华经》的西晋竺法护译本《正法华经》（还有鸠摩罗什的异译本《妙法莲华经》可供比较）。这三部经都是早期的译作，如果有指称 ZJ 的“床”，时代都比本土文献的用例早。

（A）《道行般若经》。这部经中“床”7 见，全部都在“床卧具”一语中，没有例外。如：

（4.5）卷 3：“复次，须菩提！三千大千国土人，悉作阿耨多罗三耶三菩，便如恒边沙佛刹人，皆供养是菩萨，震越衣服、饮食、床卧具、病瘦医药，如恒边沙劫供养，随其喜乐作是布施。”（CBETA, T08, no. 224, p. 439, b10-13）

（4.6）卷 3：“复有异恒边沙佛刹人，都共供养是辈菩萨摩诃萨，震越衣被、饮食、床卧具、病瘦医药，供养如恒边沙劫。”（CBETA, T08, no. 224, p. 440, a3-5）

辛嶋静志（2011：147 页注 161）将“床卧具”解释为“bedding”（寝具，包括床、被褥枕），可商。根据辛嶋静志（2010，2011），“床卧具”的平行梵文是 śayanāsana。这是个复合词由 śayana（床）和 āsana（坐具）两个成分构成，辛嶋给这个梵文词的英文注解是“bed and seat; a lodging”（床和坐具；住处），可见这个合成词指称的不仅仅有寝具，还有坐具，其实指称的是所有的生活用家具。这个理解可在其他译经中得到证明。东晋佛陀跋陀罗共法显译《摩诃僧祇律》卷 3：“……‘随盗物’者，物有八种：一者时药；二者夜分药；三者七日药；四者尽寿药；五者随物；六者重物；七者不净物；八者净不净物，是名为八。……‘重物’者，床卧具及余重物。‘床卧具’者，卧床、坐床、小褥、大褥、拘氍枕；‘及余重物’者，一切铜器、一切木器、竹器、一切瓦器。”（CBETA, T22, no. 1425, p. 245, a12-28）前面已经提到过，作为法律文件，律藏常常对法律中的术语进行解释。其中对“床卧具”解释包括“卧”的床，还有“坐”的床以及褥和枕之类铺垫物。

下面是“床卧具”在支谶的其他译经中的用例：

（4.7）《文殊师利问菩萨署经》：“若求乞瓦钵、震越、床卧具、病瘦医药，若欲求饮食，离于迦罗蜜，亲附于恶师，于本佛所无功德者，常有怖惧于本际。”（CBETA, T14, no. 458, p. 437, a11-13）

（4.8）《阿閦佛国经》下："舍利弗！若菩萨摩诃萨于是陂陀劫中皆供养诸所佛、天中天，衣被、饭食、床卧具、病瘦医药供养已，便出家学道。"（CBETA, T11, no. 313, p. 758, c16-19）

但支谶并不是第一个使用这个说法的译者，因为更早的安世高的译经中已经有其踪迹。如：

（4.9）《八正道经》："第五谛受为何等？是闻有道弟子法求，不可非法，饭食、床卧、病瘦正法求，不可非法，是为谛受。"（CBETA, T02, no. 112, p. 505, a13-15）

比支谶晚的康孟详也用这个词语。如：

（4.10）《修行本起经》下："山中多有毒虫虎狼师子，谁当供养饮食水浆床卧之具？"（CBETA, T03, no. 184, p. 468, a15-16）

"床卧"或"床卧（之）具"在同期以及更早的本土文献里没有用例，可以相信，译经中的用例都是梵语 śayana-āsana 或者其中亚语形式的翻译。可见从一开始，外来的佛经译者已将"床"作为 SJ 和 ZJ 的通称。

（B）《维摩诘经》。这部经中"床"共 6 见，其中单独的"床"2 次，在"床座"中 3 次，在"师子床"中 1 次。如：

（4.11）卷 1"弟子品"："于是，长者维摩诘自念：寝疾于床，念佛在心。"（CBETA, T14, no. 474, p. 521, b29）

（4.12）卷 1"诸法言品"："文殊师利既入其舍，见其室空，除去所有，更寝一床。"（CBETA, T14, no. 474, p. 525, c1-2）

在平行的梵文里，以上两个"床"对应的都是名词 mañca（睡卧的床）。

（4.13）卷 1"诸法言品"："贤者舍利弗心念：'无床座，是菩萨大弟子当于何坐？'维摩诘知其意，即谓言：'云何贤者，为法来耶？求床座也？'舍利弗言：'居士！我为法来，非利所安。'维摩诘言：'唯，贤者！其利法者，不贪躯命，何况床座。'"（CBETA, T14, no. 474, p. 526, c20-25）

在平行梵文里，以上三个"床座"对应的都是名词 āsana（某种坐具）。

（4.14）卷 2："化菩萨既受饭，与诸大人，俱承佛圣旨，及维摩诘化，须臾从彼已来在维摩诘舍。维摩诘即化为九万师子床，严好如前。”（CBETA, T14, no. 474, p. 532, b17-20）

在平行梵文里，“师子床”一词对应的是复合词 siṃha-āsana。其中 siṃha 是狮子，与“床”对应的也是坐具 āsana。[46]

值得注意的是，例（4.11）和（4.12）的“床”，鸠摩罗什和玄奘的异译，也都作“床”；（4.13）的三个“床座”，鸠摩罗什和玄奘的异译也同样作“床座”。但是，（4.14）的“师子床”，鸠摩罗什和玄奘的异译则分别译为“师子之座”和“师子座”，即将“床”改译为“座”。这也说明支谦也是把坐具译成“床”的。

（C）《正法华经》。这部经中“床”共39见。其中33见用在“师子床”“法床”“床榻”“床座”和“床卧（具）”等复合形式中。如：

（C_1）“师子床”（包括师子之床、师子金床和师子宝床）共14见。如：

（4.15）卷3：“遥见势富，极大长者，在于门前，坐师子床，无数侍卫，眷属围绕，出入财产，及所施与。”（CBETA, T09, no. 263, p. 81, c14-17）

（4.16）卷6：“欲令能仁佛坐我所有师子金床，讲《正法华》开化一切，使蒙其恩。”（CBETA, T09, no. 263, p. 103, a5-6）

（4.17）卷6：“十方世界各三千亿诸佛正觉，皆来诣此，如来悉坐于师子宝床。”（CBETA, T09, no. 263, p. 103, c19-21）

（4.18）卷7：“尔时他方世界无央数亿百千姟诸如来、至真、等正觉，普从十方诣能仁如来劝说法者，各各坐于七宝树下师子之床。”（CBETA, T09, no. 263, p. 111, c22-24）

所有的包含“师子床”的用例，除个别没有平行梵文之外（如“师子金床”），“床”都对应梵文的名词 āsana，指某种坐具。

同《维摩诘经》相似，竺法护《正法华经》中的师子“床”，在鸠摩罗什的异译《妙法莲华经》中，绝大部分被译为“座”。如（4.15）的“坐师子床”译为“处师子座”，（4.17）的“坐于师子宝床”译为“在宝树下，坐师子座”，（4.18）的“坐于七宝树下师子之床”译为“在于八方诸宝树下，师子座上结加趺坐”。

（C_2）“法床”1见：

（4. 19）卷 1：“大圣适说，斯经典已，能仁至尊，处于法床，加趺而坐。”（CBETA, T09, no. 263, p. 66, c8-10）

与“法床”平行的梵文是复合词 dharma-āsana，dharma 是“法”，与“床”对应的同样是 āsana。这个“法床”，鸠摩罗什异译改作“法座”。

（C_3）“床榻”5 见，其中有平行梵文的有两则。先看这一则：

（4. 20）卷 8：“卧在床榻，若着衣服，而常讲演，斯如来经。”（CBETA, T09, no. 263, p. 117, c22-24）

此处的“床榻”，平行的梵文是 śayyā，专指 SJ。大意不论睡觉还是起来，要常常讲说如来的经典。同样意义的“床榻”还有下面一例，虽然没有平行梵文。

（4. 21）卷 8：“一时得闻此经法者，若再反闻所在专精，现在生处所获福佑，常得自然无数珍宝，宫殿精舍床榻坐具，象马车乘安雅无量。”（CBETA, T09, no. 263, p. 118, b11-14)

“床榻”与“坐具”对立，只指寝具，似乎说明“床榻”是一个同义语素并列的同义连文双音词。不过，下面的用例又有不同。

（4. 22）卷 8：“佛灭度后其有得闻此经典者，持读书写若分别说，福胜无量。修慈愍哀广普受持，讲堂精舍床榻锦绣敷具，令比丘众顿止其中。”（CBETA, T09, no. 263, p. 117, a21-28）

与这个“床榻”平行的梵文却是在东汉《道行般若经》译为“床卧具”的 śayana-āsana，泛指精舍中的日用家具，包括寝具和坐具，似乎又说明“床榻”的用法要自由得多。

（C_4）“床座”3 见。具体如下：

（4. 23）卷 1：“所造珍宝，及栴檀香，多有床座，明珠诸藏。”（CBETA, T09, no. 263, p. 65, a19-21）

“床座”的平行梵文是 śayyā-āsana。与 śayana-āsana 的性质一样，śayyā-āsana 也是个复合词语，śayyā 专指 SJ，āsana 专指坐具，二者连文，表示集合的概念，指生活家具。在结构上。这两个复合词的微小区别是，表示 SJ 的，一个是 śayana，一个是 śayyā。但这两个词形有差异的都是词根 √śī（to lie, to sleep）

的派生词，也都是前述梵语中表示 SJ 的第一类词。

（4. 24）卷 7：“佛来至于，灵鹫之山，自然床座，无量姟数。”（CBETA, T09, no. 263, p. 114, c28-29）

与“床座”平行的梵文也是 śayyā-āsana。

（4. 25）卷 8：“清净法故，所建鲜明，得为天帝，梵天床座。”（CBETA, T09, no. 263, p. 119, a14-15）

这一例中与“梵天床座”平行的梵文是复合词 brahma-āsanānām，brahma 是梵天，与“床座”对应的 āsana 只是“座”，并没有“床”，与上两个用例不同。鸠摩罗什将 brahma-āsanānām 译为“梵座”。

“床座”这个说法在南北朝之前的本土文献里几乎不见。佛教文献最早见于支谦的译经，如前举《维摩诘经》，都是 āsana 的平行翻译，单指坐具 ZJ，或是支谦创造的一个译语。[47] 然而，在竺法护的译经中，“床座”有两种用法，除了沿用支谦的用法外，还用来翻译梵文的并列词组，分别指其中的 SJ 和 ZJ。这有些特别，使我们不得不留意译经中的其他“床座”是不是都指 ZJ。看到“床座”有并列 SJ 和 ZJ 的用法，仅仅表示 ZJ 的“床座”是不是所谓的“偏义复词”？但考虑并列的“床座”后出，同时“床”在汉代开始就泛指 SJ 和 ZJ，我们更相信单指 ZJ 的“床座”的内部结构是并列的，可能是大名加小名。

（C_5）“床卧、床卧具”共 10 见，其中 4 例有平行梵文：

（4. 26）卷 3：“饮食衣服，若干巨亿，诸床卧具，离垢无秽，用栴檀香，以为屋室，柔软坐具，以敷其上。”（CBETA, T09, no. 263, p. 83, a13-16）

（4. 27）卷 6：“常当供养，如奉最胜，饭食之属，诸味具膳，房室床卧，衣被亿数。”（CBETA, T09, no. 263, p. 101, a12-14）

（4. 28）卷 7：“若得供养，饮食之具，床卧所安，衣服被枕，病瘦医药，而无侥冀，不从众人，有所请求。”（CBETA, T09, no. 263, p. 108, c19-22）

（4. 29）卷 8：“供养诸缘觉，菩萨亿千姟，奉进诸饮食，衣服床卧具，榻席及屋室，皆以栴檀香。”（CBETA, T09, no. 263, p. 116, b15-17）

“床卧具”在东汉的译经中已见，是表示床榻凳椅之类家具的集合概念的复合词 śayana-āsana 的翻译。同样，例（4. 26）中与“床卧具”对应的梵文词语

同样是 śayana-āsana；其余三个用例的“床卧”和“床卧具”对应的梵语词则是与（4. 23）同样的 śayya-āsana。

在上述资料里，表示 ZJ 的梵文都是 āsana。我们也调查了这个词在竺法护和鸠摩罗什两译中的翻译情况。发现竺法护并非将这个词都译为“床”，而鸠摩罗什译为“座”。在 31 个（并非全部）具有可比性的用例中，竺法护也只有 10 处译为“床”，其他都译为“座”，“座”明显比“床”多。可以这么说，在竺法护的译文里，在翻译 āsana 的时候，“床”和“座”是同义词。

这一情形其实在东汉的译经中已经如此。在《道行般若经》中，“座”出现了 28 次，在平行的梵文中能够找到对应成分的有 16 次，真正指称坐具的有 8 次，都是 āsana。[48] 如：

（4. 30）卷 2：“如我有时与诸天共于天上坐，持异特座，乃至自我座，敢有天人来至我所承事我，我未及至座所，我不坐上时，诸天人皆为我坐，作礼绕竟已便去，是坐尊释提桓因，于是间坐受法，忉利天上诸天人为作礼。”（CBETA, T08, no. 224, p. 435, c5-10）

辛嶋静志（2011：101 页注 536）将“持异特座，乃至自我座”译为“(I) take the special seat and sit on it.”（我搬来这特别的座位并坐在上面）。因为这段文字的平行梵文是 divye svake āsane niṣaṇṇo bhavāmi，辛嶋译为“I sit on my own godly seat”（我坐在我自己的虔诚的座位上），当中有 āsane 这个字眼，它是我们熟悉的表示 ZJ 的 āsana 的依格形式。

迄今发现的东汉时期翻译佛经的“底本”很少，无法通过梵汉对勘对“床”在东汉译经中的更多用例的所指进行确认。不过我们还有些别的办法。如：

（4. 31）东汉昙果共康孟详译《中本起经》中：“尔时，世尊在舍卫国祇树给孤独园为众说法，天龙鬼神、四辈弟子严整具足。于是摩诃迦叶，垂发弊衣，始来诣佛。世尊遥见叹言：‘善来！迦叶！’豫分半床，命令就坐。迦叶进前，头面作礼，退跪自陈曰：‘余是如来末行弟子，顾命分坐，不敢承旨。’大众佥念：‘此老道士，有何异德，乃令世尊分坐命之？此人儁乂，唯佛明焉。’于是如来察众所念，欲决所疑，广论迦叶大行齐圣。”（CBETA, T04, no. 196, p. 161, a18-23）

“半床”是什么意思？其中的“床”是 SJ 还是 ZJ，有点费解。《中本起经》

迄今为止也没有发现平行的印度文本，我们无法通过梵汉对勘来弄清它的准确含义；而且，“半床”的说法在译经中仅此一例，我们也无法通过更多的用例来推知它的意义。不过，《中本起经》的“故事”在后世的译经中也有记载，其中的“半床”被译成“半座”。如：

（4.32）刘宋求那跋陀罗译《杂阿含经》卷41：“一时，佛住舍卫国祇树给孤独园。尔时，尊者摩诃迦叶久住舍卫国阿练若床坐处，长须发，着弊纳衣，来诣佛所。尔时，世尊、无数大众围绕说法。时，诸比丘见摩诃迦叶从远而来，见已，于尊者摩诃迦叶所起轻慢心，言：‘此何等比丘？衣服粗陋，无有仪容而来，衣服佯佯而来？’尔时，世尊知诸比丘心之所念，告摩诃迦叶：‘善来！迦叶！于此半座，我今竟知谁先出家，汝耶？我耶？’彼诸比丘心生恐怖，身毛皆竖，并相谓言：‘奇哉！尊者！彼尊者摩诃迦叶，大德大力，大师弟子，请以半座。’尔时，尊者摩诃迦叶合掌白佛言：‘世尊！佛是我师，我是弟子。’佛告迦叶：‘如是！如是！我为大师，汝是弟子，汝今且坐，随其所安。’尊者摩诃迦叶稽首佛足，退坐一面。”（CBETA, T02, no. 99, p. 302, a1-15）

“半座”的说法在译经中就十分常见了。下面是最早的用例：

（4.33）三国吴康僧会译《六度集经》卷4：“王意始然，金轮上向，七宝四兵飞行升天，入帝释宫。释覩王来，欣迎之曰：‘数服高名，久欲相见，翔兹快乎！’执手共坐，以半座坐之。”（CBETA, T03, no. 152, p. 22, a21-25）

“半座”就是座位的一半，这是印度的一种礼仪：主人把自己的座位让一半出来，请客人与自己紧挨着坐在一起，代表一种特别的亲密或者礼遇。

不过，“座”只是“座位”，未必不是SJ。正好，在《法华经》里也有“半座”的记载，而且有平行梵文可查：

（4.34）《正法华经》卷6：“时，四部众见多宝如来、至真、等正觉，闻其灭度去世以来不可称计亿百千劫，听言善哉！甚大惊怪，初未曾有。即以天华，供养散于释迦文佛、多宝如来。时多宝佛则以半座与释迦文，七宝寺中有声出曰：‘释迦文佛！愿坐此床。’释迦文佛辄如其言。时二如来共同一处，在于虚空，七宝交露坐师子床。”（CBETA, T09, no. 263, p. 104, a8-14）

这条材料的特别之处在于，译者先用“半座”，后面又用“床”来指称同一事物。鸠摩罗什的异译就没有这样的“混乱”：

（4. 35）《妙法莲华经》卷 4："即时一切众会，皆见多宝如来于宝塔中坐师子座，全身不散，如入禅定。又闻其言：'善哉，善哉！释迦牟尼佛！快说是法华经，我为听是经故而来至此。'尔时四众等、见过去无量千万亿劫灭度佛说如是言，叹未曾有，以天宝华聚，散多宝佛及释迦牟尼佛上。尔时多宝佛，于宝塔中分半座与释迦牟尼佛，而作是言：'释迦牟尼佛！可就此座。'即时释迦牟尼佛入其塔中，坐其半座，结加趺坐。"（CBETA, T09, no. 262, p. 33, b28-c8）

上面这段文字有完整的梵文可以比对，其中与法护译"时多宝佛则以半座与释迦文，七宝寺中有声出曰：'释迦文佛！愿坐此床。'"和罗什译"尔时多宝佛，于宝塔中分半座与释迦牟尼佛，而作是言：'释迦牟尼佛！可就此座。'"平行的梵文是：

atha khalu bhagavān Prabhūtaratnas tathāgatas arhan samyak-saṃbuddhas bhagavatas Śākyamunes tathāgatasya arhatas samyak-saṃbuddhasya tasmin eva siṃha-āsane ardha-āsanam adāsīt tasya eva mahā-ratna-stūpa-abhyantare evam ca vadati / iha eva bhagavān Śākyamunis tathāgatas niṣīdatu（然后，世尊多宝如来阿罗汉等正觉就在这师子座上，把一半座位给了世尊释迦牟尼如来阿罗汉等正觉，在大宝塔中对他说道："请世尊释迦牟尼如来就坐这里吧。"）

与例（4. 10）一样，"师子座"的梵文也是 siṃha-āsane。其中 siṃha 是"狮子"；āsane 是 āsana 的依格形式，在师子座上。"一半座位"的梵文是 ardha-āsanam，其中 ardha，是"半、一分"；āsanam 是 āsana 的单数宾格形式。

接下来与法护译"释迦文佛辄如其言。时二如来共同一处，在于虚空，七宝交露坐师子床"和罗什译"即时释迦牟尼佛入其塔中，坐其半座，结加趺坐"平行的梵文是：

atha khalu bhagavān Śākyamunis tathāgatas tasmin ardha-āsane niṣasāda tena eva tathāgatena sārdham ubhau ca tau tathāgatau tasya mahā-ratna-stūpasya madhye siṃha-āsana-upaviṣṭau vaihāyasam antarīkṣasthau saṃdṛśyete（于是，释迦牟尼如来与此如来一起坐在半个座位上。两位如来坐在虚空中这大宝塔中的师子座上。）

与前一个例子一样，"半个座位"的梵文是 ardha-āsana，"师子座"的梵文是 siṃha-āsana。

这样，通过异文，我们知道了《中本起经》的"半床"就是"半座"；又通过“半座”的对勘材料，知道了“半床”之“床”就是 ZJ。

以上的对勘材料应该足以让我们了解译经中的“床”与平行梵文的关系，并且可以确定，佛经的译者的确用汉语的“床”来翻译梵语指称 ZJ 的专用词。

5. 讨论和结语

至此，我们可以对上面的材料做一简单的讨论并结束此文。

从语料中观察到的重要现象有以下三个：

第一，在梵文里，SJ 和 ZJ 各有不同的词语指称，二者划然有别，虽然亦有少数的词有兼指的情形；

第二，在几部梵语佛教文献里，与动词“坐”相关的主要是指称 ZJ 的 āsana，与动词“睡眠”相关的主要是指称 SJ 的 śayana；

第三，但在上述梵语典籍的早期汉译文里，意义是 SJ 的 śayana 大都译为“床”，意义是 ZJ 的 āsana 则有三种译法——“座（坐）”“坐具”和“床”。也就是说，译者在翻译指称 ZJ 的词语时，也译成“床”。“床”有了两个义项，一指 SJ，一指 ZJ。

明明是两个不同的词，指称的也是两种不同的家具，为什么译经的人会将二者混同？要说原因，自然先会想到源头语言中，存在同一个词既可指称 SJ，又可指称 ZJ 的情形；特别是，这样的词的“本义”大都是 SJ。正好汉语中又没有指称印度 ZJ 的专用词，译者就趁势用汉语的“床”来翻译指称 ZJ 的词语。这样的可能性当然不能完全排除。不过，考虑到从总的方面看，SJ 与 ZJ 在梵文中分属不同的范畴，多由不同的词语指称；同时也考虑到早期译经的平行梵本中，指称 SJ 和 ZJ 的基本上是两个不同的词，我们更倾向于另外的解释。

汉语只有指称 SJ 的“床”，却没有指称 ZJ 的专用词。“座”（指坐的地方，不一定是 ZJ）和“坐具”（上位概念词）都不是理想的选择，虽然有时不得不用。为什么混用“床”？这大概与早期翻译时普遍采用“格义”之法有关，即用汉语中相近的词来“硬译”。中国的“床”在战国时代已与今天的床无大异，有腿架离地面。[49] 这与印度的 ZJ 在某些方面有相似之处。首先，印度的 ZJ 都是带腿的。这是由印度特殊的气候条件决定的。印度的气候属于热带季风气候，一年分为两个季节，雨季和旱季。雨季虽然只占一年的三分之一左右的时间，但几乎天天有雨，而且常为暴雨，一时之间积水四溢，水退之后地面非常潮湿。因此，坐的时候必须坐在与地面隔开的地方，这就有了对于椅凳之类专用坐具的必然需求。而且，当地上有水或者泥泞不堪时，两只脚也只能抬高，放在架高的坐具上，这时盘腿的坐式当然是最平稳和最节省地方的一种。其次，印度的ZJ有单人的、双人的，还有三人甚至多人的。因此，在那些关于坐具名称的英文定义中，常会看到bench（长凳）甚至couch（长沙发）的字眼。这些特征可能会让汉语是第二语言的外来传教者有足够的理由用汉语的“床”来翻译并不是床的ZJ，就像将用“（花）椒”来翻译pepper（胡椒）一样。

值得补充的是，早期被译成汉语经典的主要是经藏，这是宣传佛教宗教哲学和信仰的理论性著作。其中涉及ZJ最多的，是在讲经听经的场合描写中用来指称讲经者（通常是释迦牟尼）和听讲者（通常是佛教比丘）使用的坐具。佛教僧侣的坐式就是盘腿坐，最为典型的结跏趺坐，用来进行“禅定”的修行时，不但盘腿，脚心还要朝上。为了适应长时间盘腿坐的需要，座位上通常会有垫子，天冷时还有防寒保暖的被褥围在身体的四周。作为佛教的中心，佛经中对于释迦牟尼使用的ZJ的描写常常铺张奢华，而且“个头”很大。将这样的坐具翻译成“床”，大概也不会引起汉语使用者的过分疑惑或抵触。

汉代以降，随着中外文化交流的日渐繁盛，中国本土的文化面貌持续发生着“日新月异”的变化。印度佛教这种巨大精神文化产品和“胡床”“胡坐”“胡椒”“胡琴”之类使用者用“胡”来标记的域外物质文化产品的传入逐渐改变了中国人原有文化样态。这个历史性的大变动也必然会反映到汉语中来。原本指称SJ即睡觉用家具的“床”，在保留原来的用法的同时，又用来指称新传入的带腿的坐具。虽然“床”的这种用法在唐代之后，就随着这些“胡式”坐具的专名的出现而被淘汰，在过去并没有引起太多的注意，但是的确值得我们问问为什么。

本文根据表示坐具的“床”的最早用例见于东汉时代的汉译佛经，以及表示坐具的“床”在中古各个时代译经中的用例要远多于本土文献这一事实，推断这种用法的产生，很可能源于东汉肇始的汉译佛经，或者至少在东汉的佛经翻译中被大量使用；而这种用法之所以能够进入一般汉语，也与佛教的影响、翻译佛经的流布有很大的关系。如果这个推断不误，“床”这个词在中古时代指称对象的变化，就是佛经翻译对汉语影响的又一例证。

附录：梵语中表示床和坐具的词语一览表

说明：

一、本表的梵文词语来自主要的梵英词典和荻原云来《汉译对照梵和大辞典》(以下简称《大辞典》)。

二、本表梵文词语的“英文释义”来自梵英词典，或有删略；“荻原释义”是荻原《大辞典》的日本释义的中文翻译，参考了林光明、林怡馨编译的《梵汉大词典》。该词典是荻原《大辞典》的中文编译本；“古代汉译”是荻原《大辞典》所收录的该梵文词语在古代译经中的译词，具体出处请查荻原原书或者林氏词典；“类型”指该词语属于SJ，ZJ，还是SJ与ZJ的混合（SZ或ZS），或者是表示寝坐用具的集合的概念（S+Z）。这主要是根据英文释义做出的大致分类。

三、本表的梵文词语排序纯粹按照所含的拉丁字母顺序，以方便查找。

梵文词语	英文释义	荻原释义	古代汉译	类型
adhi-ṣṭhāna	- a position, site - residence, abode - a seat	立足点，立场，地点，座位	座，处，依，处所，依处……	ZJ
adhy-āsana	- settlement - a seat	住处，席，座；坐……之上		ZJ
āsa[50]	- a seat	座；接近		ZJ
āsadana	- a seat	坐；座席		ZJ
āsana[51]	- abiding, dwelling - sitting, sitting down - a seat, stool	坐；端坐的姿式；休止，扎营，居住；座，席，位置，王位	住处；座，踞座；坐处，床座，坐具	ZJ
āsandikā	- a little/small chair	小椅子		ZJ
āsandī	- a chair or stool (generally made of basket work)	椅子	交椅	ZJ
āśaya[52]	- sleeping, lying down - resting-place, asylum - a place of residence, abode, bed-chamber - a seat			SZ
āsita	- seated, being at rest - one who has sat down - one who is seated or dwells - sitting, sitting down - a seat - way or manner of sitting	使坐，使就位，使住；坐；座位		ZJ

续表

梵文词语	英文释义	获原释义	古代汉译	类型
āspada	- abode - a seat	地位，座，住居，用地；……的场所	依，依止；处，往处，靠处，安足处	ZJ
āśraya	- resting-place - a seat	依靠……，保护处；座，住居……	依，依止，所依	ZJ
āstara	- covering - a coverlet, blanket, carpet - a bed - cushion	被单；稻秆；卧床，坐垫		SJ
āstaraṇa[53]	- the act of spreading - a layer of sacred grass spread out at a sacrifice - a carpet, rug - a cushion, quilt, bed-clothes - a bed	扩展	张，展	SJ
āstaraṇaṃ praty-āstaraṇam			卧具	SJ
auśīra	- a bed (used also as a seat) - a seat, chair, stool			SZ
āyatana	- resting-place - home, house, abode - a seat	处，住处，领域；座；……	处，入处……	ZJ
dhāna	- receptacle, case - a seat	包含，容纳；容器，住处；座位		ZJ
dhāsi	- dwelling-place, home - a seat	住所，家		ZJ
dhiṣaṇa	- dwelling-place, abode - a seat	寓所，座位		ZJ
dīrgha-pīṭha	- a long seat			ZJ
jāhaka	- a hedge-hog, … - a bed, a cot	刺猬		SJ
keli-śayana	- a pleasure-couch	卧床，安乐睡椅		SJ
khaṭvā	- a bedstead - a couch, a cot - a swing, hammock	床，睡椅，病床	床	SJ
khaṭvāṅga	- club shaped like the foot of a bedstead	状如床脚的棍棒	床足，交床	SJ

续表

梵文词语	英文释义	获原释义	古代汉译	类型
kṣaya	- an abode, dwelling-place, house - a seat	住的，居住的；住居，家，席		ZJ
kṣetratā	- place of residence - the state of being a seat or residence - a seat	居住的，住处		ZJ
laghu-khaṭvikā	- a small couch, easy chair			ZJ
mahā-śayana		高的卧床	大床	SJ
malli	- a seat			ZJ
mañca[54]	- bedstead, bed - a couch, sofa - a raised seat, dais, - a platform resting on columns - a seat of honour or state, throne	（圆柱上的）舞台，（宫殿上的）平台，看台；高坛，王座；卧床；台座	床，床座，卧床，座，座子，床褥卧具	SJ
mañcaka	- a stage or platform - a couch, bed	同上	床座	SZ
mañca-pīṭha[55]		坛上的座席	床，床座，绳床	ZJ
mañcikā	- a chair	椅子		SZ
mandurā	- a mattress, sleeping-mat - a bed			SJ
nibandhana	- a seat - receptacle	捆绑……	连缚，执著	ZJ
nikhaṭvā	- a kind of chair or couch			ZJ
niṣadyā	- a small bed or couch	市场	坐，同居	SZ
niṣaṇṇaka	- sitting, seated - a seat		安坐，安住	ZJ
ni-ṣīdana（佛教术语）	- act of sitting - rug for sitting on, - seat (specially rug or mat for sitting on)		坐，坐具，卧敷具，尼师坛，尼师但那	ZJ
padma-niṣaṇṇa[56]			坐莲座	ZJ
paly-aṅka	- a bed, couch - bedstead	床，睡椅		SJ

续表

梵文词语	英文释义	荻原释义	古代汉译	类型
pary-aṅka （亦作 paly-)	- a bed, couch, sofa - litter, palanquin, etc. - a particular mode of sitting on the ground (a squatting position assumed by ascetics and Buddhists in meditation)	卧铺，床铺；盘腿坐式	床，大床，座，高座，端座，结跏，跏趺坐，结跏趺坐[57]	SZ
pary-aṅkika		寝椅子，卧床		SJ
pary-astikā	- sitting upon the heels or hams - a bed	盘腿坐	两交搭于肩上，拊，肩上搭衣	SJ
paṭṭa	- a chair or stool	细长的布片，绷带	板，叶；绢，缯，……细氎；衣，衣服	ZJ
pecaka （同 paryaṅka-)	- an owl; - a couch, bed	枭，猫头鹰		SJ
pīṭha	- a stool, seat, chair, bench - a religious student's seat - royal seat, throne - case, pedestal	凳子，椅子，座席，（无褥垫的）长椅子；基础，底座；地区，地方，衙门	座，坐床，小床，交床，床座，坐具，榻席，辇舆	ZJ
pīṭhaka	- a seat (a stool, chair, bench, sofa, etc.) - the seat of a religious student made of Kuśa grass - the seat of a deity, an altar - a particular posture in sitting - a pedestal in general, basis	椅子，长椅子	［轿子的一种］，台[58]	ZJ
pīṭhika	- a seat, chair, bench, stool	长凳子，底座	机，机子，椅子，梯	ZJ
pralayana	- a place of repose - a bed			SJ
pra-stara[59]	- anything strewed forth or about - a couch of leaves and flowers - (esp.) a sacrificial seat - a couch of any material - a flat surface, flat top, level, a plain	麦秆床，草或叶床，铺稻草的；……的卧床；……平面，高台，平野，高原……	放，石，平	SJ
pra-stāra	- a couch or bed in general			SJ

续表

梵文词语	英文释义	获原释义	古代汉译	类型
pra-staraṇa[60]	- bed, couch - seat	卧床，坐席		SZ
stariman	- “that which is spread”, a bed, couch			SJ
prastāra	- strewing, spreading out, extension - a layer - a flat surface, plain - a litter, bed of straw, couch	散落，流布；丰富；铺稻草，麦秆床；卧床		SJ
praty-āstaraṇa		覆盖，床单，铺盖物	草垫，坐垫，坐具	SZ
sadas[61]	- residence, abode, dwelling - place of meeting, assembly - a seat	座位，地点，住处，住宅；小屋		ZJ
sadana	- dwelling, residence, house, home - a seat			ZJ
sadman	- abode, dwelling, house, place (especially of sacrifice), temple - a seat	就坐者，陪席者，旁观者；座位，场所，住处，寓所；庙堂；家；小屋；寺院；台，桌子	宫	ZJ
saṃ-niveśa[62]	- position, situation - a seat	进入，就坐，……位置，住处，集合	住，居，众生，安立，安住，居处……	ZJ
sam-upaveśa	- a seat	座位		ZJ
sam-upaveśana	- a seat	座位		ZJ
saṃ-śrita[63]			趣，座，依止，依处；侍者，仆人	ZJ
saṃ-stara	- spreading, extension, propagation (of laws or customs) - a covering, cover - scattering, strewing - a scattered mass (of flowers etc.) - a layer (of grass or leaves) - bed, couch	（草或叶的）层，床	座，敷，蓐，铺，布，散，坐具，敷具，卧具，坐卧具; tṛṇa ~ 草座，铺草，草铺地，草布地	SZ

续表

梵文词语	英文释义	荻原释义	古代汉译	类型
saṃstara/saṃstāra	- a layer (of grass or leaves) - a bed of leaves - bed, couch			SZ
saṃ-veśa[64]	- approaching near to, entrance - lying down, sleeping - dreaming, a dream - a bedchamber - a chair, seat, stool	接近，进入；躺下，卧，睡眠；卧室		ZS
saṃ-veśana	- a seat, bench	使躺下，横卧，睡眠，同居		ZS
stariman	- "that which is spread", a bed, couch			SJ
sthāman	- station, seat, place			ZJ
śaya[65]	- a bed, couch	卧床		SJ
śayana	- lying down, resting, sleeping - the act of lying down or sleeping, rest, repose, sleep, - a bed, couch, sleeping-place - copulation, sexual intercourse	休眠的，睡着的；寝具，床铺，横卧，睡眠，休息	卧,卧具,床卧具,床;床，床榻，茵蓐	SJ
śayanāsana	- sleeping or resting place, a dwelling, cell	睡觉（就寝）或就座；住处，庵	卧具，床卧，床卧具，床褥	S+Z
śayanāsan-gata			安处卧具	SJ
śayanāsan-vastu			卧具分，卧具相分	SJ
śayanāsan-vārika			管卧具者	SJ
śayanīya/ śayanīyaka	- to be slept or lain on, fit or suitable for sleep or rest - a bed, couch	适合躺在或睡在上面的；可躺着休息或睡觉的；床，卧铺		SJ
śayyā	- lying, reposing, sleeping - a bed, couch, sofa	卧铺，床（普通之义）；躺下，休息，睡觉	卧；卧具；铺，卧处	SJ
śayyāsana		卧床与座席[66]	卧具，床卧	S+Z
śira	- a bed, couch			SJ

续表

梵文词语	英文释义	获原释义	古代汉译	类型
talpa[67]	- a couch, bed, sofa, - the seat of a carriage - an upper story, room on the top of a house, turret	卧具，床；马车的座位；塔楼		BA
talpa-viddha[68]			穿孔床	SJ
talpya		属于床的；从夫妻床上产生的		SJ
upa-talpa	- an upper story, a room on the top of a house - a kind of wooden seat or stool			ZJ
upāsana	- a seat	随侍，尊敬，归依，……座席	承事，近事	ZJ
upaveśana	- a seat	就座，坐下，入席；座位		ZJ
vedi	- a stand, basis, pedestal - a bench	坛，台，长凳子		ZJ
vedikā	- a seat, bench	坛，长凳子	栏楯，轩槛，轩陛，栏杆，边框，台	ZJ
vi-stara	- spreading, extension, expansion, prolixity, diffuseness - a layer - a bed, couch			SJ
viṣṭara[69]	- anything spread out, a handful of rushes or grass for sitting on - any seat or couch, chair, stool etc.	当作座位的一把稻草，禾捆；座位		ZJ

附注

1. 据《现代汉语词典》(第6版)，“家具”指“家庭用具，主要指床、柜、桌、椅等”(页621)，“坐具”指“供人坐的用具，如椅子、凳子等”(页1747)。但在中国古代，“坐具”固然是供人坐的用具，但最初主要是中式的席、荐之类，甚至可以包括扶几；椅子、凳子之类的家具是后来才从异域传入的。中、西“坐具”经历过一段长时间的共存期后，西式的坐具才“一统天下”。因此，在本文中，“坐具”泛指所有供人坐的用具，再另外用ZJ来指称古代的椅凳类家具，它们只是当时“坐具”中特别的一类。

2. 两部辞书指称供人坐的用具时用的分别是“坐［卧］具”和“坐具”。不知编者是否意识到上面提到的“坐具”这个词古今的词义差别，也不知道他们的“坐具”是泛指的，还是专指ZJ的。这里写作ZJ是“按道理”来处理的，下同。

3.《辞海》爿部“牀”条的义项（1）“卧具也；古坐具亦曰床。诗小雅斯干：‘载寝之床’，此谓卧具。《商君书》：‘人君处匡床之上而天下治。’此谓坐具。”（合订本，上海：中华书局，1948；巳集页109，总页865）认为《商君书》“人君处匡床之上”的“床”指坐具，不知何据。

4. 我们利用“中研院”的“上古汉语标记语料库”（西汉及之前，不收词典字典）和“中国哲学书电子化计划”（先秦两汉部分，兼收词典字典）为检索工具，对其中收录的先秦两汉所有文献（不包括佛教文献）中的“床（牀）”做了逐一检视。结果是：“上古汉语标记语料库”中，写作“牀”的2条，写作“床”的5条；“中国哲学书电子计划”中，写作“牀”的13条，写作“床”的218条，都没有发现可以确定其所指为坐具的“床”的用例。

5. 藤田丰八（1922）对古代中国人的坐式有深入的讨论。李济（1953）认为远古人以蹲踞和箕踞为主。跪坐是商人统治者的坐姿，后被商化的周人继承下来，成为“正坐”。

6. 按，“卩”像人跽跪之形。

7. 当然，我们也不能回避作为“一床说”来源的《释名》和《说文解字》对“床”的训释。首先，不得不承认的是，今天我们看到的《释名》和《说文解字》都是太田辰夫所谓的“后时材料”。在宋代采用雕版印刷术来复制或“出版”文献之前，文献典籍的流传靠的是手抄。这些数量很少的手抄本不仅会有字句的讹误，有些还会出现残损。宋代以降，对传世的手抄本进行了文献学的抢救性整理，但大部分已经无法完全恢复其原貌。今本《说文解字》是北宋徐铉的校订本，而对《释名》的整理刊刻更晚至明代。因此，对于这一类古代字书的记载，我们不能忽视，但也不可全信，需要当时具体文献用例的验证。《汉语大字典》的具体文献用例，古代部分只有三条。第一条《诗·小雅·斯干》：“乃生男子，载寝之床。”时代为先秦，其中的“床”指SJ，当无疑问；第二条《水经注·湘水》：“［井］傍有一脚石床，才容一人坐……相承云，［贾］谊宿所坐床。”时代为北魏，其中的“床”指ZJ，也基本可信。然而，读者不会不注意到，作为“床”指称坐具的最早书证，郦道元（466或472—527）的《水经注》在时间上与东汉的《释名》和《说文》有两百到三百年的差距。虽然古代字书释义与实际文献用例在时代上不相匹配的情形并不少见，但毕竟这是不能视而不见的瑕疵。更何况，今本《说文》“安身之坐”的定义本身就非无懈可击。不论“床”在许慎的时代是不是既指称SJ又指称ZJ，《说文》仅仅提到ZJ，而绝口不提SJ，本身就非常不合理。段玉裁或许意识到这一点，在他的《说文解字注》里，根据异文，断定《说文》原文应是“安身之几坐”，辩称“床之制略同几而庳于几，可坐，故曰‘安身之几坐’”。可惜的是，段氏不但没有为许慎不提SJ用法的“硬伤”找到理由，还要将指称席地而坐的人用来凭扶的家具“几”拉进来，似乎有“越描越黑”之嫌。

8. 前人对“胡床”及相关问题有许多研究。藤田丰八1922年发表的《胡床考》和1924年写的《胡床考补遗》，是近代“胡床”研究的奠基之作。有关“胡床”的形制，这里补充一条材料。失译（《开元释教录》附秦录）《毘尼母经》卷8：“一人相应法者，胡床唯得一人坐，故名一人相应法也。二人相应法者，绳床唯受二人，是名二人相应法。三人相应法者，大床唯容三人，是名三人相应法。四人相应法者，若极大床得安四人，是名四人相应法。”（CBETA, T24, no. 1463, p. 845, a3-7）其中的“床”均为寺院中供僧侣坐的坐具。从“胡床”只能坐一个人的描写看，其与“独坐床”（详下）在用法上相似，是单人座，与绳床有别。

9. 藤田丰八《胡床考》对“胡床”的文献用例搜罗甚夥。其中有三个用例被其目为“三国时代”，时间最早，“入晋则证据稍多”。这三个用例包括《汉语大词典》用的《曹瞒传》，此外还有两例，一是《后汉书·五行志》“灵帝好胡服、胡帐、胡床、胡坐、胡饮、胡箜篌、胡笛、胡舞，京都贵戚皆竞为之，此服妖也”。《后汉书》的作者是南朝人范晔，不能目为三国时的文献；一是《太平御览》卷706“胡床”条下引东汉人应劭《风俗通》：“灵帝好胡床，董卓权胡兵之应也。”藤田云：“今传《风俗通》本已残缺，《隋书·经籍志》谓三十一卷，现仅存十卷，且此十卷似亦不完整，故今本《风俗通》未见其文，而原本或确有此条。可见东汉灵帝（168—189）时，胡床已用于宫掖，而京城贵戚皆竞相效颦。应劭与灵帝为同代人，故当可确信。”所谓“或确有此条”表明藤田并不敢把话说死，因为在传世的其他汉魏文献里，均没有看到这个词语。又，在汉译佛经里，“胡床”一语罕见，只有两个很晚的用例，值得玩味。或许这是一个带有歧视意义的说法，被蔑称为“胡僧”或“胡人”的弘法高僧有意避之？

10.《汉语大词典》：“即黄瓜。北魏贾思勰《齐民要术·种瓜》：‘种越瓜胡瓜法：四月中种之。胡瓜宜竖柴木，令引蔓缘之。’明李时珍《本草纲目·菜三·胡瓜》：‘张骞使西域得种，故名胡瓜。按杜宝《拾遗录》云：隋大业四年避讳，改胡瓜为黄瓜。’”

11.《汉语大词典》：“古时豌豆亦别称‘胡豆’。明李时珍《本草纲目·谷三·豌豆》：‘胡豆，豌豆也。’又《蚕豆》：‘此豆种亦自西胡来，虽与豌豆同名，同时种，而形性迥别。’《太平御览》云：张骞使外国，得胡豆种归。指此也。今蜀人呼此为胡豆，而豌豆不复名胡豆矣。”

12.《汉语大词典》：“草名。《尔雅·释草》‘菤耳、苓耳’晋郭璞注：‘《广雅》云：枲耳也。亦云胡枲……形似鼠耳，丛生如盘。’”

13.《汉语大词典》：“亦作‘胡荾’‘胡葰’。即芫荽，俗称‘香菜’。唐玄应《一切经音义》卷十五：‘胡荾，又作葰、荽，三形同私佳反。’《韵略》云：‘胡荾，香菜也。’晋陆翙《邺中记》：‘石勒讳胡，胡物皆改名，名胡饼曰麻饼，胡荽曰香荽。’《齐民要术·种蒜》引晋张华《博物志》：‘张骞使西域，得大蒜胡荽。’”

14.《汉语大词典》：“胡杨的别名。《汉书·西域传上·鄯善国》：‘国出玉，多葭苇、柽柳、胡桐、白草。’颜师古注：‘胡桐亦似桐，不类桑也。虫食其树而沫出下流者，俗名为胡桐泪，言似眼泪也。可以汗金银也，今工匠皆用之。流俗语讹呼泪为律。'”按，中国“桐”属的植物有“梧桐”“泡桐”，等等，不知颜氏所谓“似桐”为何物。或者《汉书》之“胡桐”为“胡杨”之误。

15.《汉语大词典》：“又称核桃。晋张华《博物志》卷六：‘张骞使西域还，乃得胡桃种。’宋孙奕《履斋示儿编·杂记·因物得名》：‘胡人常食核桃而名胡桃。’”

16.《汉语大词典》：“即芝麻。相传汉张骞得其种于西域，故名。《神农本草经》卷一：‘胡麻，一名巨胜。’晋葛洪《抱朴子·仙药》：‘巨胜一名胡麻，饵服之不老，耐风湿补衰老也。’”

17.《汉语大词典》：“原产热带亚洲，我国南方有栽培。果实可做香辛调味品（胡椒粉），亦可入药。唐段成式《酉阳杂俎·木篇》：‘胡椒。出摩伽陁国，呼为昧履支。’明李时珍《本草纲目·果四·胡椒》：‘胡椒，今南番诸国及交趾、滇南、海南诸地皆有之。’”

18.《汉语大词典》：“大蒜。《东观汉记·李恂传》：‘为兖州刺史，所种小麦、胡蒜，悉付从事，一无所留。’《齐民要术·种蒜》引晋郭义恭《广志》：‘蒜，有胡蒜，小蒜。’……明李时珍《本草纲目·菜一·蒜》：‘胡国有蒜，十子一株，名曰胡蒜，俗谓之大蒜是矣。’”

19.《汉语大词典》：“即钩吻。又名野葛、断肠草。根茎叶有剧毒，误食每致命，然可作杀虫药剂。唐刘恂《岭表录异》卷中：‘野葛，毒草也，俗呼胡蔓草。误食之，则用羊血浆解之。’宋沈括《梦溪补笔谈·药议》：‘[钩吻]闽人呼为吻莽，亦谓之野葛。岭南人谓之胡蔓。俗谓断肠草。此草人间至毒之物，不入药用。’”

20.《汉语大词典》：“一、二年生草本植物。茎直立，羽状复叶，开白色小花，果实长圆形。根圆锥或圆柱形，肉质，有紫红、橘红、黄色等多种，是营养丰富的蔬菜。明李时珍《本草纲目·菜一·胡萝卜》：‘元时始自胡地来，气味微似萝卜，故名。’”

21.《汉语大词典》：“胡人的吹乐器。唐吴兢《乐府古题要解》卷上：‘又有胡角者，本以应胡笳之声，后渐用之，有双角，即胡乐也。’唐李贺《塞下曲》：‘胡角引北风，蓟门白于水。’宋王灼《碧鸡漫志》卷一：‘汉代胡角《摩诃兜勒》一曲，张骞得自西域。’”

22.《汉语大词典》：“古乐器名。古代泛称来自北方和西北各族的拨弦乐器，有时指琵琶，有时指忽雷等。约宋元开始，亦为拉弦乐器之称。唐段安节《乐府杂录·琵琶》：‘文宗朝，有内人郑中丞善胡琴，内库有二琵琶，号大小忽雷，郑尝弹小忽雷。’”

23.《汉语大词典》：“即羌笛。五孔。《后汉书·五行志一》：‘灵帝好……胡笛、胡舞，京都贵戚皆竞为之。’”

24.《汉语大词典》：“古代北方民族的乐器。用手拍击。《旧唐书·音乐志二》：‘腰鼓，大者瓦，小者木，皆广首而纤腹，本胡鼓也。’”

25.《汉语大词典》：“我国古代北方民族的管乐器，传说由汉张骞从西域传入，汉魏鼓吹乐中常用之。汉蔡琰《悲愤诗》之二：‘胡笳动兮边马鸣，孤雁归兮声嘤嘤。’”

26.《汉语大词典》：“刃旁有曲支的戈戟。《周礼·夏官·序官》‘司戈盾’唐贾公彦疏：‘汉时见戈有旁出者为句孑，亦名胡孑。’”

27.《汉语大词典》：“胡地产制的瓶。唐王昌龄《从军行》之六：‘胡瓶落膊紫薄汗，碎叶城西秋月团。’……《新唐书·李大亮传》：‘太宗报书曰：“有臣如此，朕何忧！古人以一言之重订千金，今赐胡瓶一，虽亡千镒，乃朕所自御。”’”

28.《汉语大词典》：“藏矢的器具。《玉篇·竹部》：‘簶，胡簶，箭室。’……《史记·魏公子列传》‘平原君负韊矢’唐司马贞索隐：‘韊音兰，谓以盛矢，如今之胡簏而短也。’”

29.《汉语大词典》：“唐代妇女骑马外出时所着不障面之帽。《旧唐书·舆服志》：‘开元初，从驾宫人骑马者，皆着胡帽，靓妆露面，无复障蔽。士庶之家，又相仿效，帷帽之制，绝不行用。’”

30.《汉语大词典》：“指古代西方和北方各族的服装。后亦泛称外族的服装。《后汉书·五行志一》：‘灵帝好胡服、胡帐、胡床、胡坐、胡饭、胡空侯、胡笛、胡舞，京都贵族皆竞为之。’”

31.《汉语大词典》：“犹今之烧饼。《释名·释饮食》：‘胡饼，作之大漫冱也，亦言以胡麻着上也。’晋陆翙《邺中记》：‘石勒讳胡，胡物皆改名，名胡饼曰麻饼。’”

32.《汉语大词典》：“方言。土坯。胡国瑞《跃进歌声飘过河》：‘打着胡基唱山歌，跃进歌声飘过河。’”按，今甘肃河西走廊武威一带方言称成形的土块为“土基”或“胡基”。颇疑“基”为记音字。“胡基”或指用木质模具制成的泥砖。

33.《汉语大词典》：“铅粉。用于傅面或绘画。《释名·释首饰》：‘胡粉：胡，餬也，脂合以涂面也。’《后汉书·李固传》：‘固独胡粉饰貌，搔首弄姿。’晋张华《博物志》卷四：‘胡粉、白石灰等，以水和之，涂鬓须不白。’晋葛洪《抱朴子·论仙》：‘愚人乃不信黄丹及胡粉乃化铅所作。’”

34.《汉语大词典》：“盘腿而坐。《后汉书·五行志一》：‘灵帝好胡服、胡帐、胡床、胡坐。’郭沫若《李白与杜甫·李白与杜甫在诗歌上的交往》：‘古人席地而坐，坐取跪的形式。打盘脚坐叫“胡坐”，是外来的坐法。’”

35.《汉语大词典》：“古代僧人跪坐致敬的礼节，右膝着地，竖左膝危坐，倦则两膝姿势互换。又称互跪。南朝梁慧皎《高僧传·神异上·耆域》：‘以晋惠之末至于洛阳，诸道人悉为作礼，域胡跪，晏然不动容色。’”

36.《汉语大词典》：“胡人拜坐之法，右膝跪地，竖左膝危坐。《宣和遗事》后集：‘亦有巫者，彩服画冠，振铃击鼓，于前罗列，血流布地，请为首者，皆跪膝胡拜，言尤不可辨。’”

37. 本文有关植物分类的知识，源自中国科学院植物研究所系统与进化植物学国家重点实验室专业网站“植物智”（http://www.iplant.cn/）的资料。

38. 明李时珍《本草纲目·菜一·胡萝卜》云：“气味微似萝卜，故名。”恐非。

39. 梐指木条。可能这种床的床板是木条状的，粗和细代表木条的强度，因此能够承受的重量也不一样。有的版本梐作陛，恐非。

40. 荻原云来（1970）收汉译词“独坐”，其平行的梵文是 ekākin，亦译为“独”“独一身”“单”“单一”，等等（页296）。由于译经里有“坐床”一词（见后），“独坐床”的内部结构很可能是“独+坐床”。

41. 这部经的出经时代和译者学术界有不同的意见。参看辛嶋静志《〈撰集百缘经〉的译出年代考证》，载浙江大学汉语史研究中心编《汉语史学报》第六辑，上海教育出版社；陈秀兰《梵汉对勘〈撰集百缘经〉表示复数的第一、二人称代词——兼论汉译本〈撰集百缘经〉的翻译年代》，见《圆融内外，综贯梵唐——第五届汉文佛典语言国际学术研讨会论文集》，台湾：花木兰文化出版社，2010年。Nattier（2008）对这部经的时代和译者也有讨论。又，据对这部经的语言做过长时间系统研究，并做了完整的梵汉对勘的陈秀兰教授告，这里的“小床”，平行梵文是复合词 nīcatara-āsana。其中 nīcatara 的英文释义是 lower（矮小的），āsana 就是坐具，板凳。关于这个词的解释和使用，详后。

42. 在东汉支曜译《成具光明定意经》中还有一个“床座”，但是不是指ZJ，难以断定。居士善明要请二千比丘来家饭食，但是担心没有那么大的地方。“于是，力办众有明士及诸天神王答言：‘莫忧。’因各左右顾视，屋室自然长广高大，像天之殿。于屋下，便有千亿万座，皆是众宝变地之形，绀瑠璃色。室中床座，亦复如是。如弹指顷，即有百千亿万人饭具，而皆足毕。”（CBETA, T15, no. 630, p. 452, b2-10）

43.《八正道经》（T112），《七处三观经》（T150A），《修行本起经》（T184），《中本起经》（T196），《道行般若经》（T224），《阿閦佛国经》（T313），《法镜经》（T322），《般舟三昧经》（T418），《文殊师利问菩萨署经》（T458），《道地经》（T607），《伅真陀罗所问经》（T624），《阿阇王经》（T626）《成具光明定意经》（T630），《阿弥陀三耶三佛萨楼檀过度人道经》（T362）《诸菩萨求佛本业经》（T282）。参看朱庆之《“R为A所见V”式被动句式的最早使用年代》附录《东汉译经速查表》和《三国译经速查表》，载吴福祥、洪波编《梅祖麟教授八秩寿庆学术论文集》，首都师范大学出版社，2015年。

44. 这项工作得到了李博寒和吴泽瑶二位的协助，特此致谢。其中的梵文，主要是非佛教典籍的语言，不包括佛教梵文。之间的区别，可参看维基百科的 Buddhist Hybrid Sanskrit 条目的相关内容（https://en.wikipedia.org/wiki/Buddhist_Hybrid_Sanskrit）。

45. 荻原云来（1970）原文如此。“蹦”“加”都是音译词，用字或有不同。“蹦”是受到后边的“趺”的类化才出现的新字形。

46. 暨远志有《金狮床考——敦煌壁画家具研究之二》一文，载《考古与文物》2004年第3期，可参看。

47. 支谦是月支移民的后代，汉语或是第一语言。李博寒博士在给初稿的修改意见中说：“支谦作为生长在中国的移民后代，将坐具译为‘床’，是不是更好地反映了中国本土的认知中没有与 āsana 完全对应的形式，所以支谦用‘床’也用‘座’。”所言极是。

48. 这个统计是陈秀兰教授提供的。

49. 湖北荆门包山楚墓出土有战国时期带围子的大床，原物今藏湖北省博物馆（https://kknews.cc/zh-hk/culture/k2e45gr.html）。

50. 这个词的词根是 √ās，坐。

51. 荻原云来（1970）收录两个复合词，梵文工具书未收：(1) āsana-prajñapta（āsana 座具 + prajñapta 安排），汉译“敷置（高）座，敷座”，动宾关系；(2) āsanopaviṣṭa（āsana 座 +upaviṣṭa 坐），汉译“坐座，处座”，动宾关系。

52. 词根是 √śī，意思是 sleeping, to lie down to sleep, fall asleep, sleep（睡觉，躺下睡觉，进入梦乡）。

53. 这个词与 staraṇa 同义，词根可能也是 √stṛ，铺开，展开。

54. 这个词在词典和汉译中都有 SJ 和 ZJ 两种意思，但这个词的词根可能是 √mand，即睡觉（to sleep）。与这个词有关的两个复合词，mañcakagata，意思是 gone to bed（上床，睡觉）；mañcakāśraya，字面意思是 bed-infesting（床铺感染），a bed-bug（床虱、臭虫），house-bug，还保留了其早期的意义。

55. 词典无。

56. 即“莲花座”，汉译为“坐莲座”，似读为动词。梵文工具书未见录。

57. 梵文 nyaṣīdat-paryaṅkam ābhujya, 或者 paryaṅkam ābhujyopaviśati。

58. 此处荻原原文有夺文，不可读。

59. Apte 的解释是：1. a couch of leaves and flowers. 2. a couch or bed in general; …。stara 的词根是 √stṛ，铺开，展开。按，人躺在床上做四肢展开状，故可指称睡觉的床。参看 stariman。

60. staraṇa 的意思是 the act of spreading or strewing，与 āstaraṇa 同义。同源的 stariman 的字面意思是 that which is spread，实际指床（bed）或者长沙发或可睡人的长凳（couch）。

61. 词根是 √sad，坐（sit down）。

62. 词根是 √viś，有坐（to sit down upon）之义。

63. 词干 śrita，Apte 列有 clung to, resting or sitting on 的意义。

64. veśa 的词根同上。Apte 的释义是 to sit or settle down upon。

65. 词根是 √śī，有 sleep 的意思。

66. 荻原云来（1970）将这个合成词的内部结构解释为并列关系。

67. 这个词有 SJ 和 ZJ 两种意思，但其最早的意义似应是 SJ。荻原云来（1970）收录的与该词同源的几个词可证。如 tālpa，嫡出的。字面的意思是“在洞房床上出生的”；talpa-sadya，在睡椅上休息；talpya，属于床的；从夫妻床上产生的。

68. 这个词梵文工具书未见，汉译“穿孔床”形制不详。talpa 是床，viddha 的英文意思是 pierced, penetrated; wounded, stabbed，即“穿孔”之义。

69. 词根是 √stṛ，与 vi-ṣṭara 相同。

参考文献

陈　振　2000 《再谈中古汉人从跪坐到垂脚高坐的演变》，《北大史学》第 7 期，北京：北京大学出版社。

荻原云来　1970 《汉译对照梵和大辞典》，京都：讲谈社。

高建华、刘文金　2007 《中国古代“坐”姿与坐具形式的演变》，《家具与室内装饰》第 3 期。

李　济　1953 《跪坐、蹲居与箕踞——殷墟石刻研究之一》，原载《历史语言研究所集刊》第二十四本，收入傅杰编《二十世纪中国文史考据文录（上册）》，昆明：云南人民出版社（2001 年版）。

林光明、林怡馨编译　2004 《梵汉大词典》，台北：嘉丰出版社。

藤田丰八　1922 《胡床考》，《东洋学报》第十二卷第四号。最新的汉译文《胡床考——附〈胡床考〉补遗》，《文物春秋》2020 年第 2 期，为王策、程利根据氏著、池内宏编《东西交涉史研究——西域篇及附篇》（东京星文馆，1943 年）的日文本翻译的。

辛嶋静志　2010 《道行般若经词典》，The International Research Institute for Advanced Buddhology, Soka University, Tokyo.

辛嶋静志　2011 《道行般若经校注》，The International Research Institute for Advanced Buddhology, Soka University, Tokyo.

朱大渭　1994 《中古汉人由跪到垂脚高坐》，《中国史研究》第 4 期。

朱庆之、梅维恒编　2004 《荻原云来汉译对照梵和大辞典汉译词索引》，成都：巴蜀书社。

Monier, W. 1899. *A Sanskrit-English dictionary*, revised by Leumann, E., Cappeller, C. et al. Oxford: Clarendon Press.

Nattier, J. 2008. *A guide to the earliest Chinese Buddhist translations: Texts from the eastern Han and Three Kingdoms Periods*, Bibliotheca Philologica et Philosophica, Tokyo: Soka University.

Study Group on Buddhist Sanskrit Literature. 2004. *Vimalakīrtinirdeśa: Transliterated sanskrit text collated with Tibetan and Chinese translations*, SGBSL, The Institute for Comprehensive Studies of Buddhism, Tokyo: Taisho University.

Vaidya, L. (Ed.). 1960. *Saddharmapuṇḍarīka*, Darbhanga: The Mithila Institute.

语料来源

网络版 *Sanskrit Dictionary*（梵文词典）（https://sanskritdictionary.com/）

“中研院”上古汉语标记语料库（http://lingcorpus.iis.sinica.edu. tw/ancient/）

中国哲学书电子化计划（https://ctext.org/zh）

汉译佛经梵汉对比分析语料库（http://ckc.eduhk.hk:8080/）

作者单位：香港教育大学中国语言学系 / 中国语言及中文教育研究中心

作者邮箱：qingzhi@eduhk.hk

Why the word *chuang* (床) for sleeping was able to refer to the furniture for sitting in the Middle Chinese: On the role of the Chinese translation of Indian Buddhist scriptures

Qingzhi Zhu

Abstract: In ancient Chinese, *chuang* (床) is the name of furniture used for sleeping, which is the same as today' s usage, but in the Middle Ages, *chuang* (床) can also refer to a certain kind of seat. This article discusses why there is such a change and what caused this change. Our preliminary conclusion is that the foreign monks who translated Buddhist scriptures in the Eastern Han Dynasty first used *chuang* (床) to translate the words referring to sitting utensils in the Buddhist scriptures, and this usage affected the Chinese at that time along with the spread of Buddhist scriptures.

Keywords: Bed (Furniture for sleeping, SJ), Seat, Furniture in the seat (ZJ), Buddhist scripture translation, Sanskrit

Author work unit: Department of Chinese Language Studies/Centre for Research on Chinese Language and Education, The Education University of Hong Kong

Author email: qingzhi@eduhk.hk

“们”的分布限制问题研究 *

林若望 汤志真 张永利 舒志翔 廖伟闻

摘要：本文在前人的研究基础上，进一步分析出现在名词后的“们”的句法分布和语义解释问题。本文提出“们”是个句法上的虚范畴中心语，是一个非强制性的复数个体标记，词类上选择 DP 名词短语为其补语，但语义上该 DP 必须是类别 <e> 或是可透过选择函数机制形成个体的广义量词名词短语（类别 <<e,t>, t>），因而排除“们”与语义类别为 <e,t> 的 NP 名词短语或是数量名词短语 NumP 共现。同时本文也解释为何有些泛指句允许“们”的出现，有些又不允许，以及“们”和无定量化词的共现为何会有接受度的差异和主宾语不对称现象。

关键词：们，句法分布，语义解释，现代汉语

1. 引言

有关“们”的语法性质及分析，有些人把“们”视为复数标记，有些人将它视为集合或不定数之群体标记，也有些人认为“们”除了复数义，还表达了有定义，各家看法不同，目前的文献尚未达成共识。本文的目的是在前人的研究基础上，进一步探索分析出现在名词后的“们”的句法分布限制问题，我们认为前人的文献有些观察尚不够精确，也无法真正地全面解释“们”的分布限制，因此，本文提出另一个新的尝试，主张将“们”分析成句法上的虚范畴中心语，并且词类选择完整名词短语 DP 为其补语且该 DP 在语义上必须是个体，因而排除“们”与 NP 名词短语或是数量名词短语 NumP 共现。

---

* 本文部分内容曾于 2017 年在香港中文大学 The International Symposium on Chinese in the Maritime Silk Road 研讨会，2018 年台湾中山大学 The 12th Workshop on Formal Syntax and Semantics 研讨会以及 2019 年北京大学语言研究中心博雅讲座上发表，我们感谢研讨会及讲座听众所提出的问题和建议。另外两位匿名审查人也提供了非常有价值的评论，更加完善了本文，我们在此致谢。最后，本研究是在林若望的台湾“科技部”计划（编号 MOST 106-2410-H-001-043）资助下完成的，我们感谢这项计划的资助。

本文组织如下。第 2 节回顾文献中有关“们”的基本认识、语法性质和主张。第 3 节探索“们”和数量词的不相容问题。第 4 节评论前人分析的潜在缺点。第 5 节简单介绍本文的提案及所主张的假设。第 6 节讨论在本文的假设下不可和“们”共现的名词短语及原因。第 7 节介绍和“们”共现的名词短语。第 8 节处理种类名词和“们”的共现问题。第 9 节说明关系从句和“们”的互动。第 10 节解释“N+ 们”的有定解读是怎么来的。第 11 节讨论“们”的主宾语不对称现象。最后一节是结语。

2. 文献回顾与“们”的基本认识

2.1 “们”的复数标记说

“们”通常用在指人名词、代名词或名词短语的后面，被认为有复数义的主要原因就是人称代词如“你”“我”“他”原本指称单数个体，但带上“们”后，如“你们”“我们”“他们”就变成指称复数个体；同样地，普通名词不带“们”，如“孩子”，单复数不定，但带上“们”后，“孩子们”仅能指两个或两个以上的复数的孩子（参看吕叔湘，1949），如下面的例句：

（1）a. 我们一起回家的。　　　　b. 孩子们都回家了。

根据这样的观察，有些学者如吕叔湘（1985），袁梅（1996），陶振民（1991，2000），张斌（1998），Li（1999），储泽祥（2000），李艳惠、石毓智（2000），梅艳（2003），陈小红（2005），Yang（2005），Ueda & Haraguchi（2008），伍雅清、胡明先（2013）等，认为“们”是个复数标记或是表复数义的语法成分。

但是有另外一些学者如胡裕树（1981），陈光磊（1987），袁梅（1996），储泽祥（2000），陈小红（2005）等指出“名词 + 们”不能再受表确切的数量结构修饰，因此，（2）这个例句是不能说的。这个语言事实又让人怀疑“们”是否真的是一个复数标记。

（2）*三个孩子们回家了。

虽然说“名词 + 们”不能被确数修饰，但却能被许多表不定数或是概数的词语修饰，比方说“一群”“所有”“很多”“一些”等，如下面的例句（参看邢福义，1965）：

（3）a. 为了回答一批青年同志们的要求……

b. 这几年来，有些朋友们，要我谈谈写作的经验……

c. 我们在这里向所有为和平、民主、民族独立和人类进步而真诚奋斗的文艺家们表示崇高的敬意。

d. 由于我们的杂志印数有限，好多关心语文问题的同志们对已经出版的各期还没有完全看到，或者没法补齐。

根据上述例句，邢福义提出跟“们”共现的表数词语都表示不确定的数量。戴耀晶（1987）也认为“们”是表示不确定的复数助词，储泽祥（2000）则提议“们”是不定数量的复数标记，杨炎华（2015）也持同样看法，认为“们”只能表示不定数的复数。

然而有的研究发现也不是所有的概数（不确定数）均可自由地和“们”并用。西原史晓（2009：58）对“们”与概数的共现频率多寡做了研究统计，得出下面（4）所示的规律。

（4）确数结构 < 数词连用型概数结构 < 使用概数词“多、来”的概数结构 < 使用不定数词“几”的概数结构 < 不使用量词的概数结构 < 使用集体量词的概数结构

（4）表示与“们”共现的难易程度，最左侧的确数结构完全不能与“们”共现，越是右侧的概数结构则越容易与“们”合用。

在储泽祥（2000）的基础上，张欢（2010：36—37）通过收集大量的语料也同样指出“们”与“不定数结构”的共现有强弱之分：

（5）不可共现的

A. 界指词语 → 两百字左右、五十岁上下

B. 两个数目接近的数词合用 → 两三个人、三五百个人

C. 数词 + 概数词 + 量词 + N → 二十来个人、三百多本书

可共现的

①这 / 那 + 不定量词 + N → 这 / 那些先生们

②这 / 那 + 不定数集合量词 + N → 这 / 那群 / 伙 / 帮孩子们

③这 / 那 + 不定数词 + 量词 + N → 这 / 那几个孩子们

④全量词 + N → 所有 / 全体 / 各位 / 诸位同学们

⑤不定数词 + N → 好些 / 多数 / 部分孩子们

⑥一 + 不定数集合量词 + N → 一群 / 伙 / 帮孩子们

⑦一 + 不定量词 + N → 一些朋友们

⑧不定数词 + 量词 + N → 几个孩子们

根据张欢的调查，“们”与“不定数结构”的共现程度由强到弱，可用下面的序列表示为：

（6）①/②/③ > ④ > ⑤ > ⑥ > ⑦ > ⑧ > A/B/C

加“们”………渐弱……………不加“们”

有关概数是否可以跟“们”共现的问题，不同的说话者，语感判断其实常有所不同，而且“们”出现的语境也是影响判断的一个很大的因素，比方说，下面例句是陈玉梅（2015：1）搜集到“几”、连用型数位和“们”共现的句子。

（7）a.《市场报》的几位前辈们共同寄予本报同人：超越自我，加倍努力，为办出一张可读、可信、可用、可亲的新型经济报纸做出更大的贡献。（1994 年《市场报》）

b. 还有七八个姑娘们齐声附和：“是呀，你今年的头水要抢了挑到哪里去呀？”（1994 年《人民日报》）

可见，概数是否可和“们”共现，是倾向性，不是绝对性。

此外，陈玉梅（2015：24—25）根据她所收集的语料，认为确数也可以和“们”共现，这一点和一般的认知不一样。她举了很多例子来支持确数可以和“们”共现，比如：

（8）a. 三个孩子们大哭大叫。哭一会，大孩子不哭了，到处翻找，在母亲枕头里找出了五斤白面。（严歌苓《第九个寡妇》）

b. 当年的十八位汉子们又重新坐在一起，讨论他们面临的新问题。（1994 年报刊精选）

c. 天坛这边，刘增身中数十箭，和其余的三个兄弟们倒地而亡，在他们的四周躺满了死伤的明军。（民国齐东野人《武宗逸史》）

d. 还有那七个抢犯，全都精武术，贺照雄也是练家子，师傅总得先跟那七个小辈们交一回子手，然后才能在四外放火，也得个工夫呢。[清张杰鑫《三侠剑（下）》]

以上这些例子虽然全带有确数，然而就语义解释而言，都是有定或是殊指解释而不是无定解释。这些例子也都隐含着数量短语所指称的个体就是语境里的所有相关个体，比方说（8a）隐含着“三个孩子”就是家里的那三个孩子，不隐含还有其他孩子的存在，（8b）隐含十八位汉子就是所有的汉子，（8c）也类似。从这个角度来看，（8a—c）中的例句其实都不是真正的无定用法。而（8d）的“那七个小辈们”更是不折不扣的有定名词短语。

2.2 “们”的集合说、群体说

除了把“们”看成复数的标记外，另外有些学者主张把“们”看成具有“群体”的语法意义，如胡裕树（1981，1985），宋玉柱（1982），张谊生（2001）等。陈光磊（1994）认为“们”表示非计量的论群称数法，是个体的集合，所以“学生们＝若干名或众多学生的集合”，这个集合不在于计算学生的数量，而在于指称学生的某一群。西方学者 Iljic（1994，1998，2001）也是主张“们”是个“集合”标记。

2.3 “们”的混合说

Chao（1968），Norman（1988）认为代词之后的“们”是复数标记，名词之后的“们”是集合标记。Cheung（2003）认为代词和专有名词之后的“们”是集合标记，Hsieh（2008）则认为代名词、专有名词和光杆名词之后的“们”是集合名词，被带有量化成分修饰的普通名词则是复数标记。黄伯荣、廖序东（1996）认为普通名词后的“们”是复数标记，代词或专有名词后的“们”是集合标记。杨炎华（2015）的看法类似，也是认为“们”应该分为两个，在普通名词或普通名词短语后面的“们”是复数标记，而且是个表概数或不确数的复数标记，在代词、专有名词或专有名词短语后面的“们”则是集合标记。

2.4 “们”的有定说

文献上有关“们”的另一个常见说法是“们”除了标记复数，也表达了有定性（参看 Iljic，1994；Yang，2005；Li，1999；童盛强，2002；Kurafuji，2004 等）。有定性的主要证据一方面来自于带“们”名词短语的语义解释，比方说下面例句（9）的“孩子们”只能指称你我都知道的孩子。

（9）我去找孩子们。（Li，1999：78）

另一方面，则是带“们”的名词短语不能充当谓语或是出现在某些句式里，如下面的例句（转引自童盛强，2002：275）：

（10）*他们是我的朋友们。

（11）*汉语系有很多留学生们。

（12）*去北京旅游的同学们很多。[1]

“们”是否真的标记有定性呢？所谓有定，表示的是说话者和听话者双方都熟悉的个体或对象。我们不否认（9）中的“孩子们”指称有定的对象，听说双方都知道孩子指的是哪些孩子，然而有许多“们”出现的语境是无定语境。名词短语的无定解释有两种情形：一种情形是殊指，说话者知道指称的对象，但听话者不知；另一种情形是未指或泛指，即名词短语所指称对象未必存在或没有特定指称。以下“们”的用例都是无定用法，例句全部取自网络：

（13）a. 让更多孩子们接受好的教育是我们的目标。

b. 孩子们通常信任他们的家长。

c. 在社会角落里，许多孩子们想要有安心长大的机会和未来的盼望，但环境使他们没有办法如此。

d. 在英国，大部分的孩子们在7岁的时候开始进入英国小学（prep school）进行小学课程的学习，小学一般为6年。

e. 我们去的时候，有几个孩子们正在做手工，都是些4岁左右的孩子，都挺认真。

f. 妈妈不是上陈董家打牌，就是和一些阔太太们逛街买舶来品。

g. 我自己从未在孩提时代受过什么苦，可是我却有机会碰到很多穷苦的孩子们。

h. 今年陆续接到一些孩子们的讯息，大家都纷纷表示以前练团超有趣的。

i. 在十五区吃过晚饭后，约四十来个孩子们再次回到了排练大厅。

例句（13a—d）中的“孩子”并不指称任何特定的孩子，所以不管说话者还是听话者都无法指出是哪些孩子，这些例句里的“孩子们”显然是无定的。同样地，（13e）中的“有几个孩子们”也不指称说话者和听话者都能辨认的特定对象，所以是无定的。（13g—j）中的“名词短语-们”则是殊指用法，是说话者首次把名词短语所指称的对象引入对话中，这些对象是说话者知道但听话者未必知道的指称对象，所以也是无定用法。上面的例句很清楚地显示“名词短语-们”未必是有定解释。

文献上有关“们”指称有定的对象的例句其实很多都是“光杆普通名词+们”，如例句（9）或是下面的句子：

（14）他还有三个弟弟（*们），他母亲给人家帮工当佣人，弟弟们就得由他照顾。

或是名词前有关系从句修饰的时候，也常得到有定的解释，如例句（15）：

（15）我们对于［今天特地远道赶来的］家长们，致上十二万分谢意。

这些“(关系从句)+名词+们”的有定用法，不管是说话者还是听话者都知道所指称的对象是哪些人，但一旦名词短语内部有其他概数修饰语，像是“很多”“一些”“大部分”等，无定解释就很容易产生，如（13）里的众多句子，或是带有像“通常”“很少”“偶尔”等量化副词的句子，带“们”的名词短语就未必是定指。

总而言之，带“们”的名词短语，其语义解释未必指称听说双方都能指认的有定对象，特别是有量化词修饰语时，语义解释通常是无定的，这一点和一些文献上有关“们”的认知很不一样。

2.5 “们”的语法性质

有关“们”的语法性质，各家说法不一，有人看成是词缀、语缀或词尾，有人看成是助词，我们在这节简略回顾不同的看法。前者有丁声树（1961），吕叔湘（1949，1985），朱德熙（1982），陶振民（1991），郭良夫（1983），袁梅（1996）等；后者有邢福义（1965），胡裕树（1981），戴耀晶（1987），张斌（2002）等。另外则有人持两分论，认为“们”具有词缀和助词两种性质。比方说，宋玉柱（1982）认为指人名词后面的“们”是助词，人称代词后面的“们”是词缀。张谊生、张爱民（1991）则是用“构形后缀”来表示指人名词后的“们”，用“构词后缀”来指代名词后面的“们”。孔凡涛（2004），郭华（2013）也有类似的看法。

把“们”看成是助词或构形语素而非词缀或词尾的一个重要因素是“们”可加在名词短语的后面，这一点，许多人都有类似的观察。邢福义（1998），陶振民（2000），张谊生（2001），张欢（2010）就指出，“们”可以和名词性短语包括联合短语、偏正短语以及同位短语等组合。杨炎华（2015）和陈玉梅（2015）也举出非常多的例子证明“们”可加在整个名词短语而不是名词上。以下是一些不同作者的例子：

（16）a. 一座繁华的都城突然消失得无影无踪，这样的事情不仅会引起［历史学家

和考古学家们］的浓厚兴趣，而且……（张谊生，2001：209）

b. 在［善男信女们］的眼里，这巨石是上苍神力使然。(= 在善男以及信女们眼里)（张谊生，2001：209）

c. 据［我伯父、父亲们］的说法……（张谊生，2001：209）

d.［没有结婚的小伙子和老光棍们］，付不起娶当地姑娘的彩礼，就去求四川来的妇女。（童盛强，2002：275）

上面的例子都很清楚地显示“们”是加在整个名词短语上，而不是加在名词上。比如（16b），比较合理的解释是“们”贴在“善男信女”上而不是在“信女”上，毕竟“善男”和“信女”是对等的。再以（16c）来说，父亲只有一个，根本不可能是复数，只有伯父，父亲两者相加才会是复数，所以“们”的辖域应该是“我伯父、父亲”而不是只有“父亲”。

另外，“们”加在名词短语上的证据中还有陈玉梅（2015：12—13）提供的下面的例句：

（17）a. 大厅上热闹非常，男的们彼此嘲笑，女的们挤眉弄眼地犯小心眼。（老舍《老张的哲学》）

b. 走了几步，又把盒子打开。回头看了看，拉车的们并没把眼看着他。（老舍《眼镜》）

上面两例，虽然是文学作品中的句子，口语较少见，但却是证明“们”是附加在整个名词短语上，而不是名词上的好证据。

此外，“们”也常和称呼语共现，如“各位先生、女士、记者、朋友们”中的“们”，其辖域显然不仅是“朋友”，而是也包含“先生、女士、记者”，此时的“们”应该是对整个名词短语“各位先生、女士、记者、朋友”起作用。

可见，或许代名词后的“们”是词缀，直接由词库产生，但名词后的“们”应该是短语的后附成分。有关这个结论，一位匿名审查人指出，“历史学家和考古学家们”就算是做“［历史学家］和［考古学家们］”的分析，照样可以得到许多历史学家和许多考古学家的解读，另外，他也认为“我伯父、父亲们”的例子很费解，因为爸爸只可能有一个，他并且认为（16）、（17）中的例子仅能证明“的”可以贴在短语上，且这个短语应该是 NP 而不是 DP，他还认为“三个学生”中 Num Cl 后边是一个 NP，因为 N 可加上修饰语如“三个［$_{NP}$［学习很用功的］学生］”，所以（17）也仅能证明“的”加在NP后面。

为了解释审查人的上述疑问，首先，考虑下面互联网上的例句：

（18）宴会之上，娜迦女皇带着安吉公主一一接受了水岛之上各族族长的敬礼和祝福，然后是百官以及三军统帅们的祝贺。

我们知道三军统帅只有一个，就如同“父亲”只有一个一样，所以（18）中的“们”不可能是加在“三军统帅”上，而是加在整个对等结构“百官以及三军统帅”上。所以“们”的辖域可及于整个名词对等结构并无问题。

至于“们”是否只加在Num Cl之下的NP上，而不是整个名词短语上，一个有趣的语言事实可以证明，互联网上有大量的“每一个N”加“们”的例子，如下面的例句：

（19）a. 希望每次的消防队参观都能让每个孩子们有满满的收获。

b. 每一个孩子们的学习能力也都很棒。

c. 祝福芦苇的每一位老师们……教师节快乐!!

这些例子显示“们”的辖域是整个名词短语，“每一个孩子”在语义上是复数的，所以可和“们”共现，不这样分析的话，“们”会和数词“一”有所冲突。

最后一点是，如果“们”是贴在数量词下的NP上，而不是数量词之上的整个名词短语上，那么有定数量名词短语可接“们”，而无定数量名词短语不可，这个语言事实将很难说明，下文会详述这个问题。

3. 数量词和“们”的不相容问题

和“们”相关的一个最重要问题是“们”和精确数量结构的不相容现象，这个现象，邢福义（1960），赵元任（1980），胡裕树（1981），程观林（1985），陈光磊（1987），Li（1999），袁梅（1996），储泽祥（2000），陈小红（2005），Yang（2005），郭华（2013），李亚非（2015）等都早已观察到。

赵元任（1980）认为“N们”指集体，所以不能加数词修饰。

胡裕树（1985）则认为汉语有两种表数范畴的手段，一种是词汇手段，在名词前用上表示复数的数词和量词，如“三个学生”，“三个”是计量定数；另一种是词法手段，在名词上加后缀“们”，表示不定复数，是不计量的，表

"群"的意义。在这样的看法下，"三个学生"和"学生们"能说，而"三个学生们"不能说的原因是"计量"与"不计量"产生了矛盾，表"数"与表"群"不相一致，群是不计算数量的多数。

张斌（1998：216—217）的看法也很接近，他认为加数量词是把事物一个一个来计算的，"们"则是把事物当作一个整体，因此不能说"三个同学们"。有关张斌的"把事物一个一个来计算"，储泽祥（2000）认为从个体化的角度来理解更为合适，也就是汉语的"数量+N"中的数量使N个体化，要求N必须是个体性的，所以N就不能以集体身份出现，而"们"表集体，所以"三个同学们"不能说。如果数量不要求N个体化，N就可以加上复数标记，如"一些新来的同志们""一教室的学生们"。除此以外，他还认为"十几个丫头们"近代可以说但现代不能说，根本原因就是"十几个"对"丫头"个体化。

储泽祥也指出，能与"们"共现的表数词语都是不定量的数量词语，包括"一些、一帮、一班、这些、那些"，"许多、任何、所有、好多"，"全体、全部、各位、诸位"等，这是因为"N们"本身表现的数量都是不定量性的，是复数标记的不定量性阻碍了确数词的出现。

最后，储先生也从信息角度来解释为何确数不能和"们"共现。根据他的看法，N前表示数量的词语越精确，越容易成为新知信息，而"们"则是负载已知信息，因此"们"和精确数字并存的可能性很小。这是从信息结构角度所做的解释，西原史晓（2009）也有类似的主张，他认为确数结构所表示的信息量较大，故常成为句子中的重要新信息，概数结构所表示的信息量相对较小，不能成为一个句子中的重要信息，而"们"字结构所承担的信息是旧信息，所以"们"可以与概数结构共现，而不与确数结构共现。

宋玉柱（2003）也是主张"们"的语法意义就是表示"群体"概念，与数量无关，所以凡是与数量有关的词都不能与"们"同现，即使是模糊的数量也不行。

陈小红（2005）不使用群的概念，改为使用整体多数义，即"N们"这个整体是由多数个体组成，但依旧是不计量的多数的观点，所以不可和计量数词共享。除了确数外，她认为像"几个""大部分""三分之一"等不可用来修饰"们"。

除了以上传统分析方式，形式分析则以Li（1999）为代表。她是从生成语法的角度来解释“们”和确数不能共现的原因，她认为“们”是个复数标记而表示单复数的标记在基底结构是位于 NumP 的中心语 Num 的位置上，数词则是 NumP 的指示语，NumP 之上是 DP，代表指称性短语，NumP 的下方是 ClP 量词短语，再下来则是 NP 短语，如（20）所示：

（20）

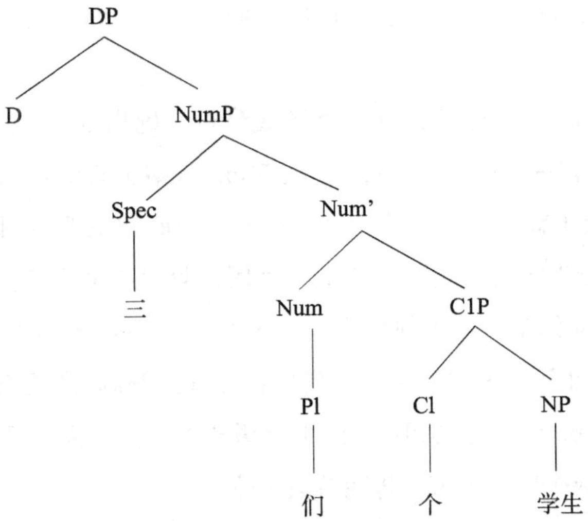

Li 主张中文的复数标记虽然基底结构在 Num 的位置上，但必须在虚范畴 D 上实现，所以“们”必须从 Num 这个位置移位到 D 的位置上，而 D 带有 [+def] 这个有定属性，此属性会激发名词的移位，所以普通名词要得到有定的意思就会从 Num 的位置移位到 D 的位置，而“们”就嫁接到位于 D 上的普通名词，所以“孩子们”语义上一定是指称有定的孩子。

（21）

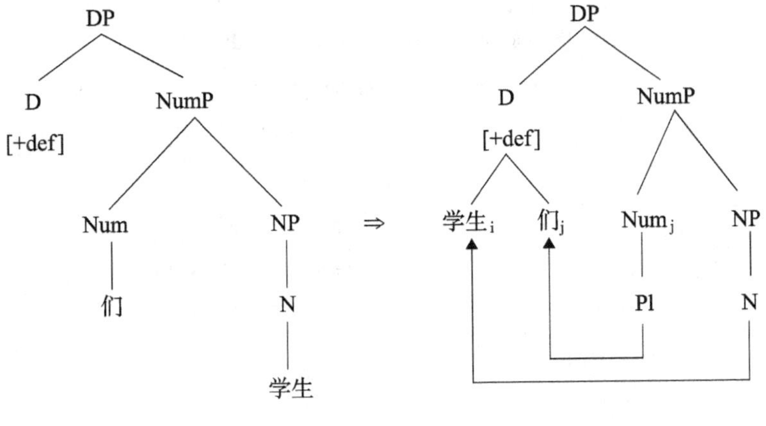

另一方面，如果普通名词有数量词修饰如（20），则普通名词“学生”无法移位到D的位置，因为中心语到中心语的移位会被量词中心语“个”阻碍而违反中心语到中心语的移位限制，因此在（20）中，“们”无法嫁接到名词“学生”上，导致“三个学生们”的不合法。另一方面，Li也注意到“这些学生们”是可说的，原因是“这些”占据D的位置，所以“们”反而必须实现在N上而不是D上。

Yang（2005）的分析也是另外一个形式分析。她提议DP和NP之间除了NumP和ClP外还有一个小nP在NP之上。Yang采纳了Chierchia（1998）有关中文名词指称种类（概念）的想法，这个小n的功能就是把名词所指称的概念转换成指称个体用法的短语。以“孩子”为例，假设原来只有三个孩子a、b、c，那么“孩子”指称整体孩子的概念，小n则是将“孩子”的概念变成个体，可以是单数个体，也可以是复数个体，所以小nP的指称通常是{a, b, c, {a, b}, {a, c}, {b, c}, {a, b, c}}。但是小nP的中心语若由“们”来实现，则“们”会把nP指称中的复数个体挑出来，排除单数个体。

有关“们”的句法结构，她的具体主张如下（Yang，2005：123—124）：

（22） a. 学生们

b.

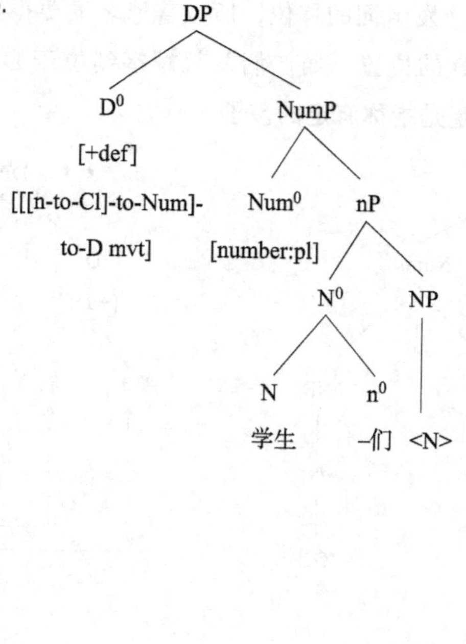

根据 Yang，N 到 n 的移位是个必要移位，而且满足“们”的词缀用法，接下来的 n 到 Num 到 D 的移位则是受 D 的 [+def] 触发，并且将 Num 的复数特征一并带上。

在上面的假设之下，Yang 解释了为何数量词不可以和“们”共现。根据 Yang（2005：124），量词的功能是要从 nP 的指称中把单数个体挑出来，但是当 nP 的中心语是“们”时，nP-$_{们}$所指称的集合只包括复数个体，因此量词的语义功能和 nP-$_{们}$冲突，也就是，Cl 和 nP-$_{们}$组合起来时会产生空集合，所以数量词不能和“们”共现。Yang 的分析虽然和大陆学者的传统分析不完全一样，但思路一致，也就是，名词和“们”先组合，因此阻碍了数词的使用，只是她透过形式工具更加具体化了分析的内容。

另外一个形式分析则是李亚非（2015）所提出的。他指出 Li（1999）的分析预测只要名词短语有量词出现，“们”就不可出现，但这与事实不符。他举出不管是个体量词还是群体量词，都完全可和“们”共享的例子，如：

（23）a. 十几名还没有学过代数的学生们都没能回答这个问题。

b. 一群新员工们在礼堂里聊天。

李亚非指出李文分析的另一问题是她的分析会错误地允许关系从句出现在被修饰的名词后，如例（24），因为关系从句不是核心语，不会阻碍名词与量词的移位。

（24）* 老师接待了学生们没有学过代数的。

因此，李亚非提出下面（25）所示的另外一组假设以及汉语的名词短语结构［如（26）所示］：

（25）a. 汉语名词性短语是核心成分后置结构。

b.“们”不是名词后缀，而是依附于短语的附着语素（clitic）；其语义含义为表达含混数量（vague quantity）的复数。

c. 数量组合作为一个句法成分，处于 NumP 的详指位置（Spec）。

（26）

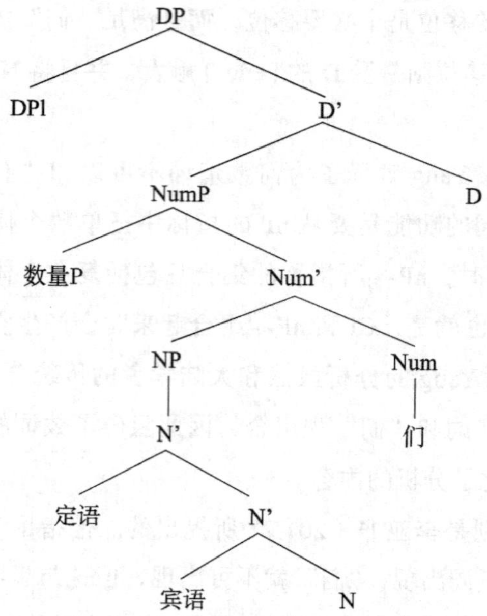

上面假设（25b）可由例句（27）中的“们”既涵盖“要退休的老师”也涵盖“新来的学生”获得证明：

（27）[新来的]学生和[要退休的]老师们

根据李亚非（2015：103）的说法，“们”在语义上表达含混数量，和“们”相冲突的不是量词而是表达精确数量的数词。

Jiang（2017）也提出另一套形式分析。句法上，她提出“们”是个复数词缀，是 AssPlP 短语的中心语，并以 NP 为其补语，如（28b）所示，名词中心语则必须移位到“们”上来实现名词的复数性。语义上，她则假设普通名词指称种类，语义类别是 <e^k>（请参看 Carlson，1977），“们”的语义功能则是将名词短语所指称的种类，转换成个体数大于或等于 2 的复数群体集合，语义类别是 <e,t>，种类转换成群体是透过一个群体函数 G 来运作，但是不同于 Yang（2005），Jiang（2017）认为“N–们”的定指及殊指用法不需要透过投射 DP 结构来达成，而是透过隐性算子比如 iota 来获得（Chierchia，1998；Dayal，2004）。其主张的分析如下（Jiang，2017：224）：

（28）a. 学生们

b. 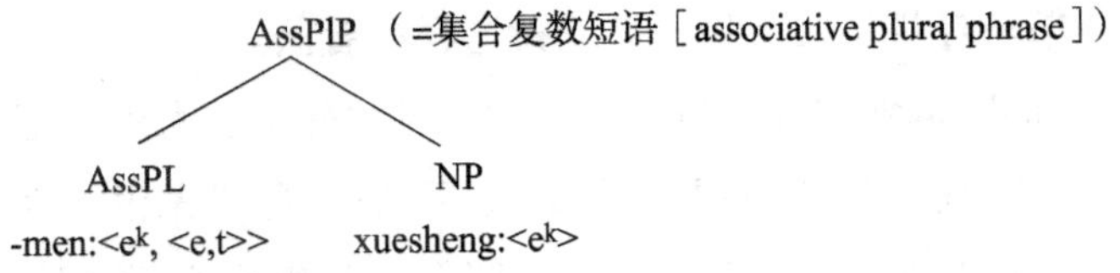

c. $[[\text{xuesheng}]] = {}^{\cap}\text{students}$ $\quad <e^{k}>$

d. $[[\text{-men}]] = \lambda k \lambda Y[{}^{\cup}k_{human} \ \& \ |Y| \geqslant 2 \ \& \ G(k)= Y]$ $\quad <e^{k}, <e,t>>$

e. $[[\text{xuesheng-men}]] = \lambda Y[{}^{\cup\cap}\text{students} \ \& \ |Y| \geqslant 2 \ \& \ G({}^{\cap}\text{students})= Y]$ $\quad <e,t>$

f. $\iota([[\text{xuesheng-men}]]) = \iota Y[{}^{\cup\cap}\text{students} \ \& \ |Y| \geqslant 2 \ \& \ G({}^{\cap}\text{students}) = Y]$

$<e>$(via iota)

此外，根据 Jiang（2017：230）的看法，“*三个学生们”的结构是 $[_{\mathrm{ClP}}$ $[_{\mathrm{NumP}}$ 三 $[_{\mathrm{Cl}}$ 个 $[_{\mathrm{AssPlP}}$ 们 $[_{\mathrm{N}}$ 学生]]]]]，也就是量词“个”以（28b）为补语，但是“个学生们”无法做语义合成，因为个体量词的语义功能和“N-们”的指称有所冲突，冲突产生的原因是个体量词的功能是把种类转换成实现那个种类的原子个体的集合，然而名词一旦和“们”结合后，其语义指称就不再是种类，而是复数的群体，也就是说，“个”要求其补语是类别 $<e^{k}>$，但“学生们”的语义类别却是 $<e,t>$ 如（28e）所示，所以有类别冲突问题。换句话说，根据 Jiang 的分析，其实不是数词让确数结构和“们”不相容，而是量词和“们”的用法不相容。另一方面，根据 Jiang（2017：228），群体量词如“那一群孩子们”中的“群”可和“NP-们”组合运算，因为群体量词有一派生用法，使得它们可以和群体名词短语做语义运算。总而言之，Jiang 对确数结构和“们”的不相容问题做出了具体解释，她的解释在精神上和传统说明其实也相差不远。

4. 前人分析的问题

前人有关数量词和“们”的不相容问题，除 Li（1999）外，大部分都架构在一个假设上，也就是名词（短语）会先与“们”组合得到集合量、模糊量或是复数义，然后再与表个体化的数量词语组合，因而导致语义冲突，然而诚如陈玉梅（2015）指出，这个假设应该是错的，许多语言事实告诉我们“们”的辖域应该是整个名词短语而不仅是名词，也就是，当名词有修饰语时，包含关系从句、概数修饰语等，应该先与修饰成分组合，然后整体再与“们”组合，我们在 2. 5 节已经举了很多例子来支持这样的看法。

此外，“们”也常和称呼语共现，如“各位先生、女士、记者、朋友们”中的“们”，其辖域显然不仅是“朋友”，而是包含“先生、女士、记者”，但“们”如果是跟“先生、女士、记者、朋友”先组合完后再跟“各位”组合的话，那么前人的分析应该判定此用法不恰当，因为“各位”的功能正是个体化，和“们”的集体化、群体化或复数化功能是冲突的。同样地，“每个孩子们”也显示“们”是附着在完整名词短语“每个孩子”上，而不是只在“孩子”上或“个孩子”上。

如果上面的讨论正确的话，这表示当“们”和确数结构或概数结构同现时，应该也是数量词先和名词组合后再与“们”组合，也就是结构上应该是（29a）而不是（29b）：

（29）a. [[Num Cl N] 们]　　　　b. *[Num Cl [N 们]]

如果这个结构才是正确的话，那么传统分析或是 Yang（2005）的形式分析就不可能是对的，因为“Num Cl”的个体化功能是针对名词而不是“名词 + 们”来做运算。

数量词的个体化和“们”的集体、整体或群体义不一致，因而导致“们”和数量名词短语的不相容，这样的说法还有一严重问题。在讨论“们”和数量名词短语的共现问题上，前人文献都聚焦在无定确数名词短语不可和“们”共现，但模糊数量词或群体数量词则可，但少有人特别观察有定名词短语中确数和“们”的共现情形，有趣的是，我们发现数量词前头，不管是确数还是概数，只要带上指示词“这”或“那”，“们”的使用并无问题，前人文献就有相关例句，比方说前面章节已经讨论的例句（8d）：

（8d）还有那七个抢犯，全都精武术，贺照雄也是练家子，师傅总得先跟那七个小辈们交一回子手，然后才能在四外放火，也得个工夫呢。

又比如（30）中的例句，全部是取材自互联网的实例，虽然都带有确数，但都是合格的句子，实际上，读者若在互联网上搜寻，可发现大量有定确数名词短语和“们”共现的例句，这表示这种类型的语料是真实存在的，而不是笔误或口误。[2] 不过我们也要提醒读者，如本文注释 2 的说明，部分人的方言可能不接受有定精确数量名词短语和“们”共现，这部分的差异或许表示“们”的语法在变化中或方言上有差异。

（30）a. 后面的话是说给今天招来的那六个孩子们听的。

b. 这么一想我好对不起我的那三个朋友们。

c. 我能理解那三个孩子们为何敢不听话不打扫教室，因为有家长支持他们不扫地。

d. 昨天熬夜网上看的，太心疼松鼠迅哥了。都没人选他，最后还一个人去救那五个兄弟们。

如果数量词的个体化和“们”的群体或集体义不相容，为何上面的例句都能说呢？为什么有定的“这 / 那 +Num+N+ 们”和无定的“Num+N+ 们”会形成对比呢？文献上的既有传统分析无法解释这个区别，利用现代语言学方法为分析工具的研究如 Yang（2005）、李亚非（2015）、Jiang（2017）等也都无法区分带有精确数量的有定和无定名词短语，他们的分析都会把（8d）和（30）中的例句错误地判定为不合格，但真正不合格的结构是带有表精确数量的无定结构，比方说，李亚非主张“们”附着在短语上而不是在名词上，按他的分析，“那三个孩子们”的结构如下：

（31）[DP 那 [$_{D'}$ [$_{NumP}$ 三个 [$_{NP}$ 孩子们]]]]

但“孩子们”的模糊量不是应该和“三”的精确数量产生冲突而不能说吗？为何可说呢？又比方说，全称量化名词组“每一个孩子们”，按照我们所收集的大量资料，也是可说的，前文已经给了一些例子。按李亚非的分析，这个名词短语的结构应是（32）。

（32）[DP 每 [$_{D'}$ 一个 [$_{NP}$ 孩子们]]]

（32）引发了两个问题。第一，“们”的模糊量和数字“一”的精确数量是冲突的。第二，“们”的复数义和“一”的单数义是冲突的。所以按照李文的分析，全称量化名词组“每一个孩子们”是不可说的，这和语言事实明显不合。所以即便李文的分析是把“们”当作短语附着词而不是名词附着词，他的分析和其他传统分析以及前文所提及的审查人建议都面临同样的问题。

至于 Jiang（2017）的分析，虽然她正确地指出一些前人观察的缺失，但是其分析也面临一些问题。她的分析预测，只要有个体量词出现，“们”就不能出现，这和前文所讨论的许多语言事实显然不合。另外，Jiang（2017）把“NP–们”处理成语义类别为 <e,t> 的群体集合，这又表示，“NP 们”可当谓语，显然也是有违语言事实，因为“*他们是学生们”是不合格的句子。[3]

前人的分析似乎只关注无定的确数名词短语，而把有定的确数名词短语给忽略了，但如何解释有定确数名词短语为何可以和“们”共现其实和解释“们”为何和无定确数名词短语不相容同等重要，这应该是同一问题的两面。

至于用“们”的已知信息和数量所表达的新信息冲突来解释数量和“们”不可共现也有其局限性。我们前文提到，和确数不一样，许多概数其实可以和“们”共现，而且那些概数所出现的语境代表了新信息，这表示“们”并非本质上表示旧信息，否则大部分概数和“们”共现的句子应该都是不合格的。

5. 本文的提案

根据前文的讨论，指人名词或名词短语后的“们”，其辖域是整个名词短语，基于此，我们提议“们”在结构上的位置在 DP 外头，以 DP 为其补语，如下所示：[4]

（33）

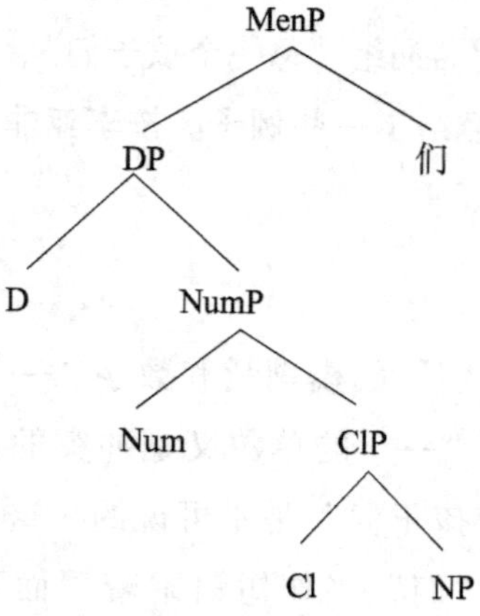

这个结构表示“们”是个虚范畴中心语并选择 DP 当补语[5]，因此“们”可对其补语做句法或语义选择限制，比如有生名词要求，就可透过中心语和补语间的选择限制关系表达出来。至于“们”到底表达什么意思？我们认为“们”的语义和复数义的确有很大关联，我们主张它是个非强制使用的复数个体标记，因为是个体标记，“们”所选择的 DP 名词短语就必须是能引介类别 <e> 的名词短语。请注意复数个体标记和复数化的概念是不同的，前者只能贴在类别 <e> 的个体上，后者则是对类别 <e,t> 的谓语产生作用，比如英文的 -s 标记，其作用的名词就是类别 <e,t>，将原本只指称单数的个体集合变成也包含复数的个体集合，比如从 {a, b, c} 变成 {a, b, c, a⊕b, b⊕c, a⊕c, a⊕b⊕c}，这也解释了为什么中文的“们”和英文的 -s 行为是不同的。

“们”必须以 DP 为其补语的一个重要影响就是“们”不会直接和 NP 或 NumP 组合。文献上，特别是形式语法的相关文献，有关 DP 和 NP/NumP 的一个重要区别是 DP 在语义上是指称性成分，可指称类别 <e> 的个体，NP/NumP 则是述谓成分。所谓述谓成分，就是用来描述个体论元的谓语，语义类别是 <e,t>，也就是个体的集合，是个带上个体论元后会输出真假值的函数，典型的例子就是大家所熟悉的不及物动词如“笑”“哭”等，但普通名词也属于此类别，以“学生”为例，这个名词基本上是在描述个体论元是否具有学生的特征，有此特征的，就在“学生”的外延集合里，所以“学生”也是类别 <e,t> 的谓语。[6]

各式名词性短语和语义类别间的对应关系文献上早有讨论，如 Szabolcsi（1987），Stowell（1989，1991），Longobardi（1994，2001）等。Zamparelli（2000）的多层次 DP 假设（Multi-Layered DP Hypothesis）就主张数量名词短语的语义是数量谓语（cardinality predicate）时，就会出现在 DP 结构中的较低位置，其语义类别是 <e,t>。Guillemin（2011：231）也做了类似假设，根据他们的看法，较高的 DP 会对应到类别 <<e,t>,t>（或是类别 <e>），被数量词修饰的名词短语则是对应到类别 <e,t>，最低的 NP 对应到 <e,t>（或是类别 <e>，如果中心语名词被解释成种类的话）。

（34）

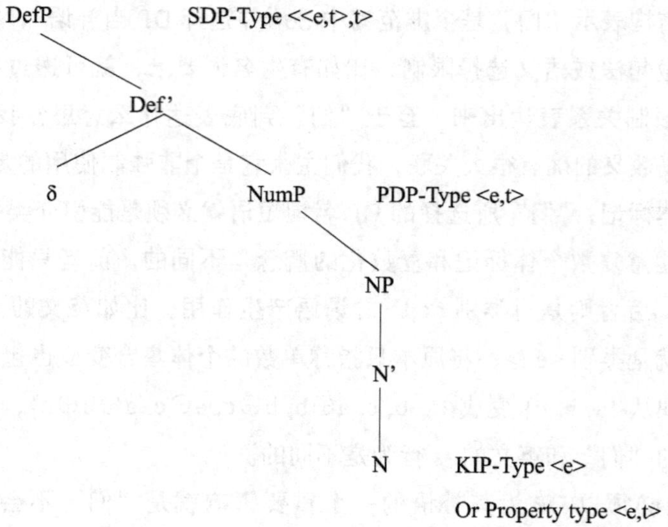

认为 NumP 的语义类别是 <e,t> 的语言学家还有很多，如 Matthewson（2001），Landman（2003，2004），Mathieu（2009），Gebhardt（2009），Rothstein（2013）等，仅举几例。

本文采纳上述学者的观点，提议将汉语数量名词短语分析成 <e,t> 的语义类别，NumP 的具体语义运算如下：

（35）a. 三本书

b. $[\![\text{本}]\!] = \lambda P.\ \lambda n \lambda x.\ P(x) \wedge OU_{\text{本}}(x) = n$ (OU = object unit)

c. $[\![\text{三}]\!] = 3$

d. $[\![\text{书}]\!] = \lambda x.\ books(x)$

e. $[\![\text{本书}]\!] = \lambda n \lambda x.\ books(x) \wedge OU_{\text{本}}(x) = n$

f. $[\![\text{三本书}]\!] = \lambda x.\ books(x) \wedge OU_{\text{本}}(x) = 3$

我们有理由相信这样的分析是有道理的。众所周知，无定数量名词短语在主语位置前必须加上“有”字，句子才合格，如例句（36）。

（36）*（有）三个孩子在哭。

根据林若望（撰写中），“有”字的出现正是因为无定数量名词短语的语义类别是 <e,t>。所以“三个孩子”的语义是“$\lambda x.\ kids(x) \wedge OU_{\text{个}}(x) = 3$”，因为这个语义不是类别 <e>，也不是类别 <<e,t>,t>，因此无法和语义类别也是

<e,t> 的动词短语“在哭”（λx. x cry）做语义上的函数运算，但两个互为姐妹节点的 <e,t> 短语却可透过 Heim & Kratzer（1998）的述语修饰规则（predicate modification）来做语义组合运算，得到另一个也是 <e,t> 的述语，也就是“$\lambda x.\ x$ are kids $\wedge$ $OU_{\uparrow}(x) = 3 \wedge x$ cry”。因为变项 x 尚未被算子闭锁形成命题，整个句子无法表达真假，所以“有”字就出现了。“有”的功能就是用存在算子来闭锁 x 这个变项，让原本语义上表 <e,t> 的谓语表达式成为可表真假的命题（亦请参阅 Cheng，1994）。“有”的语义可定义如下：[7]

（37）$[\![\text{有}]\!] = \lambda P_{\langle e,t\rangle} \exists x.\ P(x)$

如果上面有关 DP 和 NP/NumP 的区别正确的话，一个可以用来解释“们”句法分布的假设是：“们”只能选择指称性的 DP 为其补语，我们姑且称之为“们”的指称性假设。

（38）“们”的指称性假设

和“们”共现的名词短语必须是指称性的 DP，而不是述谓性的 NP/NumP。

根据 Montague（1973）以及 Partee（1987），指称性 DP 的类别可以是类别 <e>，指称个体，或是类别 <<e,t>,t>，指称特征的集合，也叫作广义量词（generalized quantifier）。广义量词以 <e,t> 类别的谓语当论元，然后得到真假值。举专有名词“马云”为例，专有名词的典型语义解释是类别 <e>，指称独一无二的个体，所以“马云”就指称马云那个独一无二的人。但是每一个个体都有其特征，比方说马云的特征是类似下面的一个集合：

（39）{是中国人，出生于杭州，亚洲大富豪，阿里巴巴集团，淘宝网创始人……}= λP. P（马云）

具有（39）那个集合里特征的人就是马云那个人，所以专有名词的语义也可以不看成个体，而看成定义那个个体的特征的集合，这种特征的集合就是 Montague（1973）所谓的广义量词，语义类别是 <<e,t>,t>。

其他的 DP 表达式都一样，“那三个人”可指称由特定三个人所构成的复数个体，语义类别是 <e>，也可看成“那三个人”都具有的特征的集合，类别是 <<e,t>,t>。

量化性的DP如“每（一）个人”通常被分析成指称每一个人都具有的特征的集合，语义类别是<<e,t>,t>。不过后文会进一步说明，部分量化名词短语其实可透过选择函数机制来抽取出个体，包含全称量词，“大部分”，“很多”等。总而言之，DP的语义可以指称个体，也可以指称表特征集合的广义量词。

在Montague-Partee的假说以及（38）这个“们”的指称性假设下，我们可推论：

（40）和“们”共现的名词短语必须是指称类别<e>的个体或是可抽取出个体的<<e,t>,t>广义量词。

下文的重点就是要探讨如何利用（38）和（40）这样的假设来解释名词短语后的“们”的分布。

在此之前，我们先提醒读者专有名词和代名词后的“们”不是本文要讨论的对象，这两种用法都有不同于“名词短语+们”的独特性。首先考虑“你和他们”这样的联合短语。这个名词短语只有一个语义解释，也就是“你”是单数，“他们”是复数，换句话说“们”并非在句法部门才附着在“你和他”这个名词短语上，由此可见，“他们”很可能是在词库里就直接产生，不是在句法上才衍生出来。

至于“专有名词+们”。文献指出像“马云们”这样的短语有两个意思，一个表示马云和其他人，另一个表示具有和马云同样特征的人。我们认为“马云们”会有两个意思可能是因为“马云”可以解读为专有名词，指称个体或是转类为普通词，指称具有马云特征的人。当“马云”指称个体并和“们”合用时，因为“们”的复数性要求无法被单一个体满足，迫使“马云们”产生语义延伸的用法，表达出马云和其他人的语义，以满足“们”的复数要求。我们认为专有名词加“们”是“们”复数语义要求下的语义延伸特殊用法，并不是典型的“们”的语义，因为有定名词短语加“们”不会得到类似的意思，比方说，Lan（2010：8）就指出“你的那个朋友们”并无你的那个朋友及其他人的语义。同样地，“那班学生们”这个名词短语也不会有“那班学生和其他人”的语义，这表示专有名词加“们”的这个语义是必须另外处理的结构，本文不讨论这个用法。第二个语义则可当成一般名词来处理，产生像（41）的例句：

（41）这场历时20年的互联网运动中，马云和马化腾们以技术和模式创新，改变了很多产业的资源和利益分配方式，再造了秩序和游戏规则。

6. MenP假设下不可和"们"共现的名词短语

如果"们"必须选择指称性DP当它的补语，其结果就是"们"应该无法和语义类别为<e,t>的述谓性NP或NumP并用，这个预测是正确的。一个常被观察到的现象就是当名词短语表示判断、属性或做谓语使用时，"们"就不能出现，比方说下面例句都是不好的句子。

（42）我真想不出，彼此不能交谈，怎能成为朋友（?们）（张谊生，2001：204）

（43）论年龄，他们几个都快老太婆（*们）了。（张谊生，2001：203）

（44）他们是学生（*们）。

上面这些例子不好的原因正是名词短语表示判断、属性或做谓语使用时，其句法投射是NP，而不是DP，语义类别是<e,t>，而不是<e>或<<e,t>,t>。[8]

（38）或（40）这条限制的另一个重要预测就是"们"不能和数量名词短语（NumP）一起使用，因为数量名词短语的语义类别是<e,t>。也就是，数量名词短语和属性或谓语名词短语不可以和"们"共现的原因是同样的：它们的语义类别都是谓语性的<e,t>，而不是指称性的<e>或<<e,t>,t>。这样分析的一个很大的好处是把不同的两个现象归并于同一个因素，实现语言的经济性解释。

童盛强（2002）所讨论的"*汉语系有很多留学生们"的情形类似。当"有"作为存现动词时可带宾语，但宾语不可以是有定宾语，也就是不能是DP，但可以是普通名词如"汉语系有留学生"或是数量名词短语如"汉语系有三个留学生"。从语用角度来说，有定名词短语常预设所指称个体的存在，个体既已存在，就不适合再用存现句来说明他们的存在。但光杆名词或是数量无定名词短语并不预设个体之存在，因此适合用存现句来表示他们的存在。又光杆或无定名词短语语义类别属<e,t>，所以童盛强的例句"*汉语系有很多留学生们"不能说，这也符合我们假设的预测。

不过"有"字句带有定宾语的情形并不是没有，甚至也可带"们"，如例句（45），这又是为什么呢？

（45）那里有我的父老乡亲们。

要回答这个问题，我们不妨来看一下英文存现句的有定效应。英文表存在的“there be + NP + XP”句型，“there be”后的名词短语只能是无定，而不能是有定。

（46）a. There are two books on the table.

b. *There are the two books on the table.

但很多语言学家也指出，有定名词短语在特定语境下，句子也是合格的，如（47）和（48），两组例句皆取自 Abbott（1993）。

（47）A: Is there anything to eat?

B: Well, there’s the leftover chicken from last night.

（48）A: I guess we’ve called everybody.

B: No, there’s still Mary and John.

根据 Abbott 的看法，（47）和（48）的句子有定宾语之所以合格是因为这些例句语用上已经不再预设指称个体的存在，所以可出现在存在句里。以例句（47）为例，说话者可能已经忘了剩饭剩菜的存在，所以剩饭剩菜就不在预设中存在，因此听话者可用有定宾语“the leftover chicken”来宣称剩饭剩菜的存在。我们认为（45）应该类似，“我的父老乡亲”如果不被存在预设，就不会有宣称存在与预设存在的冲突，所以（45）反而可用来进一步支持“们”只能和 DP 一起使用这样一个假设。

7. MenP 假设下可和“们”共现的名词短语

我们的分析预测了类别 <e> 或可从 <<e,t>,t> 抽取个体的名词短语可以和“们”共现，接着我们就来看看是否如此。

基本上，专有名词除外，名词短语是否为类别 <e> 或 <<e,t>,t> 主要是看是否有 D 的出现，如果有 D 的成分而且其类别是 <<e,t>,e>，或是 <<e,t>,<<e,t>,t>> 的话，那么那个名词短语就会是类别 <e> 或 <<e,t>,t>。指示词“这”和“那”就是属于前者，它们的语义功能基本上和英文的定冠词“the”差异不大，所以“那些孩子”或是“那三个孩子”都可以和“们”共现，如（49）：

（49）

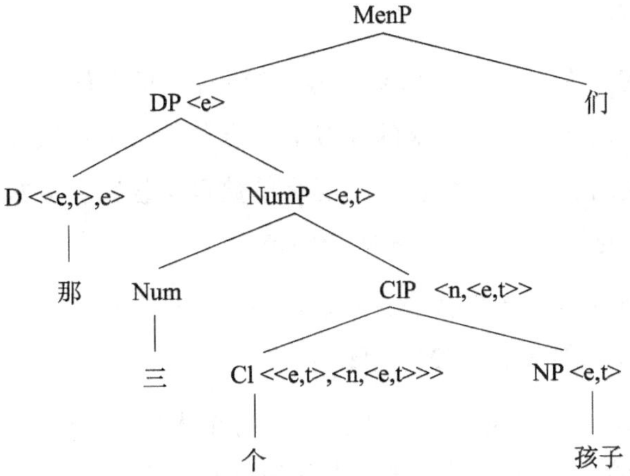

"那些孩子"的情形也类似，"那三个孩子"及"那些孩子"都是指称复数的有定个体，语义类别都是 <e>，所以都可以和"们"共现。

我们在此强调，因为"们"看的是其邻近姊妹节点的最终语义类别，所以有定名词短语中的数量词，如例（49）中的"三个"，并不会影响"们"的使用，这是我们和前人分析的一个极大的差异之处。前人的分析会把"那三个孩子们"这样的有定名词短语判定为不合格，本文的分析则判定为合格。

前文我们提到可以和"们"共现的名词短语的频率，有定名词短语是排在最前头的，这或许是因为类别 <e> 是最典型的指称性类别。

接着我们来看 <<e,t>,t> 类的名词短语，此类名词短语基本上是量化性名词短语，表特征的集合，通常是以一个类别为 <<e,t>,<<e,t>,t>> 的 D 为中心语，典型的例子是全称限定词，如"每个孩子"中的"每"。当"每"和"（一）个孩子"组合后，其语义类别就变成 <<e,t>,t>，表达了每个孩子都具有的特征的集合，也就是下面的广义量词语义。

（50）⟦每（一）个孩子⟧ $= \lambda P.\ \forall x[child\ (x) \rightarrow P\ (x)]$

根据陈玉梅（2015：21）的语料调查，"每"可以和"们"共现。前文例句（19）我们也提供了三个例证。下面是另外两个互联网上搜集到的句子：

（51）a. 在与她相处三年多的时间里，婆婆让我惊讶的是，她做到了每个母亲的梦想：她的**每个孩子们**感情都非常地亲密，就算他们有不同的父亲。

b. 藉由歌声传递爱与温暖，直达**每个孩子们**的心中，让每个孩子都有动力继续改变。

有关上面例句，有两个问题需要回答。第一，“每个孩子”是单数还是复数？第二，为什么在与“们”共享的梯级上，全称量词的梯级会比有定名词短语的梯级低呢？我们认为“每个孩子”既是单数也是复数。单数是句法上的单数，复数是语义上的复数。请看下面两个例句。

（52）每个被骗的人都不相信是老张欺骗了他。

（53）每个农夫都说是政府欺骗了他们。

（52）句用句法上单数的“他”来回指“每个人”，此时，“他”和全称量化词在句法上的数保持一致，并充当后者的约束变项（bound variable），因此，“他”所指称的个体会随着“每个被骗的人”所指定的对象变动。（53）则不同，“农夫”由复数代名词“他们”回指，因为说话者把“每个农夫”所引介的一个个农夫整合成言谈中的一个复数个体，所以可以指称语义上的复数，正是因为这个原因，（51）中的“们”并没有单复数的不一致冲突。稍后我们会说明，部分量化名词短语其实可透过 Reinhart（1997）的选择函数机制来抽取复数个体，而全称量化名词短语正是允许选择函数运作的一种广义量词。[9]

我们要特别强调，根据我们的分析，“们”是位于“每一个 N”的外头，所以很多个“一个 N”可以构成语义上的复数，满足了“们”的复数要求。但是传统分析或 Yang（2005）、李亚非（2015）、Jiang（2017）的分析方式，就会把“N-们”先组合起来，再跟“一个”组合。这种分析，无可避免地会产生“数”的冲突。从这个角度来看，（51）中的例句支持了本文的提案，也反驳了传统分析或 Yang（2005）、李亚非（2015）、Jiang（2017）等的分析方式。

第二个问题，全称量化词和“们”的连用可能性为何较低？这有可能是因为全称量化名词短语的核心意义本来是语义类别为 <<e,t>,t> 的广义量词，并不直接指称个体，而是要透过其他机制，比如下文将讨论的选择函数机制来抽取个体，因为这个过程是额外的复杂过程，不如直接指称个体来得直接，因此 <<e,t>,t> 类的全称量化名词短语与“们”的共现性较弱。

除了“每”外，还有其他一些表全体的量化词如“全体”“所有”，也都可以和“们”共现，只是这些全称词不需使用量词，而是会加上“的”来修饰名词，如"所有的孩子们"或"全体（的）弟兄们"。虽然这些全称量化词是不是出现在D的位置比较有争议，但就语义分析而言，他们的确是可被归类为<<e,t>,<<e,t>,t>>。或许不带量词的全称量化词可分析成DP的详指语。

除全称量化词外，汉语还有一些非全称量化词也是带"的"的修饰语，如"大部分的""少部分的"，这些量化词和"们"的共现频率似乎较全称量化词低，且百分比越低的，越不易和"们"共现，如：

（54）a. 在英国，**大部分的孩子们**在7岁的时候开始进入英国小学（prep school）进行小学课程的学习，小学一般为6年。

b. 虽然大部分的孩子都排挤她，但依旧有**少部分的孩子们**愿意包容她。

"大部分的"的分析可以和全称量化词的分析一样，把它们视为DP的详指语，和名词组合后得到<<e,t>,t>的意思，但一样可透过选择函数机制来抽取复数个体，因为<<e,t>,t>不直接指称个体，所以和"们"共现的使用频率也较低，而且低于全称量化名词短语，这可能是因为"大部分的N"这类的名词短语比全称量化名词短语在语用上更不易抽取出所指的复数群体是哪个群体，"少部分"则又更加不容易指认出是哪个复数群体。

"们"的使用和高辨识度的复数群体相关这点可由下面的事实获得证明。有关全称量化词和"们"的共现分布，陈玉梅（2015：21）发现在她所收集的所有语料里，"们"和"任何"共现的例子数目是零。为什么"任何"就不能和"们"共现呢？我们认为一个重要原因是"任何N"比任何一个全称量化名词短语更不具指称性。"任何N"有两个含义，一个是用作否定极项词，如"我不认识任何语言学家"，此时"任何N"不指称任何个体，其范域在否定词之下，其语义较像是无定名词短语，其引介的变项会被否定词下的存在算子所约束。"任何N"的第二个含义是任指用法，如"任何人都可以参加"，此时不指称具体的个体，而是指称可能世界中的可能个体，但此个体未必存在，也就是，内涵性个体，不管是哪一种含义，"任何N"的语义都无法指称现实世界的具体个体，所以和"们"无法共现。

除了上面这些量化词外，我们还有一些量化词如"很多""一些"等需要说明，如下面网络上搜到的例句。

（55）a. 这也代表（有）很多孩子们即将踏上高中的第一年。

b. 由于现在的信息很容易取得，（有）一些学生们会有一些学习上的误解，就是以为“学的东西很难，都看不懂”才叫作学到东西。

这类型的概数无定名词短语和确数无定名词短语一样都可和“有”共现，然而此时的“有”常常是可有可无的，我们猜测这里的“有”可能是定语性的“有”，所以“有很多孩子”和“有一些孩子”其实是DP短语，我们后文会有较详细的讨论，另外按照Reinhart（1997），some、many这样的无定量化词可透过选择函数来抽取出所指称的个体。

一位匿名审查人指出，不能和“们”共现的名词短语还包括否定名词短语，如（56a），我们发现被“很少”修饰的名词短语似乎也不能带“们”，如例句（56b）。

（56）a. 没有孩子（*们）喜欢那位老师。

b. 很少孩子（*们）喜欢那位老师。

这两种单调项特征向下蕴涵的名词短语都是允许指称为空集合的名词短语，无法透过选择函数来抽取个体的量化名词短语，属极低个体辨识度名词短语。

总而言之，我们认为“们”的分布和语义指称有相关性。类别 <e> 是典型指称个体的名词短语，最容易接受“们”，类别 <<e,t>,t> 的广义量词有的容易，有的不易接受“们”，全凭形成个体的辨识难易度而定。类别 <e,t> 则是谓语成分，不可当指称性论元，因而不可和“们”共现，我们可用下面的梯级呈现这个差异：

（57）<e> > <et,t> > ?<et,t> > ??<et,t> > *<et,t>
*<e,t>

这个梯级相当程度上反映了前人文献有关“们”的观察。

问题是为什么会有这样的一个梯级呢？Jin（2020）近来有一篇有关“为什么”问句中量化词导致的干扰效应的研究，或许可给我们提供一个技术上的解答。根据Soh（2005）及Yang（2012）的研究，当疑问词“为什么”受某类型的量化词C-统治时，比如单调性特征为向下蕴涵的量化词，此时疑问句不合格，而量化词的单调性特征为向上蕴涵时，如“每个人”“大部分人”就无类似干扰效应。以下例句取自Jin（2020：348）。

（58）# 没有人 / 很少人 / 最多两个人为什么要辞职？

（59）大多数人 / 所有人 / 每个人为什么都要辞职？

同时 Jin 还观察到，部分向上蕴涵的量化词会产生较弱的干扰效应，且这个弱干扰效应在一些特定语境或语用环境中，比如补语子句，可能会消失，如下面对比显示（Jin，2020：348—349）：

（60）? 至少三个人 / 超过三个人 / 三个人 / 几个人为什么要辞职？

（61）小李（已经）知道了三个人 / 至少三个人 / 几个人为什么要辞职。[10]

向下蕴涵的量化词则是即便在补语子句中也同样不合格，如（62）：

（62）# 我（已经）知道了没有人 / 很少人 / 不到三个人为什么辞职。

有趣的是，我们发现“任何人”也同样有干扰效应，且无法在特定语境中被拯救。

（63）a. * 任何人为什么都要辞职？

b. * 我已经知道了任何人为什么都要辞职。

Jin 认为量化词是否会产生干扰效应和其本身可否指称可主题化的个体有很大的关联性，他认为不会产生干扰效应的量化词，基本上都是单调性特征向上蕴涵的量化名词短语，这些名词短语都可透过 Reinhart（1997）的选择函数机制来产生符合该量词比例的个体，所谓选择函数就是一个函数 *f*，其论元是一个集合 S，*f* 运用到 S 就会从 S 这个集合挑出其中一个元素来当作值。Reinhart 原始分析是将选择函数运用到像 some、a、a certain 这样的无定量化词，但 Jin（2020）举证同样分析可运用到其他单调性向上蕴涵的量化名词短语，根据他的看法，这类量化词名词短语会在 D 的位置引介出选择函数变项 *f*，以“大部分人”为例，就是 $[_{DP}\ [_{D}\ f_1]\ [_{NP}$ 大部分人]]，Jin（2020：358—359）提议其语义解释如下：

（64）a. ⟦ 大部分 ⟧= $\lambda P_{<e,t>}\lambda x_e[P(x) \wedge |Atoms(x)| > 1/2|\{y: atom(y) \wedge P(y)\}|]$

(where Atoms (x) returns the set of atomic elements of the plurality x: $Atoms(x) = \{y: atom(y)$, ie., $y \leqslant x \wedge \forall z. [z \neq y \rightarrow z \leqslant y]\})$

b. ⟦[f_1[大部分人]]⟧^{g} = g (1) ⟦most people⟧^{g}

= g (1) $(\lambda x_e[people(x) \wedge |Atoms(x)| > 1/2|\{y: atom(y) \wedge person(y)\}|])$

（*f* 表选择函数，选择出一个包含大部分人的复数个体）

其他如“每个人”“所有人”“很多人”“一些人”等都可透过类似手段来抽取出复数个体，这些量化名词短语不会有干扰效应。

根据 Jin 的分析，“为什么”基底结构就产生在 [Spec, CP]，所以要出现在此位置以上的名词短语只能是主题化的名词短语，个体可被主题化，但因为只有单调性非向下蕴涵的名词短语可透过选择函数机制来产生指称性个体，单调性向下蕴涵特征的不行，因为这些短语允许空集合，但在假设上空个体不存在，所以只有前者可产生可主题化的个体，后者不行，又因为选择函数机制的个体选择受语境影响，所以部分单调性向上蕴涵的名词短语需有特定语境支撑，才容易产生特定个体，这是为什么（60）的句子较差的缘故。有关 Jin 文的详细内容，读者可参阅原文以做更好的理解。

如果 Jin 的分析正确的话，我们可得出结论：“们”只能贴在表复数个体的名词短语上，不同的量化词转换成个体的可能性不相同，因此和“们”的共现情形就不同。越容易透过选择函数机制在语用上抽取出个体的量化名词短语，就越容易和“们”共现，这就说明了（57）那个梯级，也说明了为何量化名词短语和“们”的共现接受度常因人而异，毕竟选择函数是否能成功抽取个体出来和语境也有相当程度的关系。

8. 种类名词和“们”的共现问题

我们的分析预测了只要是“个体”应该都可以接受“们”的出现，这就预测了种类名词可以和“们”共现，因为根据 Carlson（1977），像“dogs”这样的光杆复数名词可以分析成指称种类的个体，其类别也是 <e>，比方说下面例子中的“dogs”和“mammals”就是种类的专名，因为“widespread”和“are mammals”属于种类谓语，只能运用到种类名词短语上：

（65）a. Dogs are widespread.

b. Whales are mammals.

然而根据文献上的观察，比如 Iljic（2001）等，种类名词似乎不能接受“们”，所以例句（66b）是不好的句子。

（66）a. 人是从猴子演化来的 / 总有一天会灭绝。

b. *人们是从猴子演化来的 / 总有一天会灭绝。

不过我们同时也发现并非泛指名词就不能带"们"，比方说，从网络上找到的下面的例句就是合格的句子。

（67）a. 孩子们总是对任何事物好奇。

b. 女孩子们通常会把旅行幻想得很Fancy。

（66）和（67）的最主要区别是在谓语上。前者的谓语"从猴子演化来的"或是"总有一天会灭绝"是所谓种类谓语（kind-level predicate），后者的谓语则是个体谓语（individual-level predicate）。个体谓语可运用到个体上，但种类谓语就不行，因此有如下对比：

（68）a. *张三是从猴子演化来的。

b. 张三总是对任何事物好奇。

有了这个基本认识，我们就可以说明为何（66b）不合格，而（67a，b）合格。所谓种类名词，就是那个名词指称的是整个种类，这个种类的个体既可在真实世界里体现，也可在可能世界里体现，但语义上种类属于一个整体，无法透视构成整体里的个体，因而是语义上的内涵性单数，因此（66b）不合格。但（67）里的泛指名词不一样，因为泛指句里的泛指名词是个体的累积，是一种概括，语义上可视为复数，所以可以带"们"。

9. 关系从句和"们"

前文提到光杆确数词修饰名词时不可带"们"。然而这些光杆数量词前头若加上一个关系从句，句子就会变好，而且比加在光杆数量词后头还要好，如（69b，c）和（70b，c）。

（69）a. *我见了三个孩子们。

b. ?我见了三个我教过的孩子们。

c. 我见了我教过的三个孩子们。

（70）a. *我们对五位家长们致上十二万分谢意。

b. ?我们对五位今天特地远道赶来的家长们致上十二万分谢意。

c. 我们对今天特地远道赶来的五位家长们致上十二万分谢意。

有关关系从句的位置，Chao（1968）就已经观察到其可出现在数量词后头或定指词前头，如下面例句（71a，b）。我们同时也注意到，关系从句不能出现在数量词前、详指词后的位置，如（71c）：

（71）a. 那一位戴眼镜的先生

b. 戴眼镜的那一位先生

c. *那戴眼镜的一位先生

这表示在（69c）和（70c）里头的关系从句必须在DP外头，虽然句中并未出现定指词。我们认为正是此因素认可了（69c）和（70c）中的“们”。此二句中的“们”，其姊妹节点是DP而不是NP，DP外头的关系从句表示有一个隐性的D在结构里，因而也就认可了“们”。

至于（69b）和（70b），此二句的关系从句位于数量词下面，所以是附加在NP上，照道理此二句的名词短语并非DP，但或许是因为关系从句的使用增加了描述性，使得指称对象更为明确，让“们”的使用也变得较可以接受。

10.“N+们”的有定性

文献上一个有关“们”的普遍认知是“N+们”的语义解释是有定的，比方说（72a）中的“家长们”就是有定而不是无定解释，或是说名词前头有关系从句时，如（72b），也都是有定解释。

（72）a. 校长接见了家长们。

b. 校长接见了前来拜访的家长们。

然而我们已经指出，“们”的出现不能保证有定解释，特别是当无定量化词出现的时候，如（13）中的诸多例句。既然“们”的无定解释是允许的，那为何（72a）中的“N+们”只能获得有定解释呢？下面我们就来回答这个问题。

前文我们指出，光杆名词可以有两种语义类别，当作种类名词解释时，是类别<e>，另一可能性是当作谓语，此时类别为<e,t>。然而种类名词是单数义，而不是复数义，所以不可和“们”共现。但是<e,t>类别也不能和“们”共现，所以理论上（72a）应该是不合格的句子。

我们认为（72a）之所以合格而且会获得有定解释是因为“们”要求其补足语是DP，所以名词“家长”必须由N的位置移位到D的位置，这种移位就将原本不能带“们”的NP结构延伸为DP结构。在许多其他语言里，N到D的移位是光杆名词获得指称的手段[11]，我们认为这正是（72a）的情形，所以（72a）中的“家长”因为N到D的移位获得了有定指称并且可以带上“们”。在此请注意，如果名词有数量词修饰如“三位家长们”，句子就变得不合格，因为数量词会阻碍N到D的移位，在这点上，我们的分析和Li（1999）利用N到D的移位来解释“N+们”的有定解读是相似的。

光杆名词必须从N的位置移位到D来获得有定解释，本来类别为<e,t>的NP也因而变成类别<e>的DP，同时创造了“们”的使用条件。这个分析表示不是“们”本身具有有定解释，而是“们”要求其补语必须是DP，因而迫使N到D的移位，才产生有定解释。这个分析不仅说明为何（72a）“家长们”是有定解释，同时也可说明为何像（73b）这种存现结构是不合格的。

（73）a. 来客人了。　　　　　　b. *来客人们了。

（73a）中“客人”只能是无定解释，不允许有定解释，因为前面的讨论已经说明存现结构有无定宾语限制的要求，所以（73a）的“客人”只可以是NP。然而在（73b）里，因为“们”的出现，名词“客人”一定要从N移位到D，产生一个有定DP，否则“们”的指称性DP补语要求无法满足，然而为了满足“们”的指称性DP补语要求所产生的有定DP却和此句型的无定宾语限制互相冲突，因此造成（73b）的不合格。

如果（72a）中的N必须移位到D来获得有定解释的话，（72b）中关系从句的出现是不是表示没有N到D的移位呢？如果是这样，那（72b）中“前来拜访的家长们”的有定指称解释又从何而来？

上一节我们已经说明关系从句可以附加在DP外头，所以（72b）中的关系从句可以是在DP的外头，在此假设下，N到D的移位依旧是可能的。另外一个可能性则是N到D的移位没发生，但是透过关系从句的存在认可了一个隐性的有定D以及DP的投射。DP既已存在，“们”的使用就没问题，也就是说，（72b）的语义解释其实是等同于“校长接见了前来拜访的那些家长们”。

有位匿名审查者指出，如果“*三位家长们”不好是因为数量词阻碍了N到D的移位，但是在“我教过的三个孩子们”中却因关系从句的存在而让隐性

D来认可“们”，那么一个疑问是为什么“*三位家长们”不可有隐性的D来认可“们”呢？根据这位审查人的语感，（74）是不合格的句子：

（74）中文系有三位留学生，而且三位留学生（*们）都是从日本来的。

有关无定数量名词短语为回指有定用法的语感判断，我们在互联网搜寻，其实可以轻易地找到例子：

（75）a. 一日偶遇同在公园中散步的西尔维娅（Kate Winslet 饰）和她的四个孩子，四个孩子们的天真无邪以及小彼得忧郁孤僻的气质深深吸引了他。
b. 手掌妈妈有五个孩子，五个孩子们都互相瞧不起。

换句话说，无定数量名词短语在适当的环境下，比方说有关系从句出现或是有主题认可的情形下，隐性的D就可被允准并进而透过选择函数机制来使“们”的使用合法。

11. 主宾语的不对称现象

在2.2节，我们提到有些学者认为除了确数外，连用型数字，数字加概数，或是像“几”这样的词语不可和“们”一起出现，然而前人文献或是网络上的语料中都可发现类似下面的例句：

（76）a. 有几位孩子们在回答问题的时候没有把话说完整的习惯。
b. 还有七八个姑娘们齐声附和：“是呀，你今年的头水要抢了挑到哪里去呀？”（1994年《人民日报》）

这些语料有一个重要特征，也就是这些概数（或确数）无定名词短语都出现在主语位置并且常伴随着“有”字，在语义解释上则隐含着部分指称（partitive）或分指义。另一方面，如果这些无定名词短语出现在宾语位置，就不容易得到分指义，也不能和“们”共现，如下面的例句：

（77）a. *?? 我们只认识几位前辈们。
b. * 我们附和了七八位姑娘们的意见。
c. * 校长一共接见了三位家长们。

为什么会有这种主宾语的不对称现象是本节要回答的问题，但在回答问题前，我们要先来简单介绍一下蔡维天（2004）有关“有”字的看法。

一般都认为表呈现的“有”字句如“有人来了”中的“有”是助动词（比如黄正德，1988），是一元述语，位于动词短语之上，如（78）：

（78）

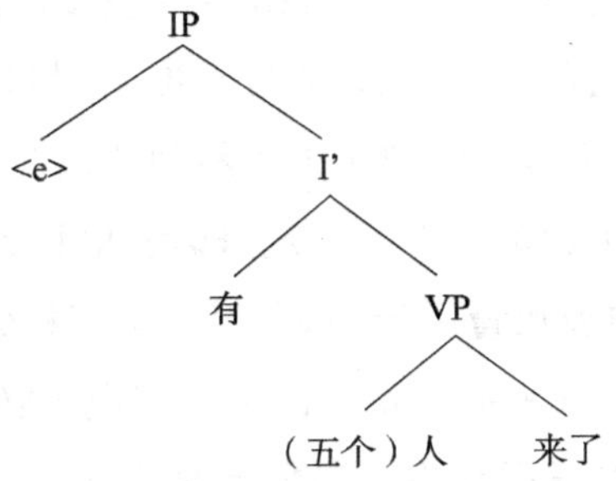

此时的“有”结构位置较高，和数量短语“（五个）人”并不构成一名词短语，所以“*张三骗了有（五个）人/*张三把有（五个）人骗了”是不合格的句子。

除了助动词用法，蔡维天认为在“有的人没来/有些人没来”的句式里，“有”其实是定语，是名词短语里的一部分，如（79）：

（79）

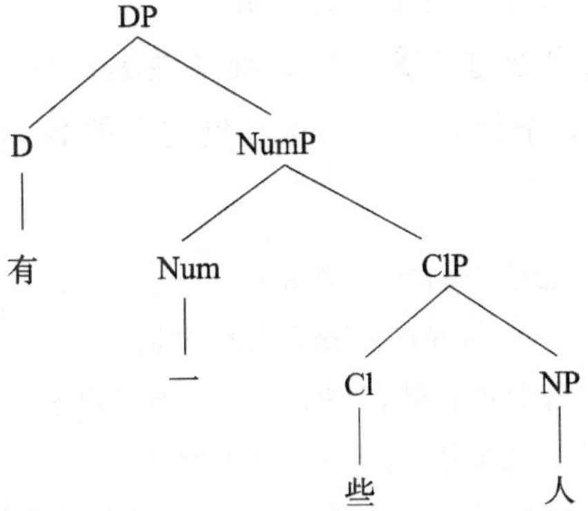

所以可说“张三把有的人/有些人骗了”。此外，他还认为在语义上，“有的人”转化成“some of the people”的意思，也就是分指义；“有些人”则转化成殊指义。定语的“有”是从呈现“有”虚化而来，此虚化过程使得和邻近助动词“有”主语并入，动前宾语次之，动后宾语则因为和“有”字较远，合并不易。

假设蔡维天有关“有”并入定语的主张是正确的话，或许我们就可以解释为什么类似（76）的例句在合格度上，不同的学者常有不同的判断。我们认为接受（76）句里“们”用法的人，其实认为“有”已经不是助动词的“有”，而是被重新分析成定语性的存在量化词“有”，占据D的位置，语义上因此具备了量化词D常有的量化预设，也就是分指义，所以允准了“们”的使用。另一方面这样的分析也可解释为什么（77）中的宾语不易和“们”共现，这个主宾语不对称可能正反映蔡维天先生所提的“有”的定语语法化和距离有关。

我们在此要特别强调，真正的表数量无定名词短语其句法投影是NP，不是DP，语义类别是<e,t>，而不是<e>或<<e,t>,t>。比方说（80）这种句型，数量名词短语“三个学生”并不指特定学生，即使出现在主语位置也不可加“有”，如（81a），或是和“们”共现，如（81b）。

（80）（老师规定）三个学生睡一张床。

（81）a. *（老师规定）有三个学生睡一张床。

b. *（老师规定）三个学生们睡一张床。

所以真正表数量的名词短语，也就是NumP（参看Li，1998）和指称性的DP名词短语，在和“们”的合用上的确是有所区别。

最后，有位匿名审查人指出通过“有”来论证某些名词短语也是DP，有一个潜在问题是和前文所举的如下例句有关，这些例句中的名词短语都不可加“有”但却可加上“们”。

（3a）为了回答（*有）一批青年同志们的要求……

（13a）让（*有）更多孩子们接受好的教育是我们的目标。

（13d）在英国，（*有）大部分的孩子们在7岁的时候开始进入英国小学（prep school）进行小学课程的学习，小学一般为6年。

（13f）妈妈不是上陈董家打牌，就是和（*有）一些阔太太们逛街买舶来品。

（13g）我自己从未在孩提时代受过什么苦，可是我却有机会碰到（*有）很多穷苦的孩子们。

“有”不可以出现在上面（3a）、（13a）、（13f）、（13g）中，那是句法因素使然，因为“有”只出现在无定主语的前面，但是这些句子里的无定名词短语是宾语。（13d）的“大部分的孩子们”虽然在主语位置，但因为它是个强名词短语（strong NP），而不是弱名词短语（weak NP），所以不能出现在表存在的

“有”字句中［请参看 Milsark（1974，1977）及 Barwise & Cooper（1981）］。可是“有”如果不能出现在这些句子里，那么为何这些句子的名词短语可被视为 DP 呢？我们认为这是因为表不定量的量化词如“大部分”“很多”“一些”等，和英文的 most、many、some 一样，可直接出现在 D 或是 DP 指示语的位置，或是它们出现在 NP 里，但是 D 的位置是隐性的选择函数变项。

12. 结语

普通话“们”字相当特殊，具有复数的语义要求，但分布上又不完全像是个典型复数标记。本文主张“们”是个非强制性的个体复数标记，而不是复数化标记，所以只能以指称性的 DP 且语义类别为 <e> 或是可透过选择函数机制来抽取个体的 <<e,t>,t> 名词短语为补足语，因而排除语义类别为 <e,t> 的数量名词短语，谓语性名词短语，称谓性名词短语与部分量化名词短语和“们”的共现。我们也对“们”的共现梯级做了一个可能且合理的解释。

附注

1. 根据我们搜寻的互联网资料，和（12）类似的下面这几个例句都是合格的，所以本文会将（12）当作合格句。

（i）a. 最近视力不好，戴眼镜的孩子们很多。

b. 今天搅浑水的孩子们很多嘛，是不是没有仔细看这事？

c. 11 月要拍摄 753 或租借衣服的孩子们很多！

2. 陈俊和（2009：93）讨论了带精确数量的有定结构，认为是不合格的句子，并举（i）为例：

（i）*那三个女人们只顾拍摄，一点都没察觉到四周的变化。

例句（i）的合格度，我们留给读者自行判断，但（30）里的句子我们听起来的确都是合格的。

3. Jiang（2017）自己注意到了这个问题（p.224：ft.23），她指出这个问题也同样会出现在主张 DP 的分析，这个论点并不完全正确，在下节，我们会提出“–们”只会选择语义类别为 <e> 或是可透过选择函数机制来产生个体的类别 <<e,t>,t> 的名词短语为补语。在句法结构上，语义类别 <e> 或类别 <<e,t>,t> 会对应到带有 DP 或 QP 的定词短语或量词短语，因此，将“–们”当作 DP/QP 以外的中心语不但不需要将“N 们”分析为述语，而且最能直接反映语义–句法的对应关系。

4.“们”也有可能只是个附着语，本文不讨论附着语和中心语的差别。

5. 汉语中心语在后的虚范畴还有“呢”“吗”等句末助词。

6. 普通名词在语义上充当谓语，语义类别是 <e,t> 这样的观点，请读者自行参看形式语义学的诸多文献介绍，本文采纳这个被人广为接纳的假设。但若把普通名词当作种类专名来看的话，语义类别就变成类别 <e>（请参看 Carlson，1977；Chierchia，1998）。

7. 请注意，宾语位置的无定数量名词短语也需存在闭锁，但不是透过“有”，而是透过 Diesing（1992）的隐形存在算子在 VP 层次做存在闭锁，或是透过动词的语义做存在闭锁，本文不对此做深入讨论。

8. 一位审查人问，为什么“学生们”不能借由类别转换由 <e> 变成 <e,t>。如果假设普通名词基本语义类别是 <e,t>，那么一开始，“们”就不能使用，也就没有后续的类别转换。如果普通名词要先类别转换为 <e> 或是移位到 D 来获得 <e> 的解读，之后再转回类别 <e,t>，这可能有经济性考虑而不被允准。

9. 根据 Lin（1998）的分析，“每”的语义功能正是要形成类别 e 的复数个体，详细分析，请参看 Lin（1998）。

10.（61）中的句子听起来好像也不是完全自然的句子，但的确比（60）好，比起（62）则是好得多。

11. 请特别参看 Longobardi（1994，1996，2001）。

参考文献

蔡维天　2004《谈“有人”、“有的人”和“有些人”》，《汉语学报》第 2 期。

陈光磊　1987《关于“们”与“-S”》，《复旦学报》第 5 期。

陈光磊　1994《汉语词法论》，上海：学林出版社。

陈俊和　2009《现代汉语“X+们”的语义功能研究》，复旦大学博士学位论文。

陈小红　2005《论“们”的语法意义和“N 们”的指称特点》，《中山大学学报论丛》第 6 期。

陈玉梅　2015《“们”的辖域、性质、意义及“X + 们”的指称类别研究》，华中师范大学硕士学位论文。

程观林　1985《“们”的一种有生命力的用法及其修辞作用》，《汉语学习》第 1 期。

储泽祥　2000《数词与复数标记不能同现的原因》，《民族语文》第 5 期。

戴耀晶　1987《论助词“们”》，《吉安师专学报》第 1 期。

丁声树　1961《现代汉语语法讲话》，北京：商务印书馆。

郭　华　2013《中英复数对比研究》，《语文学刊》第 3 期。

郭良夫 1983 《现代汉语的前缀和后缀》,《中国语文》第4期。
胡裕树 1981 《现代汉语》,上海:上海教育出版社。
胡裕树 1985 《从“们”字说到汉语语法的特点》,《语文园地》第12期。
黄伯荣、廖序东 1996 《现代汉语》,北京:高等教育出版社。
黄正德 1988 《说“是”和“有”》,《中央研究院历史语言研究所集刊》第59本第1分。
孔凡涛 2004 《试论汉语“们”及“们”字短语》,《徐州教育学院学报》第4期。
李亚非 2015 《也谈汉语名词短语的内部结构》,《中国语文》第2期。
李艳惠、石毓智 2000 《汉语量词系统的建立与复数标记“们”的发展》,《当代语言学》第1期。
吕叔湘 1949 《说“们”》,《国文月刊》第79、80期。
吕叔湘 1985 《近代汉语指代词》,上海:学林出版社。
梅 艳 2003 《关于汉语名词加“们”和英语名词加-s之比较》,《新疆石油教育学院学报》第4期。
宋玉柱 1982 《关于“们”的语法意义及其他》,《语文学习》第11期。
宋玉柱 2003 《“们”的定指意义商榷》,《学语文》第4期。
陶振民 1991 《物类名词后用“们”的语法现象——兼论修辞现象和构词现象的差异》,《华中师范大学学报(哲学社会科学版)》第1期。
陶振民 2000 《“们”表复数语法意义的结构形式》,《焦作工学院学报》第2期。
童盛强 2002 《“们”的定指意义》,《中国语文》第3期。
伍雅清、胡明先 2013 《复数标记与量词同现现象的研究》,《语言科学》第4期。
西原史晓 2009 《“概数+名词+‘们’”结构与“们”的信息结构》,《言语情报科学》。
邢福义 1960 《谈“们”和“诸位”之类并用》,《中国语文》第6期。
邢福义 1965 《再谈“们”和表数词与并用的现象》,《中国语文》第5期。
邢福义 1998 《汉语语法学》,长春:东北师范大学出版社。
杨炎华 2015 《复数标记“们”和集合标记“们”》,《语言教学与研究》第6期。
袁 梅 1996 《“们”的语法意义及其实现》,《延安大学学报》第1期。
张 斌 1998 《汉语语法学》,上海:上海教育出版社。
张 斌 2002 《新编现代汉语》,上海:复旦大学出版社。
张 欢 2010 《现代汉语名词的复数表达形式及其标记问题》,南昌大学硕士学位论文。
张谊生 2001 《“N”+“们”的选择限制与“N们”的表意功能》,《中国语文》第3期。
张谊生、张爱民 1991 《“N+们”的多角度考察》,《现代汉语语法论稿》,南京:江苏教育出版社。

赵元任 1980 《中国话的文法》(丁邦新译)，香港：香港中文大学出版社。

朱德熙 1982 《语法讲义》，北京：商务印书馆。

Abbott, B. 1993. A pragmatic account of the definiteness effect in existential sentences. *Journal of Pragmatics*, 19(1): 39–55.

Barwise, J. & Cooper, R. 1981. Generalized quantifiers and natural language. *Linguistics and Philosophy*, 4(2): 159–219.

Carlson, G. 1977. *Reference to kinds in English*. Ph. D. dissertation, University of Massachusetts Amherst.

Chao, Y.-R. 1968. *A grammar of spoken Chinese*. Berkeley: University of California Press.

Cheng, L. 1994. *Wh*-words as polarity items. In Li J.-K. P., Huang C.-R. & Tang, C.-C. J. (Eds.), *Chinese languages and linguistics, vol. 2: Historical linguistics*. Taipei: Institute of History and Philology, Academia Sinica. 615–640.

Cheung, C.-H. 2003. *An investigation of the Jingpo nominal structure*. Hong Kong: Chinese University of Hong Kong.

Chierchia, G. 1998. Reference to kinds across language. *Natural Language Semantics*, 6(4): 339–405.

Dayal, V. 2004. Number marking and (in)definiteness in kind terms. *Linguistics and Philosophy*, 27 (4): 393–450.

Diesing, M. 1992. *Indefinites*. Cambridge, MA: MIT Press.

Gebhardt, L. 2009. *Numeral classifiers and the structure of DP*. Ph. D. dissertation, Northwestern University.

Guillemin, D. 2011. *The syntax and semantics of a determiner system: A case study of Mauritian creole*. Amsterdam: John Benjamins Publishing Company.

Heim, I. & Kratzer, A. 1998. *Semantics in generative grammar*. Oxford: Blackwell.

Hsieh, L. 2008. *The internal structure of noun phrases in Chinese*. Taipei: Crane Publishing Company.

Iljic, R. 1994. Quantification in Mandarin Chinese: Two markers of plurality. *Linguistics*, 32(1): 91–116.

Iljic, R. 1998. Number and Person. Paper presented at IACL-7/NACCL-10, Stanford University.

Iljic, R. 2001. The problem of the suffix *-men* in Chinese grammar. *Journal of Chinese Linguistics*, 29(1): 11–68.

Jiang, L. J. 2017. Mandarin associative plural *-men* and NPs with *-men*. *International Journal of*

Chinese Linguistics, 4(2): 191–256.

Jin, D. 2020. A semantic account of quantifier-induced intervention effects in Chinese why-questions. *Linguistics and Philosophy*, 43(4): 345–387.

Kurafuji, T. 2004. Plural morphemes, definiteness, and the notion of semantic parameter. *Language and Linguistics*, 5(1): 211–242.

Lan, H. 2010. *Possible interpretations for suffix men in Mandarin Chinese*. Master's thesis dissertation, Utrecht University.

Landman, F. 2003. Predicate-argument mismatches and the adjectival theory of indefinites. In Coene, M. & D'Hulst, Y. (Eds.), *From NP to DP volume 1: The syntax and semantics of noun phrases*. Amsterdam: John Benjamins Publishing Company. 211–237.

Landman, F. 2004. *Indefinites and the type of Sets*. Malden, MA: Blackwell Publishing.

Li, A. 1999. Plurality in a classifier language. *Journal of East Asian Linguistics*, 8(1): 75–99.

Li, Y.-H. A. 1998. Argument determiner phrases and number phrases. *Linguistic Inquiry*, 29(4): 693–702.

Lin, J.-W. 1998. Distributivity in Chinese and its implications. *Natural Language Semantics*, 6(2): 201–243.

Longobardi, G. 1994. Reference and proper names: A theory of N-movement in syntax and logical form. *Linguistic Inquiry*, 25(4): 609–665.

Longobardi, G. 1996. The syntax of n-raising: A minimalist theory. OTS Working Papers, Research Institute for Language and Speech, University of Utrecht.

Longobardi, G. 2001. The Structure of DPs: Some principles, parameters and problems. In Baltin, M. & Collins, C. (Eds.), *The handbook of contemporary syntactic theory*. Malden and Oxford: Blackwell. 562–603.

Mathieu, E. 2009. From local blocking to cyclic agree: The role and meaning of determiners in the history of French. In Ghomeshi, J. Paul, I. & Wiltschko, M. (Eds.), *Determiners: Universals and Variation*. Amsterdam: John Benjamins Publishing Company. 123–158.

Matthewson, L. 2001. Quantification and the nature of crosslinguistic variation. *Natural Language Semantics*, 9 (2): 145–189.

Milsark, G. 1974. Existential sentences in English. Ph. D. dissertation, MIT.

Milsark, G. 1977. Toward an explanation of certain peculiarities of the existential construction in English. *Linguistic Analysis*, 3: 1–29.

Montague, R. 1973. The proper treatment of quantification in ordinary English. In Hintikka, J.,

Matthew, J., Moravcsik, E. & Suppes, P. (Eds.), *Approaches to natural language*. Dordrecht: D. Reidel. 221–242. Reprinted in Montague, 1974. 247–270.

Norman, J. 1988. *Chinese*. Cambridge: Cambridge University Press.

Partee, B. 1987. Noun phrase interpretation and type-shifting principles. In Groenendijk, J., de Jongh, D. & Stokhof, M. (Eds.), *Studies in discourse representation theory and the theory of generalized quantifiers*. GRASS 8, Foris, Dordrecht. 115–143.

Reinhart, T. 1997. Quantifier scope: How labor is divided between QR and choice functions. *Linguistics and Philosophy*, 20(4): 335–397.

Rothstein, S. 2013. A fregean semantics for Number Words. In Aloni, M., Franke, M. & Roelofsen, F. (Eds.), *Proceedings of the 19th Amsterdam Colloquium*. Amsterdam: University of Amsterdam. 179–186.

Soh, H.-L. 2005. *Wh*-in-situ in Mandarin Chinese. *Linguistic Inquiry*, 36(1): 143–155.

Stowell, T. 1989. Subjects, specifiers, and X-bar theory. In Baltin, M. & Kroch, A. (Eds.), *Alternative conceptions of phrase Structure*. Chicago: University of Chicago Press. 232–262.

Stowell, T. 1991. Determiners in NP and DP. In Leffel, K. & Bouchard, D. (Eds.), *Views on phrase structure*. Dordrecht: Kluwer Academic Publishers. 37–56.

Szabolcsi, A. 1987. Functional categories in the noun phrase. In Kenesei, I. (Ed.), *Approaches to Hungarian vol. 2*. Szeged: Jate. 167–189.

Ueda, Y. & Haraguchi, T. 2008. Plurality in Japanese and Chinese. *Nanzan Linguistics: Special Issues*, 3(2): 229–242.

Yang, S.-F. H. 2005. *Plurality and modification in Mandarin nominal phrases*. Ph. D. dissertation, The University of Texas at Austin.

Yang, Y. 2012. Intervention effects and *wh*-construals. *Journal of East Asian Linguistics*, 21(1): 43–87.

Zamparelli, R. 2000. *Layers in the determiner phrase*. New York: Garland Publishing.

作者单位：台湾“中研院”语言学研究所

作者邮箱：林若望：jowanglin@gmail.com

On distributional restrictions on *-men* (们)

Ruowang Lin, Zhizhen Tang, Yongli Zhang,
Zhixiang Shu, Weiwen Liao

Abstract: Based on previous studies, this article further analyzes the syntactic distribution and semantic interpretation of *men* (们) appearing after the noun. This article proposes that *men* (们) is a syntactically imaginary category head, which is a non-mandatory plural individual mark. In terms of parts of speech, DP noun phrase is selected as its complement, but semantically, the DP must be a category <e> or can be passed through the selection function mechanism forms individual generalized quantifier noun phrases (category <<e,t>,t>). Therefore, the co-occurrence of *men* (们) and NP noun phrases or quantitative noun phrases with semantic category <e,t> is excluded. At the same time, this article also explains why some general demonstrative sentences allow the appearance of *men* (们) and some do not allow it, and why the co-occurrence of *men* (们) and non-quantified words has differences in acceptance and subject-object asymmetry.

Keywords: men, syntactic distributions, semantic interpretations, Mandarin Chinese

Author work unit: Institute of Linguistics, Academia Sinica, Taiwan

Author email: Ruowang Lin: jowanglin@gmail.com

The syntax and acquisition of Mandarin sluice-like constructions

Minqi Liu, Nina Hyams, Victoria Mateu

Abstract: *Sluicing* refers to an elliptical structure in which only a *wh*-phrase is overt in a CP, as in *Someone left. I don't know who.* In Mandarin, sluice-like strings ('S-strings') with argument *wh*-remnants require the presence of *shi*, a form that is ambiguous between a copula and a focus marker. This paper proposes a hybrid analysis of Mandarin S-strings as having two possible derivations, a sluice and a pseudo-sluice, unless one of the structures is independently forced. When *shi* is a copula, the S-string has a pseudo-sluice analysis, [*pro* be *wh*-phrase], involving neither movement nor ellipsis. When *shi* is a focus marker, the S-string is derived by focus movement followed by TP-ellipsis yielding a sluice analysis. Results from a comprehension experiment with 59 Mandarin-speaking children show that 3-4-year-olds have only a pseudo-sluice/copula analysis of S-strings. They acquire the sluice/focus movement derivation at approximately age 5 at which point they show the 'subject advantage' typically associated with A' -movement structures in young children.

Keywords: Ellipsis acquisition, intervention, A' -movement, Mandarin sluicing, pseudo-sluicing

1. Introduction

Ellipsis – unpronounced yet understandable elements in a sentence – is a central component of human language. One such elliptical structure is 'sluicing' (first named by Ross 1969), in which only a *wh*-phrase is pronounced, as in the embedded clause in (1a). The sluiced structure in (1a) is semantically equivalent to its un-elided counterpart, the embedded *wh*-question such as *who you called* in (1b). The missing information in the sluice is recovered under semantic/syntactic conditions connecting it to the antecedent in the main clause.

(1) a) You called someone, but I don' t know *who*.

b) You called someone, but I don' t know *who you called*.

Merchant (2001), following Ross (1969), proposed a movement+ellipsis derivation for sluices: in this account, the *wh*-phrase moves to Spec CP, as in other *wh*-constructions, and the remnant TP is deleted at PF, as demonstrated in (2a). Contrary to this derivation, a pseudo-sluicing approach (e.g., Erteschik-Shir 1977 and Pollmann 1975) suggests that the elliptical structure in (1a) is derived from a copula structure in which the subject and the copula are deleted, as shown in (2b). [1]

(2) a) Sluice: You called someone, but I don' t know *[$_{CP}$* ***who***$_i$ *[$_{TP}$* ~~***you called t***$_i$~~*]]*.

b) Pseudo-sluice: You called someone, but I don' t know ***who*** ~~***it was***~~.

Both the movement+ellipsis and the pseudo-sluicing approaches can potentially derive the surface structure in (1a). Nevertheless, in languages with *wh*-movement, syntactic evidence from case-marking, preposition stranding, and binding phenomena mainly supports the movement + ellipsis derivation (Merchant 2001). For instance, (3a) shows that the *wh*-remnant in a German sluice has to be in the same case as its un-elided counterpart in an embedded question (3b), indicating parallel structures between a sluice and an un-elided question.

(3) a) *Er will jemandem schmeicheln, aber sie wissen nicht,*

he wants someone.DAT flatter but they know not

*{*wer / *wen /* ***wem****}*.

who.NOM who.ACC who.DAT

'He wants to flatter someone, but they don' t know who. '

b) *Sie wissen nicht, {*wer/ *wen /* ***wem****} er schmeicheln will.*

they know not who.NOM who.ACC who.DAT he flatter wants

'They don' t know who he wants to flatter. '

In *wh*-in-situ languages, a sluice-like string ('S-string' henceforth) can be different from sluices in languages with *wh*-movement. In Mandarin S-strings, an element *shi* precedes the *wh*-phrase, obligatory in argument S-strings (4a) but optional in adjunct S-strings (4b).

(4) a)	*Lisi*	*jiao-le*	*yi-ge*	*ren,*	*wo*	*bu*	*zhidao*	**(shi)*	*shei.*
	Lisi	call-PERF	one-CL	person	1SG	not	know	SHI	who

'Lisi called someone. I don' t know who. '

b)	*Lisi*	*jiao-le*	*yi-ge*	*ren,*	*wo*	*bu*	*zhidao*	***(shi)***	*weishenme.*
	Lisi	call-PERF	one-CL	person	1SG	not	know	SHI	why

'Lisi called someone. I don' t know why. '

Importantly, *shi* is not only a copula, as shown in (5a), but it also functions as a focus marker (henceforth FM) that often appears in clefts, as in (5b).

(5) a)	*na*	***shi***	*shei?*
	that	**be**	who

'Who is that?'

b)	***shi***	*Lisi*	*jiao-le*	*Mali.*
	FM	Lisi	call-PERF	Mali

'It is Lisi who called Mali. '

This ambiguity of *shi* 'be/FM' has led to a debate over whether such structures in Mandarin involve sluicing, as illustrated in (2a), or rather are pseudo-sluices as in (2b) (see section 2 for more details). In this paper, we investigate the Mandarin S-strings from both a theoretical and experimental perspective. We present the results of an experimental study testing Mandarin-speaking children' s interpretation of S-strings. Our results shed light on the acquisition of this kind of ellipsis – not previously tested in Mandarin – and also have direct implications for the sluice vs. pseudo-sluice debate of S-strings in adult Mandarin.

We begin in the following section by discussing the two competing theoretical accounts of Mandarin S-strings, including new data bearing on this debate. In Section 3, we discuss our acquisition experiment as well as a follow-up CHILDES corpus study. To anticipate our conclusions, we will propose that S-strings have both a sluice and pseudo-sluice derivation and that children acquire the two analyses at different points of development. The final section concludes this paper and discusses some potential future studies.

2. Syntactic study: sluice/pseudo-sluice ambiguity in adult Mandarin

In Mandarin, sluice-like constructions with argument *wh*-phrases (such as *shei* 'who' and *shenme* 'what') require the presence of *shi*, a word that is ambiguous between a copula and a FM. This phenomenon has led syntacticians to two competing analyses of Mandarin S-strings: The pseudo-sluicing approach (as in (6)) posits a silent *pro* as the subject of the copula *shi* and involves neither movement nor ellipsis (Adams 2004; Wei 2009, 2011; Adams & Tomioka 2012; Li & Wei 2014, 2017), while the movement + ellipsis analysis (as in (7)) derives S-strings by focus movement, triggered by the FM *shi*, and TP ellipsis, parallel to the English sluicing analysis involving *wh*-movement followed by TP ellipsis (Chen 2004; Wang & Wu 2006; Chiu 2007; Song & Yoshida 2017).

(6) The pseudo-sluicing analysis:

Lisi jiao-le [yi-ge ren]$_i$, [wo bu zhidao [pro$_i$ ***shi*** *shei]].*

Lisi call-PERF one-CL person 1SG not know *pro* be who

'Lisi called someone$_i$. I don' t know who (*pro$_i$* is). '

(7) The movement + ellipsis analysis:

Lisi jiao-le yi-ge ren...

Lisi call-PERF one-CL person

... wo bu zhidao [$_{CP}$ [$_{C}$ ***shi*** *[$_{FP}$ shei$_i$ [$_{F[+Foc]}$ ~~[$_{TP}$ Lisi jiao-le t$_i$]~~]]]].*

1SG not know FM who < Lisi call-PERF>

'Lisi called someone, I don' t know who (it is that Lisi called). '

In the following sections, we compare these two competing analyses of Mandarin S-strings with respect to several properties, including island-insensitivity, *wh*-else S-strings, idiomatic reconstruction, strict/sloppy readings, the argument/adjunct asymmetry with regard to the presence of *shi*, and multiple S-strings. Based on these data, we will argue for a hybrid analysis of Mandarin sluice-like constructions: both the movement + ellipsis (i.e., sluicing) analysis and the pseudo-sluicing approach can derive S-strings and both are attested in different contexts. More specifically, in certain contexts there must be elided ('hidden') structure in an S-string, supporting a movement + ellipsis derivation (section 2. 2). However, we will also present some prosodic evidence suggesting that there are cases where an S-string must be a pseudo-sluice (section 2. 3). Therefore, we recognize the presence of both sluices and pseudo-sluices in Mandarin and conclude that a surface S-string can have two different derivations and is thus ambiguous between a sluice and a pseudo-sluice unless one of the derivations is blocked. [2]

2.1 The pseudo-sluicing analysis vs. the movement + ellipsis analysis in Mandarin

According to the pseudo-sluicing analysis, the internal structure of S-strings is [*pro* be *wh*-phrase] (see (6) above) and the silent pronoun *pro* is argued to be an E-type pronoun (Adams 2004; Wei 2011; Adams & Tomioka 2012). In this analysis, *pro* has a quantifier antecedent but is not bound by the quantifier. [3] However, in a *wh*-adjunct S-string (8b), *pro* cannot be an E-type pronoun because its antecedent is not clear. [4] Thus, in these cases, it is treated as an event-denoting pronoun (Wei 2011) or a sentential pronoun (Adams & Tomioka 2012), whose denotation is an event or a proposition.

(8) a) *wh*-argument S-string:

Lisi jiao-le [yi-ge ren]$_i$, wo bu zhidao [pro$_i$ shi shei].

Lisi call-PERF one-CL person 1SG not know *pro* be who

'Lisi called someone$_i$. I don' t know who (*pro*$_i$ is). '

b) *wh*-adjunct S-string:

[Lisi jiao-le yi-ge ren]$_i$, wo bu zhidao [pro$_i$ (shi) weishenme].

Lisi call-PERF one-CL person 1SG not know *pro* be why

'[Lisi called someone]$_i$. I don' t know why (*pro*$_i$ is). '

One argument supporting the pseudo-sluicing analysis is that Mandarin is a *pro*-drop language and the silent pronoun *pro* in Mandarin sluices alternates with the overt pronoun *na* 'that' (Adams 2004), as in (9) (cf. (8)).

(9) a) *wh*-argument sluicing:

Lisi jiao-le [yi-ge ren]$_i$, wo bu zhidao ***na***$_i$ *shi shei.*

Lisi call-PERF one-CL person 1SG not know that be who

'Lisi called someone$_i$. I don' t know who *that*$_i$ is. '

b) *wh*-adjunct sluicing:

[Lisi jiao-le yi-ge ren]$_i$, wo bu zhidao ***na***$_i$ *shi weishenme.*

Lisi call-PERF one-CL person 1SG not know that be why

'[Lisi called someone]$_i$. I don' t know why *that*$_i$ is. '

Another potential piece of evidence in favor of the pseudo-sluicing analysis comes from the island-insensitivity of S-strings. As Ross (1969) first noticed for English, the extraction proposed by the movement + ellipsis analysis in sluicing is possible out of some syntactic islands. This is also the case in Mandarin sluices, such as complex NP islands (10), adjunct CP islands (11), sentential subject islands (12), and the left branch condition (13).

(10) *Lisi zhao-le [yi-ge hui shuo liang-men yuyan de ren],*

Lisi find-PERF one-CL can speak two-CL language C person

'Lisi found a person who can speak two languages…'

dan wo bu zhidao [shi na liang-men (yuyan)].

but 1SG not know be which two-CL language

'…but I don' t know which two (languages). '

(11) *Lisi$_i$ [yinwei* <e_i> *kan-le yi-ge jiemu] hen shangxin,*

Lisi because watch-PERF one-CL show very sad

'Lisi$_i$ was very sad because <he$_i$> watched a show…'

dan wo bu zhidao [shi shenme/na-ge jiemu].

but 1SG not know be what/which show

'…but I don' t know what/which show. '

(12) *[you yi-ge ren yao cizhi de xiaoxi] chuan-le chulai…*

there.be one-CL person will resign C news spread-PERF out

'The news that a person will resign spread out…'

dan wo bu zhidao [shi shei].

but 1SG not know be who

'…but I don' t know who. '

(13) *Lisi mai-le yi-tao [fangzi], dan wo bu zhidao [shi duo da].*

Lisi buy-PERF one-CL house but 1SG not know be how big

'Lisi bought a house but I don' t know how big. '

This phenomenon casts doubt on the movement + ellipsis analysis as it would require focus-movement out of syntactic islands. By contrast, the island-insensitivity of S-strings is not a problem for the pseudo-sluicing analysis because under this approach there is no extraction.

Nonetheless, since Ross' s (1969) observation about the island-insensitivity of English sluices, some proponents of the movement + ellipsis analysis (e.g., Lasnik 2001 and Merchant 2001, following ideas of Ross 1969 and Chomsky 1972) have argued that islands are essentially a PF phenomenon and thus the PF deletion of the offending *wh*-copy/trace inside the island can repair an otherwise ungrammatical structure ('salvation by deletion'). The more recent linearization theories (e.g., Fox & Pesetsky 2005) also provide a similar solution for this apparent problem of the movement + ellipsis analysis, claiming that islands are the result of spell-out rule violations, therefore they do not arise when the island is not spelled out.

2.2 Arguments for the movement + ellipsis analysis

In the previous subsection, we saw two arguments supporting the pseudo-sluicing analysis: the overt pronoun alternation and the island-insensitivity of S-strings (cf. Lasnik 2001; Merchant 2001; Fox & Pesetsky 2005). Let us turn now to the arguments that favor a movement + ellipsis derivation over a pseudo-sluicing analysis. Because the pseudo-sluicing analysis posits no hidden structure, it fails to account for a number of properties of Mandarin S-strings including *wh*-else S-strings, the behavior of idiomatic expressions, the strict/sloppy identity ambiguity, the argument-adjunct asymmetry with respect to *shi*, and multiple S-strings. We discuss these in turn.

2.2.1 The *wh*-else S-string

The Mandarin *wh*-else S-string is illustrated in (14). Note that the existential verb *you* 'have' is obligatory before the *wh*-phrase *shei* 'who' .

(14) *Lisi jiao-le Mali, wo bu zhidao hai *(you) shei.*
Lisi called Mali 1SG not know additionally have who
'Lisi called Mali. I don' t know who else. '
(lit. 'I don' t know additionally have who. ')

The pseudo-sluicing analysis cannot account for *wh*-else S-string because *pro* cannot be the subject of the existential verb *you* 'have' , which is non-thematic, and no matter what reference is assigned to *pro*, the intended meaning cannot be derived, as shown in (15a). [5] By contrast, the movement + ellipsis analysis successfully derives *wh*-else sluices if we assume that the existential verb *you* 'there. be' is also a trigger for the extraction of the *wh*-phrase from within the TP, as shown in (15b). [6]

(15) *Lisi$_i$ jiao-le Mali$_j$, wo bu zhidao...*
Lisi called Mali 1SG not know
'Lisi called Mali. I don' t know...'
a) ... pro$_{*i/*j/*k}$ *hai you shei.*
pro additionally have who
Intended: '...who else. ' (lit. '...**pro* additionally have who')
b) ... *hai you shei [$_{TP}$ Lisi jiao-le __ / __ jiao-le Mali].*
additionally have who Lisi call-PERF call-PERF Mali
'...who else <Lisi called / called Mali>. '

2.2.2 The idiomatic reconstruction

A second argument in favor of ellipsis and against pseudo-sluicing comes from the idiomatic reconstruction in S-strings, as pointed out by Song & Yoshida (2017). The example in (16) contains the idiom *chi yi ge ren de cu* 'be jealous of someone' (lit. 'eat a person' s vinegar'). The well-formedness of the S-string under the idiomatic interpretation shows that there must be an elided structure containing the verb *chi* 'eat' (16a); without that structure the DP (*shei de cu* 'whose vinegar') in the S-string loses its idiomatic interpretation. Under a pseudo-sluicing analysis, in which the null subject *pro* takes the DP *yi ge ren de cu* 'a person' s vinegar' as its antecedent, only the unintended literal interpretation is available, which is still the case even if the null subject *pro* is replaced by the overt pronoun *na* 'that' , as shown in (16b).

(16) *Lisi zai* ***chi*** ***[yi-ge ren]-de cu...***
Lisi PROG eat one-CL person-GEN vinegar
'Lisi is jealous of someone...'

a) ...*wo bu zhidao shi shei-de cu*$_i$ ~~[$_{TP}$ *Lisi zai chi t*$_i$]~~.

1SG not know FM who-GEN vinegar Lisi PROG eat

'I don' t know who <Lisi is jealous of>. '

(lit. I don' t know whose vinegar <Lisi is eating>.)

b) ...*wo bu zhidao pro/na shi shei-de cu.*

1SG not know *pro*/that be who-GEN vinegar

'I don' t know whose vinegar that is. '

(≠ Intended: 'I don' t know who Lisi is jealous of. ')

2.2.3 Sloppy identity

Another argument showing that there must be elided structure in S-strings comes from the strict/sloppy identity ambiguity, or more precisely, the availability of sloppy readings in Mandarin S-strings. The sentence in (17), in which both strict and sloppy readings are possible, is illustrative:

(17) *Lisi*$_i$ *zhidao shei tou-le ta*$_i$*-de qian,*

Lisi$_i$ know who steal-PERF 3SG-GEN money

'Lisi$_i$ knows who stole his$_i$ money…'

Mali ye zhidao shi shei.

Mali too know be/FM who

a) strict reading: '…Mali$_j$ also knows who (stole his$_i$ (=Lisi' s) money). '

b) sloppy reading: '…Mali$_j$ also knows who (stole her$_j$ (=Mali' s) money). '

The availability of a sloppy reading for the S-string in (17), i.e., (17b) indicates the presence of the 3SG pronoun *ta* inside the elided structure, as in (18), that takes the local *Mali* as its antecedent. The strict reading is also available under an ellipsis analysis when *ta* refers to the distant antecedent *Lisi*. The ambiguity introduced by the pronoun in the elided structure is demonstrated in (18).

(18) *Mali*$_j$ *ye zhidao shi shei* ~~[*tou-le ta*$_{i/j}$*-de qian*]~~.

Mali$_j$ too know FM who steal-PERF 3SG-GEN money

'…Mali$_j$ also knows who (stole his$_i$/her$_j$ money). ' (strict reading; sloppy reading)

On the other hand, the pseudo-sluice analysis must posit that the ambiguity comes from the *pro* subject of the dependent clause (cf. 6). But if *pro* in the pseudo-sluice is the null counterpart of *na*, as we have assumed (following Adams 2004), then like *na* it should have only a strict reading, referring to the one and only pragmatically prominent antecedent; in the case of (19), *na* must be the person who stole Lisi' s money and cannot be interpreted as the person who stole Mali' s money:

(19) ... *Mali ye zhidao na shi shei.*
Mali too know that be who
'...Mali also knows who that is. ' (strict reading; *sloppy reading)

Thus, the availability of the sloppy reading shows that the S-string has more covert structure than a simple copular structure with a null subject. This is consistent with the movement + ellipsis analysis but not the pseudo-sluicing derivation. [7]

2.2.4 Other arguments

Further evidence in favor of the movement + ellipsis analysis regards the argument/adjunct asymmetry associated with *shi*, as well as the behavior of multiple S-strings.

The presence of *shi* is obligatory when the *wh*-remnant is an argument, as in (20a), but *shi* is optional when the *wh*-remnant is an adjunct, as in (20b).

(20) a) *Lisi jiao-le yi-ge ren, dan wo bu zhidao *(shi) shei.*
Lisi call-PERF one-CL person but 1SG not know be/FM who
'Lisi called someone but I don' t know who. '

b) *Lisi jiao-le yi-ge ren, dan wo bu zhidao (shi) weishenme.*
Lisi call-PERF one-CL person but 1SG not know be/FM why
'Lisi called someone but I don' t know why. '

Adams (2004), following the pseudo-sluicing approach, explains this asymmetry by claiming that *wh*-adjuncts are predicative, while the two *wh*-arguments (*shei* 'who' and *shenme* 'what') are not. Observing that *shi* is obligatory in argument fragment answers (21a), but not required in adjunct fragment answers (21b), Adams concludes that *wh*-arguments require the copula *shi* 'be' in order to predicate a property of the null subject *pro*, while *wh*-adjuncts can predicate a property of *pro* directly.

(21) Speaker A: *mama zhu-le yi-pan haochi-de cai.* (Adams 2004)
mom cook-PERF one-CL delicious-DE dish
'Mom cooked a delicious dish.'

a) Speaker B: *(*na*/pro *shi) shenme?*
that/*pro* be what
'What *(was it)?'

b) Speaker B: (*na*/pro *shi) shenme shihou?*
that/*pro* be what time
'When (was it)?'

However, a counterexample to this claim is illustrated in (22), in which the *wh*-argument *shei* 'who' is grammatical in a fragment answer with or without *shi*.

(22) Speaker A: *mama jian-le yi-ge ren.*
mom meet-PERF one-CL person
'Mom met someone.'

Speaker B: *(shi) shei?*
be/FM who
'Who?'

If Adams' (2004) argument is correct and the ability to stand alone in a fragment answer is the criterion for being predicative, given (22) we would also expect *shei* to be predicative and thus that *shi* would be optional in an S-string with *shei*, contrary to fact. As noted above, *shi* is obligatory in S-strings with *shei* 'who' and *shenme* 'what'.

Alternatively, following a movement + ellipsis derivation, we propose that the argument-adjunct asymmetry with respect to the presence of *shi* results from the different positions of *wh*-arguments and *wh*-adjuncts: *wh*-arguments are within TP while the *wh*-adjuncts, that show optionality with the presence of *shi*, are adjoined to it. [8] To escape the TP, a *wh*-argument has to be extracted, as happens, for example, through the focus movement triggered by the FM *shi*, as shown in (23). [9] That is why *shi* is always present with argument S-strings such as (20a). Absent *shi*, the argument *wh*-phrase would not be able to escape the TP-ellipsis.

(23) *wh*-arguments extracted out of the TP via focus movement:

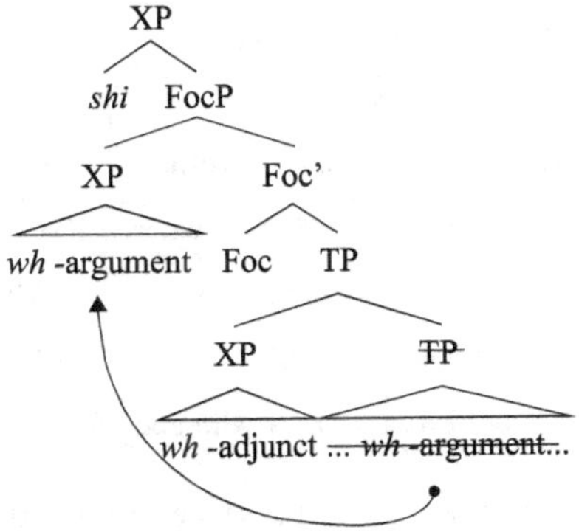

By contrast, *wh*-adjuncts like *weishenme* 'why' are adjoined to TP at the point of TP-ellipsis (which deletes the TP that they are adjoined to, but does not include them). *Shi* is optional for those *wh*-adjuncts because the focus movement triggered by *shi* is not necessary for them to escape the elided TP. In other words, focus movement of those *wh*-adjuncts is optional: when the adjunct moves to Spec-FocP the structure is (24b); otherwise the structure is (24a).

(24) a) b)

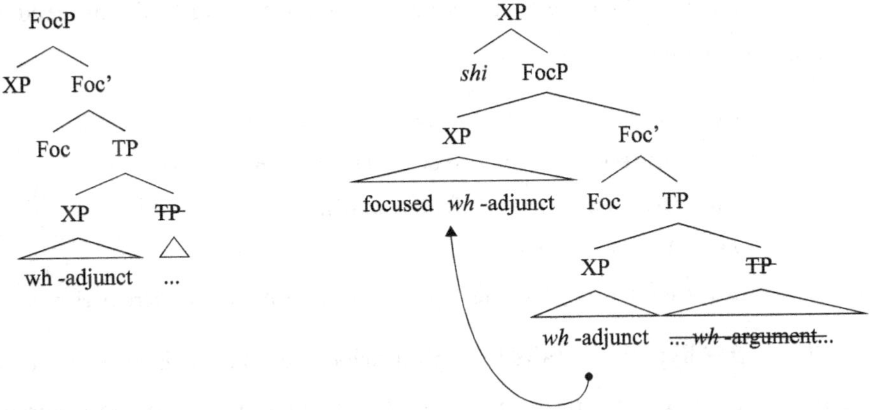

The movement + ellipsis derivation also accounts for the behavior of multiple S-strings in Mandarin. The sentences in (25) illustrate two properties of multiple S-strings: (i) the *wh*-argument must precede, not follow the *wh*-adjunct (25a), and (ii) the FM *shi* only occurs before the first *wh*-phrase but is not allowed before the second (25b). [10]

(25) *Lisi* *da-le* *yi-ge* *ren*...
Lisi beat-PERF one-CL person
a) ... **dan* *wo* *bu* *zhidao* *shi* *zai-nali* *shi* *shei.*
but 1SG not know FM at-where FM who
b) ... *dan* *wo* *bu* *zhidao* **(shi)* *shei* *(*shi)* *zai-nali.*
but 1SG not know FM who FM at-where
'Lisi beat someone but I don' t know who and where. '

These two requirements are a natural result of the movement + ellipsis derivation in (23). The *wh*-argument precedes the adjunct in multiple S-strings because the former is in the higher focus position and the latter is in its original position. That *shi* only occurs before the *wh*-argument but not before the *wh*-adjunct derives from the fact that there is only one *shi* projection in (23).

On the other hand, the pseudo-sluicing analysis cannot explain these two properties of multiple S-strings. This analysis posits a null subject in the S-string. Hence, in multiple S-strings, there should be multiple null subjects, one referring to the antecedent DP *mouren* 'someone' and one referring to the antecedent event 'Lisi beat someone' , as follows:

(26) *[Lisi* *da-le* *yi-ge* *ren*$_i$*]*$_j$ *dan* *wo* *bu* *zhidao*...
Lisi beat-PERF one-CL person but 1SG not know
...pro$_i$ **(shi)* *shei* pro$_j$ *(*shi)* *zai-nali.*
pro be who *pro* be at-where
'[Lisi beat someone$_i$]$_j$ but I don' t know who (was *pro*$_i$) and where (was *pro*$_j$). '

Thus, this hypothesis fails to explain why only one *shi* is allowed, or why the order of the *wh*-argument and the *wh*-adjunct phrases cannot be reversed. Both problems are solved by a movement + ellipsis derivation.

2.2.5 Interim summary

Summarizing the discussion thus far, we have seen that the movement + ellipsis derivation provides a better explanation for the argument/adjunct asymmetry with regard to *shi* and the two properties of multiple S-strings. More importantly, because the pseudo-sluicing analysis does not posit ellipsis in S-strings, it fails to account for various phenomena that require the presence of hidden structure: *wh*-else S-strings, idiomatic reconstruction, and the strict/sloppy ambiguity of Mandarin S-strings. Finally, the island-repair effect of S-strings – perhaps the strongest argument in favor of the pseudo-sluicing analysis, is not fatal to the movement + ellipsis derivation insofar as various syntactic solutions are available to account for the extraction out of islands.

2.3 Prosodic evidence for pseudo-sluices

The preponderance of evidence presented to this point supports the focus movement + ellipsis analysis of Mandarin S-strings (as opposed to the pseudo-sluicing approach). However, in this section we discuss cases in which a surface S-string is in fact a pseudo-sluice, that is, a copular sentence with a null subject *pro* [*pro* be *wh*-phrase].

We have seen that one crucial difference between these two derivations is how they analyze the ambiguous *shi*. The movement + ellipsis derivation recognizes *shi* as a FM of the same kind we find in clefts, whereas the pseudo-sluicing analysis treats it as a copula linking the silent subject and the *wh*-phrase. In this section, we discuss a prosodic difference between the FM *shi* and the copula *shi*: the former cannot be accented while the latter can. Since the *shi* in an S-string itself is ambiguous, we will use un-elided structures to show this difference. Example (27) shows that before the cleft-pivot *Lisi* the FM *shi* cannot be accented in un-elided clefts.

(27) **SHI* *Lisi* *jiao-le* *Mali.*
FM Lisi call-PERF Mali
'*It WAS Lisi that called Mali.'

By contrast, the accent in a copular sentence can be realized on the copula *shi,* as shown in (28), especially when *shi* 'be' is contrastive with its negative form *bu shi* 'be not', for example (29). [11]

(28) *jiao-le* *Mali* *de* *ren* *queshi* *SHI* *Lisi.*
call-PERF Mali C person indeed be Lisi
'The person who called Mali (indeed) WAS Lisi.'

(29) Context: Speakers A and B are waiting for Lisi. They see a man who looks like him but are not sure whether he is Lisi or not.

a) Speaker A: pro/*ta*/*na*[12] *haoxiang* ***bu*** ***shi*** *Lisi.*
pro/3SG/that seemingly not be Lisi
'Seemingly, <it>/he/that is not Lisi.'

b) Speaker B: *bu,* *ni* *cuo-le.* pro/*ta*/*na* *SHI* *Lisi.*
no, 2SG wrong-PERF *pro*/3SG/that be Lisi
'No, you're wrong. <It>/He/That IS Lisi.'

In S-strings, *shi* is usually not accented because it is typically the *wh*-phrase that bears the focus accent. If *shi* does get accented, it is a sign that the surface S-string is a pseudo-sluice because copula *shi* can be accented while FM *shi* cannot. (30) is an example of an accented *shi* in a S-string, where *shi* 'be' is being contrasted with *bu shi* 'not be'.

(30) Context: Someone stole Lisi's money. I don't know who did it but I know who didn't (because they have an alibi).
Mouren *tou-le* *Lisi-de* *qian…*
someone steal-PERF Lisi-GEN money
'Someone stole Lisi's money…'
wo *bu* *zhidao* *SHI* *shei,* *dan* *wo* *zhidao* *BU* *SHI* *shei.*
1SG not know be who but 1SG know not be who
'I don't know who *pro* WAS, but I know who *pro* WAS NOT.'

In this example, the S-string must be a pseudo-sluice [*pro* SHI shei] because *shi* is accented. We, therefore, derive a prediction: in those cases where *shi* is accented (hence necessarily a pseudo-sluice structure), a sloppy reading of the S-string should be unavailable, as shown in (19) above. As we see in (31), this prediction is borne out.

(31) *Lisi* *zhidao* *shi* *shei* *tou-le* *ta-de* *qian…*
Lisi know FM who steal-PERF 3SG-GEN money

'Lisi knows who$_i$ is it that stole his money...'

Mali ye zhidao SHI shei / Mali zhidao BU SHI shei.

Mali too know be who Mali knows not be who

a) strict reading: 'Mali also knows who *pro$_i$* IS. / Mali knows who *pro$_i$* IS NOT. '

b) sloppy reading: '#Mali$_j$ also knows who (stole her$_j$ money) / #Mali$_j$ knows who did not (steal her$_j$ money). '

In (30) and (31), the accented *shi* forces a pseudo-sluice interpretation of the S-string. [13] It follows that a pseudo-sluicing analysis must be available in Mandarin and hence that an S-string is ambiguous between a sluice (derived by movement + ellipsis) and a pseudo-sluice (a copula structure with a null subject), unless one of the structures is blocked. For example, idiomatic reconstruction would not be possible under a pseudo-sluicing derivation, which does not posit elided structure, while an accented *shi* would not be derivable on a movement + ellipsis derivation since only when *shi* is a copula can it be accented.

2.4 Summary

In this section, we have discussed two syntactic accounts of Mandarin S-strings: the movement + ellipsis analysis treats *shi* as a FM and proposes that S-strings derive from focus-movement of the *wh*-remnant and TP-ellipsis; whereas the pseudo-sluicing analysis treats *shi* as a copula that links a null subject *pro* and the *wh*-phrase, postulating no movement or elided structure. [14]

We argued that the sloppy readings, idiomatic reconstruction, and *wh*-else S-strings support the presence of hidden structure, hence ellipsis, in S-strings. However, the fact that *shi* can be accented also indicates that S-strings can be analyzed as containing a copula *shi*. We thus propose a hybrid analysis in which Mandarin S-strings are structurally ambiguous between a sluice and a pseudo-sluice, unless one or the other derivation is forced in certain contexts.

3. Experimental study: S-strings in child Mandarin

In the previous section, we compared the movement + ellipsis analysis and the pseudo-sluicing analysis with regard to several properties of Mandarin

S-strings. In fact, these two analyses also make different predictions with respect to Mandarin-speaking children' s acquisition of S-strings.

Mateu, Hyams, and Winans' (2017) study of the acquisition of sluicing in English found that children aged 3; 0-6; 11 (*M* = 5;03) comprehend subject sluices significantly better than object sluices – what we henceforth refer to as the 'subject advantage' . Their finding is consistent with the predictions of the Intervention Hypothesis (Friedmann et al. 2009; cf. also Hyams & Snyder 2005; Snyder & Hyams 2015), viz., that A' -dependencies that cross another potential A' -moving element are harder for children. [15] According to this hypothesis, the subject advantage results from the movement + ellipsis derivation of English sluices. As shown in (32a), there is no intervener in the movement of *who* in the subject sluice, while the embedded subject *John* intervenes the movement of *who* in the object sluice (32b). [16]

(32) a) Someone pushed John, but I don' t know [$_{CP}$ who$_i$ ~~[$_{TP}$ t_i pushed John]~~]. (subject sluice)
b) John pushed someone, but I don' t know [$_{CP}$ who$_i$ ~~[$_{TP}$ John pushed t_i]~~]. (object sluice)
intervener

Since the movement + ellipsis analysis of Mandarin S-strings postulates (focus) movement of the *wh*-remnant, it also predicts that Mandarin-speaking children will show the same subject advantage, which is to say that they would perform better on subject S-strings than on object S-strings. On the other hand, the pseudo-sluicing analysis, which proposes no movement in the derivation of Mandarin S-strings, makes no such prediction. All else being equal, children should show no subject (or object) advantage in their comprehension of S-strings.

This experiment is designed to investigate whether the subject advantage exists for 3- to 6-year-old Mandarin-speaking children. Our results should provide us with a better understanding of the acquisition of the Mandarin S-strings construction as well as its syntax.

3.1 Methods

3.1.1 Subjects

A total of 59 native Mandarin-speaking children aged 3; 0-6; 8 (*M* = 4;10) were tested, 15 in each year interval except for the 3-year-old group which had 14 subjects. Forty-seven of the children were recruited in Changsha, Hunan, China, and the remaining twelve in Los Angeles, California, all of whom had at least 80% exposure to Mandarin according to parents' reports. Fourteen additional subjects were tested but excluded because they failed five or more out of the twelve control trials, namely the full *wh*-questions.[17]

3.1.2 Design and materials

This experiment had 24 trials with a 2 × 2 × 2 design crossing three factors: S(entence)Type (S-strings vs. full (unsluiced) *wh*-questions (as control trials)), Position (subject vs. object), and Animacy (animate vs. inanimate arguments). Three out of the four transitive verbs were used in each condition: *zhui* 'to chase', *tui* 'to push', *ya* 'to be on the top of', and *kao* 'to lean on'.

Sentences (33) and (34) demonstrate the four conditions (2 Positions × 2 Types) with animate arguments. Under the animate condition, the *wh*-phrase used was *shei* 'who'. The (a) examples illustrate the S-string, and the (b) examples the full *wh*-question control:

(33) Subject extraction with animate arguments

Antecedent clause:

wo	*neng*	*kanjian*	*yi-ge*	*ren*	*zai*	*zhui*	*hongse*	*yifu-de*	*nansheng...*
1SG	can	see	one-CL	person	PROG	chase	red	clothes-DE	boy

'I can see that someone is chasing the boy in red...'

a)

... *ni*	*neng*	*kanjian*	*shi*	*shei*	*ma?*
2SG	can	see	be/FM	who	Q

'...can you see who?'

b)

... *ni*	*neng*	*kanjian*	*shei*	*zai*	*zhui*	*hongse*	*yifu-de*	*nansheng*	*ma?*
2SG	can	see	who	PROG	chase	red	clothes-DE	boy	Q

'...can you see who is chasing the boy in red?'

(34) Object extraction with animate arguments

Antecedent clause:

wo	*neng*	*kanjian*	*hongse*	*yifu-de*	*nansheng*	*zai*	*zhui*	*yi-ge*	*ren...*
1SG	can	see	red	clothes-DE	boy	PROG	chase	one-CL	person

'I can see that the boy in red is chasing someone...'

a) ... *ni* *neng* *kanjian* *shi* *shei* *ma?*
2SG can see be/FM who Q
'...can you see who?'

b) ... *ni* *neng* *kanjian* *hongse* *yifu-de* *nansheng* *zai* *zhui* *shei* *ma?*
2SG can see red clothes-DE boy PROG chase who Q
'...can you see who the boy in red is chasing?'

Our experiment also had trials with inanimate arguments to cancel a potential effect observed in previous studies, viz. that children generally prefer animate DPs to be subjects and inanimate DPs to be objects (e.g., Dahl 2000 for Swedish, Øvrelid 2004 for Norwegian, Scott & Fischer 2009 for English). More specifically, in the S-string trials such as (33a) and (34a), if children are affected by the tendency in natural language for *shei* 'who' questions to be subject *wh*-questions and the more general trend of animate DPs to be subjects, there will be a bias towards a subject answer in the S-string trials, potentially resulting in a subject advantage. Therefore, we manipulated Animacy so that the trials with animate arguments and inanimate arguments were balanced. [18] Sentences (35) and (36) exemplify the four conditions with inanimate arguments. In the inanimate conditions, the *wh*-phrase used was *shenme* 'what'. As before, the (a) examples are the S-string, and the (b) examples the full *wh*-question control.

(35) Subject extraction with inanimate arguments
Antecedent clause:
wo *neng* *kanjian* *yi-ge* *dongxi* *zai* *zhui* *huangse-de* *che*...
1SG can see one-CL thing PROG chase yellow-DE car
'I can see that something is chasing the yellow car...'

a) ... *ni* *neng* *kanjian* *shi* *shenme* *ma?*
2SG can see be/FM what Q
'...can you see what?'

b) ... *ni* *neng* *kanjian* *shenme* *zai* *zhui* *huangse-de* *che* *ma?*
2SG can see what PROG chase yellow-DE car Q
'...can you see what is chasing the yellow car?'

(36) Object extraction with inanimate arguments

Antecedent clause:

wo neng kanjian huangse-de che zai zhui yi-ge dongxi...

1SG can see yellow-DE car PROG chase one-CL thing

'I can see that the yellow car is chasing something...'

a) ... *ni neng kanjian shi shenme ma?*

2SG can see be/FM what Q

'...can you see what?'

b) ... *ni neng kanjian huangse-de che zai zhui shenme ma?*

2SG can see yellow-DE car PROG chase what Q

'...can you see what the yellow car is chasing?'

As discussed earlier (Section 2. 2. 4), S-strings with argument *wh*-phrases such as *shei* 'who' and *shenme* 'what' require the presence of *shi*, regardless of the Position. However, in full *wh*-questions in Mandarin, *shi* is optional in subject(-cleft) *wh*-questions (37a) but unacceptable in object(-cleft) *wh*-questions (37b).

(37) a) *(shi) shei zai zhui wo?*

FM who PROG chase 1SG

'Who is chasing me?' / 'Who is it that is chasing me?'

b) *wo zai zhui (*shi) shei?*

1SG PROG chase FM who

'Who am I chasing?' / '*Who is it that I am chasing?'

To avoid introducing another variable into the experiment (i. e. the presence of *shi* in subject but not object full *wh*-questions), we did not include *shi* in either the subject or object *wh*-question controls.

3.1.3 Procedure

The children were shown images on a screen and were then asked pre-recorded questions by a cartoon character, Miss Donkey. Figures 1 and 2 are examples of these images, in which three characters/items perform the same actions (e.g., chase, push, etc.) on one other. The children were required to answer the questions, illustrated in (33)–(36) above, by answering 'yes/no' or pointing to one character/item in the image. [19] In half of the images, one character/item was partially hidden so that when asked if they could see the target character/item, the children were not biased towards always responding 'yes' (or 'no'). [20]

Figure 1. Chasing event with animate characters[21]

Figure 2. Chasing event with inanimate items[22]

For example, in Figure 1, the girl in purple is chasing the boy in red, who is in turn chasing someone who is partially hidden. Miss Donkey would ask, for example (35a), 'I can see that someone is chasing the boy in red, can you see who?' A correct response to this question would be either to point to the girl in purple or to verbally answer 'yes (the girl in purple)' . Other responses (e.g., pointing to another character or saying 'no') were counted as incorrect. [23]

The test started with a brief color-naming test which eliminated one subject who failed this pretest. Next was the training session that contained 9 items designed to familiarize the children with the task. No child had to be excluded due to misunderstanding of the task. There were 24 test sentences in the 2 × 2 × 2 design, as described previously. Any child who became tired or lost interest in the tasks was given a short break. The full set of the training and testing items is provided in Appendix B.

3.2 Results

Table 1 (plotted in Figures 3 and 4) lays out the mean percentages of correct responses under four conditions ({subject, object} × {full *wh*-questions, S-strings}) and the numbers of children who performed significantly above chance in each age group. [24]

Table 1. Percentage of correct responses (standard errors in parentheses) and numbers of above-chance participants in each age group

	Full *wh*-question controls			S-strings		
	Subject *wh*-Q	Object *wh*-Q	# above-chance	Subject S-string	Object S-string	# above-chance
Age 3	73. 81% (6. 2)	69. 05% (3. 7)	13/14	63. 10% (6. 8)	59. 52% (6. 1)	10/14
Age 4	85. 56% (6. 0)	90. 00% (4. 4)	15/15	75. 56% (8. 4)	84. 44% (6. 7)	13/15
Age 5	93. 33% (5. 6)	94. 44% (2. 8)	15/15	92. 22% (3. 2)	81. 11% (4. 6)	15/15
Age 6	92. 22% (5. 6)	97. 78% (2. 6)	15/15	93. 33% (3. 2)	81. 11% (5. 8)	15/15
Average	86. 23% (3. 6)	87. 82% (2. 5)	–	81. 05% (3. 8)	76. 55% (3. 6)	–
	87. 02%		–	78. 80%		–

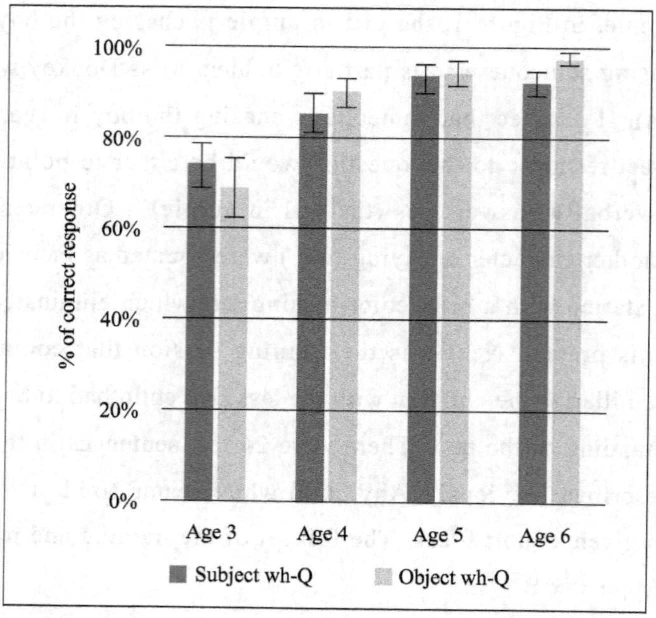

Figure 3. Mean percentages of correct responses for full *wh*-questions by age

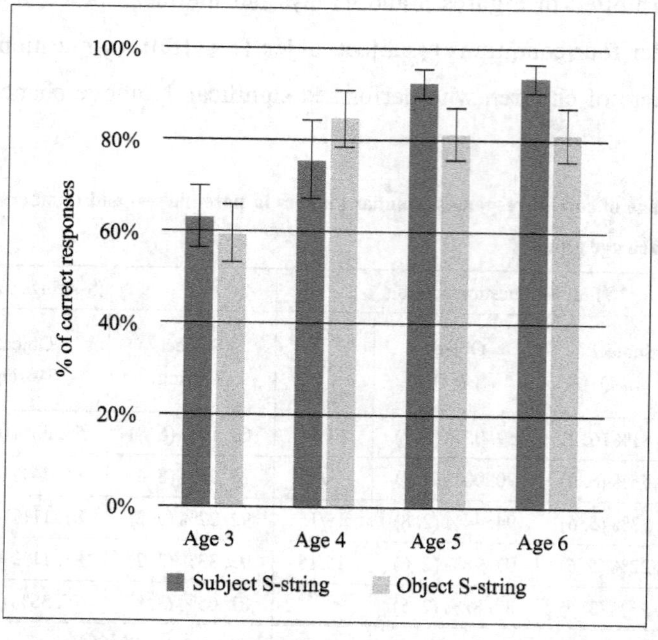

Figure 4. Mean percentages of correct responses for S-strings by age

(Error bars indicate standard errors in figures 3 and 4.)

Data analysis was conducted in R version 3. 5. 0 (R Development Core Team 2014). Because responses were binary (either correct or incorrect), a mixed-effect logistic regression (using the lme4 package, Bates & Maechler 2009) modeled the dependency of correct responses to Age, SType, Position, Animacy, the SType-Position interaction, and the Animacy-Position interaction, with Verb and Participant as random intercepts. Our results show that Age ($\chi^2(1) = 20.484$, $p < 0.001$) and SType ($\chi^2(2) = 25.495$, $p < 0.001$) both contributed significantly to the model fit according to a likelihood-ratio test, while Animacy ($\chi^2(2) = 5.595$, $p = 0.061$) and Position ($\chi^2(3) = 1.057$, $p = 0.787$) did not, neither did the Animacy-Position interaction ($\chi^2(1) = 0.700$, $p = 0.403$) nor the SType-Position interaction ($\chi^2(1) = 0.353$, $p = 0.553$). Since neither Animacy nor its interaction with Position contributed significantly to the model and is not directly relevant to our research question, we henceforth exclude it from the model. The results of all conditions including Animacy, are shown in Appendix A.

In the simplified logistic regression model with only Age, SType, Position and the SType-Position interaction as fixed effects and Verb and Participant as random intercepts, we found significant effects of Age ($p < 0.001$) and SType ($p < 0.001$). The conclusions drawn from these results are that (i) older children performed better than younger children, and that (ii) children performed better with full *wh*-questions than S-strings.

As can be seen in Figures 3 and 4, the performance of children was different across ages. To better explore this age effect, the data were divided into the younger (3- and 4-year-old) and the older (5-and 6-year-old) groups. The first difference between these two groups is the interaction between SType and Position, which is not significant in the younger group ($p = 0.673$) but significant in the older group ($p = 0.026$). The interaction in each group is demonstrated in Figures 5 and 6.

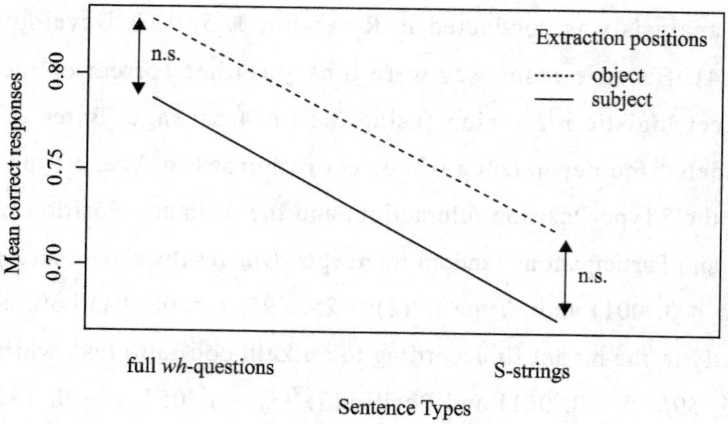

Figure 5. The SType-Position interaction in the younger group (3- and 4-year-olds)

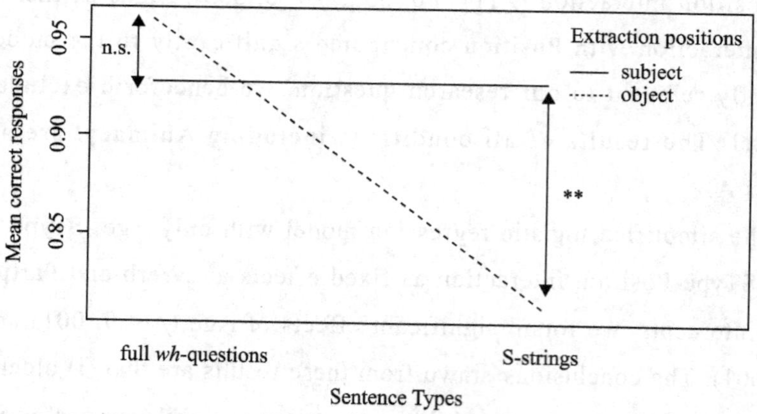

Figure 6. The SType-Position interaction in the older group (5- and 6-year-olds)

As shown in Figures 5 and 6, the younger children showed no difference in performance between subject/object trials in either S-strings or full *wh*-question controls ($p = 0.489$ and 0. 301 for full *wh*-questions and S-strings, respectively), whereas the older children showed no difference in performance on subject/object *wh*-questions ($p = 0.841$), but performed significantly better on subject S-strings than on object S-strings ($p = 0.004$). In other words, the younger children (3- and 4-year-olds) did not show any subject/object asymmetry in either sentence type, while the older children (5- and 6-year-olds) showed a significant subject advantage in their comprehension of S-strings.

3.3 Discussion

Our primary goal was to determine whether there is a subject advantage in Mandarin-speaking children' s comprehension of S-strings. Recall the different predictions of the two analyses of S-strings: if only a pseudo-sluicing analysis is available to these children, they should not show subject/object asymmetry in their interpretation of S-strings; however, given the intervention effect observed in English sluices (and other A' -movement structures, see fn. 15), we expect that if a movement + ellipsis derivation is also part of their grammar, children will perform better on subject S-strings than on object S-strings (the subject advantage).

Our results show a clear subject advantage in older Mandarin-speaking children (ages 5-6). This finding supports the hypothesis that these children, and (a fortiori) Mandarin-speaking adults, have focus movement + ellipsis as part of their grammar. In this respect, our results parallel those found for English. However, the subject advantage is not observed in younger Mandarin-speaking children (ages 3-4). Thus, another important finding of our study concerns the delayed appearance of a subject advantage in Mandarin as compared to English. As discussed earlier, Mateu et al. (2017) found that by age 3 English-speaking children show a subject advantage in their comprehension of sluices, becoming adult-like (i.e., losing the subject > object asymmetry) only at around age 5. On the other hand, using similar materials, the Mandarin experiment shows a subject advantage only in the 5- and 6-year-old groups.

Why do Mandarin-speaking children show a subject advantage later than English-speaking children? Our hypothesis is that the presence of *shi* with its copula/FM ambiguity introduces a structurally simpler, non-movement derivation for Mandarin S-strings that does not exist for English sluices. We propose that Mandarin-speaking children first analyze *shi* uniquely as a copula, thereby deriving only the pseudo-sluice. Later, they learn that *shi* is also a FM, at which point a movement + ellipsis derivation of the S-string also becomes available. Because children initially have only a copula analysis of *shi* (Stage 1), there is no movement at this stage, hence no intervention and no subject advantage. Once they acquire the focus property of *shi*, the movement + ellipsis derivation also becomes available and the subject advantage emerges as an effect of intervention (Stage 2).

In addition to the age effect just described, our experiment also shows a full *wh*-question > S-string asymmetry, viz. that the children performed better on *wh*-questions than on S-strings. This asymmetry is unsurprising: Children must recover unspoken information in the S-string (be it the elided structure in sluices or the reference of the null subject *pro* in pseudo-sluices) in order to assign an interpretation, while this is not an issue in the full *wh*-questions.

We found no subject/object asymmetry in full *wh*-questions at any age. One possible explanation is that Mandarin is a *wh*-in-situ language, viz., there is no overt *wh*-movement, thus the intervention effect is not triggered in full *wh*-questions. However, in a *wh*-movement language like English, there is also no intervention effect in full *wh*-questions among 3-6-year olds either (Mateu et al. 2017). Therefore, a more plausible account is that by age 3 children are fully adult-like with respect to *wh*-questions, and hence show no intervention effect, i.e., no subject/object asymmetry. [25]

3.4 A Follow-up Corpus Study

To further test this two-stage hypothesis, we followed up with a corpus study which included 457 children (age 0; 08–6; 11) from the CHILDES database (MacWhinney 2000). [26] We conducted a search of all instances of *shi*. The expectation given our two-stage model is that children will not produce sentences with FM *shi* until a later age, while copula *shi* should be present quite early.

As predicted, our results show that Mandarin-speaking children produce copula *shi* from age 0; 08, the earliest age in the database. For illustrative purposes, we provide several early examples in (38).

(38) a) *Xueer* ***shi*** *laoshu.* (0; 08)
Xueer be mouse
'Xueer is a mouse. '

b) *zhe bu* ***shi*** *qiu ma?* (0; 08)
this not be ball Q
'Isn' t this a ball?'

c) *zhe* **shi** *da* *qiqiu.* (1; 05)
this be big balloon
'This is a big balloon. '

d) *wo* **shi** *ni-de* *laoshi.* (2; 03)
1SG be 2SG-GEN teacher
'I am your teacher. '

On the other hand, FM *shi* appears later and is far less frequent, also as predicted. [27] Of 6235 tokens of *shi* only 13 are FMs (0. 21%). Table 2 provides the total number of FMs produced by the children in our corpus study at one-year age intervals.

Table 2. The number of FM *shi* produced by age in two structures in Mandarin

	Age 3	Age 4	Age 5	Age 6
# of sentence-initial FM *shi* in clefts	1	5	5	2
# of FM *shi* in S-strings	0	0	0	0

Note that all instances of FM *shi* that we found appeared in clefts, for example (39). There were no occurrences of argument S-strings in Mandarin-speaking children's spontaneous productions through the age of 6; 11.

(39) a) ***shi*** *shenme* *zai* *xiang* *a.* (age 3 (month unknown))
FM what PROG make.sound SFP
'What is it that is making a sound?'

b) Child 1: *dao-le.* (age 4; 03)
fall-PERF
'(It) fell down. '

Child 2: *zenme* *nong* *de?*
how do DE
'What happened?'

Child 1: ***shi*** *ni* *nong* *de* *a.*
FM 2SG do DE SFP
'It was you (who did it). '

As Table 2 shows, we found only one occurrence of FM *shi* among the 3-year-olds, given in (39a) (this one production might be an "isolate", see fn. 26) and the exact age of this child is unknown (only the year but not the month is provided). [28] The next example appears at age 4; 03, shown in the exchange in (39b). Thus, it is only after 4 years old that the FM *shi* becomes somewhat productive, with 5 examples, the same number as produced at age 5.

Thus, consistent with our hypothesis, Mandarin-speaking children produce FM *shi* much later and far less frequently than copula *shi*, supporting the claim that the focus property of *shi* is acquired relatively late. Moreover, the fact that there were no S-strings in the corpus data, even at age 6, highlights the difficulty of this structure for Mandarin-speaking children. [29] This is consistent with our experimental results: when presented with an S-string in the experiment the younger children assign the only interpretation (pseudo-sluicing) available in their grammar – with *shi* as a copula. [30] Sometime between 4 and 5 years old, the focus property of *shi* is acquired (as evidenced by the production of clefts) and the movement + ellipsis derivation also becomes available. At that point, the subject advantage emerges as a result of the intervention effects triggered by focus movement. In the comprehension experiment, we see this effect in age groups 5 and 6.

It is reasonable to ask at this point why the Mandarin-speaking child who already has the structurally simpler pseudo-sluicing analysis (with copula *be*) would add the more complex movement + ellipsis derivation. One possibility is that this development is driven by input data that are not analyzable under a pseudo-sluicing analysis but which require "hidden" structure, for example, the sloppy reading cases, idiomatic reconstruction, and *wh*-else structures discussed in Section 2. 2 (among other data). This kind of input could trigger the development from Stage 1 to Stage 2, in which both sluice and pseudo-sluice analyses are applied to S-strings.

Another, and perhaps more likely explanation, is that the movement + ellipsis analysis is grammatically-driven: Children may acquire the focus movement associated with *shi* on the basis of clefts and then extend the possibility of a movement analysis to S-strings which also contain *shi*. In an S-string of the sort in (35a), repeated as (40), the focus movement of *shei* 'who' when *shi* is analyzed as a FM, requires an extraction site, which entails a hidden TP structure. Thus, in this way children add a movement + ellipsis (sluicing) derivation to the pseudo-sluicing derivation already established in their grammar.

(40) *wo neng kanjian hongse yifu-de nansheng zai zhui yi-ge ren...*
1SG can see red clothes-DE boy PROG chase one-CL person
'I can see that the boy in red is chasing someone…'
... ni neng kanjian shi shei ma?
2SG can see be/FM who Q
'…can you see who?'

Under this proposal, it is the acquisition of *shi* as a FM in clefts that triggers focus movement, and leads to a focus movement + ellipsis analysis. This "grammar-internal" trigger for sluicing seems the most likely given the relative frequency and accessibility of structures containing FM *shi,* such as clefts, over sentences involving sloppy identity, *wh*-else structures, and idiomatic reconstruction which would force a sluicing analysis.

Note that under either scenario, at Stage 2 both derivations are possible except for cases where one or the other is blocked (see sections 2. 2 and 2. 3). When the child commits to a movement + ellipsis analysis this gives rise to the intervention difficulties associated with long-distance dependencies. When a pseudo-sluicing analysis is generated no asymmetry arises. There does not seem to be any obvious way to predict for any individual S-string what analysis the child (or adult) will choose. The choice may be random or determined by a variety of discourse and other factors.

3.5 Summary

The primary finding of our experiment is a subject advantage (subject > object) in the interpretation of S-strings among older Mandarin-speaking children. The implicatures of this finding are two-fold: First, the subject advantage observed in the older groups supports a movement + ellipsis analysis of Mandarin S-strings. Second, the delay of such a subject advantage suggests a two-stage development for Mandarin-speaking children: they initially analyze *shi* as a copula, hence apply a simpler, pseudo-sluicing derivation, and only later acquire the focus properties of *shi*. At that point, the movement + ellipsis derivation enters their grammar and the subject advantage emerges as an effect of intervention. A follow-up corpus study shows that the development of FM *shi* is later than that of a copula *shi*, consistent with the hypothesis of a two-stage development of *shi* and (pseudo-)sluicing in Mandarin.

4. Conclusion and future studies

This paper discusses the syntax and L1 acquisition of Mandarin sluice-like constructions (S-strings). The derivation of Mandarin S-strings has been controversial because of the presence of *shi*, an element that is ambiguous between a copula and a FM.

The syntactic investigation led us to a hybrid analysis in which an S-string has two possible derivations: a sluice (derived by focus movement and TP ellipsis) and a pseudo-sluice (a copula structure with a null subject), unless one of the structures is forced. In some cases, an S-string must have elided structure, e.g. in order to derive sloppy readings, idiomatic reconstructions or *wh*-else sluices, whereas an accented or negated *shi* forces a pseudo-sluice interpretation.

The comprehension experiment with Mandarin-speaking children (3; 00–6; 08, *M* = 4; 10), as well as a follow-up corpus study, support a two-stage acquisition model and thus provides converging evidence for a hybrid analysis: Mandarin-speaking children initially analyze *shi* as a copula, hence have a simpler, pseudo-sluice interpretation, and only later fully acquire the focus properties of *shi* and the sluice interpretation derived by focus movement + ellipsis at which point a subject advantage emerges as an effect of intervention. Evidence from both adult syntax and from acquisition point to the same conclusion: Mandarin S-strings have both a sluice and pseudo-sluice derivation.

There are several avenues to pursue in future studies in order to further elucidate the properties of (pseudo-)sluices in Mandarin. For example, our findings can be followed up with studies looking at adult speakers' online processing of Mandarin S-strings. In particular, we are interested in any potential subject/object asymmetry in adults, and also the relation between focus accent and strict/sloppy readings.

With respect to the S/O asymmetry, insofar as one of the two derivations of the ambiguous S-strings is parallel to the movement + ellipsis derivation of sluices in languages with *wh*-movement, we predict that Mandarin-speaking adults' performance on S-strings will show an 'object advantage' due to linear intervention between the indefinite and the remnant in subject sluices (see fn. 16) as has been found in English, Spanish and Portuguese (e.g., Frazier & Clifton 1998; Carlson et al. 2009; Harris 2015 on English; Lawn & Harris 2017 on Spanish; Lawn & Harris 2019 on Portuguese).

Another line of potential research concerns the availability of strict/sloppy readings. Because the prosodic information affects which structure is activated when we hear an S-string (see Section 2. 3), we predict an interaction between the focus accent placement and the availability of a sloppy reading: If *shi* is accented, hearers should assign the S-string a pseudo-sluice analysis and the availability of a sloppy interpretation is predicted to significantly drop compared to when the focus accent falls on the *wh*-phrase. Relatedly, young children who have not yet acquired the movement + ellipsis analysis should fail to obtain sloppy interpretations in a controlled experiment.

Finally, there is the potential interaction between sloppy interpretation and adjunct/argument asymmetry. Adams & Tomioka (2012) (see fn. 7) proposed that, sloppy readings are easier to obtain with adjunct *wh*-remnants than argument *wh*-remnants. This should be tested with both older children and adults.

Appendix A. Results of all conditions

Table 3. Percentages of correct responses by age and condition

Sentence Type	S-strings (12 trials)				Full *wh*-questions (12)			
Extraction Position	Subject (6)		Object (6)		Subject (6)		Object (6)	
Animacy	+ (3)	− (3)	+ (3)	− (3)	+ (3)	− (3)	+ (3)	− (3)
Age 3 (*N* = 14)	59. 52%	66. 67%	59. 52%	59. 52%	71. 43%	76. 19%	71. 43%	66. 67%
	63. 10%		59. 52%		73. 81%		69. 05%	
	61. 31%				71. 43%			
	66. 37%							
Age 4 (*N* = 15)	71. 11%	80. 00%	80. 00%	88. 89%	86. 67%	84. 44%	86. 67%	93. 33%
	75. 56%		84. 44%		85. 56%		90. 00%	
	80. 00%				87. 78%			
	83. 89%							
Age 5 (*N* = 15)	91. 11%	93. 33%	77. 78%	84. 44%	97. 78%	88. 89%	93. 33%	95. 56%
	92. 22%		81. 11%		93. 33%		94. 44%	
	86. 67%				93. 89%			
	90. 28%							
Age 6 (*N* = 15)	93. 33%	93. 33%	77. 78%	84. 44%	91. 11%	93. 33%	95. 56%	100. 00%
	93. 33%		81. 11%		92. 22%		97. 78%	
	87. 22%				95. 00%			
	91. 11%							

Appendix B. Test materials

Training session

a) *meige xiaohai chuan-zhe butong yanse-de yifu,*
every child wear-PROG different color-DE cloth
ni neng kanjian hongse yifu-de nansheng ma?
2SG can see red cloth-DE boy Q
'Each child is wearing a different color. Can you see the boy in red?'

b) *wo neng kanjian butong yanse-de che he butong yanse-de saoba,*
1SG can see different color-DE car and different color-DE broom

ni	*neng*	*kanjian*	*huangse-de*	*che*	*he*	*huangse-de*	*saoba*	*ma?*
2SG	can	see	yellow-DE	car	and	yellow-DE	broom	Q

'I can see cars in different colors and brooms in different colors. Can you see the yellow car and the yellow broom?'

c)

wo	*neng*	*kanjian*	*liang-ge*	*nvsheng,*	
1SG	can	see	two-CL	girl	
ni	*neng*	*kanjian*	*yi-ge*	*nansheng*	*ma?*
2SG	can	see	one-CL	boy	Q

'I can see two girls. Can you see a boy?'

d)

wo	*neng*	*kanjian*	*zise*	*yifu-de*	*nvsheng*	*he*	*fense*	*yifu-de*	*nvsheng,*
1SG	can	see	purple	cloth-DE	girl	and	pink	cloth-DE	girl
ni	*neng*	*kanjian*	*shei*	*zai*	*shu*	*houmian*	*ma?*		
2SG	can	see	who	at	tree	behind	Q		

'I can see the girl in purple and the girl in pink. Can you see who is behind the tree?'

e)

wo	*neng*	*kanjian*	*yi-ge*	*ren*	*dai-zhe*	*maozi,*
1SG	can	see	one-CL	person	wear-PROG	hat
ni	*neng*	*kanjian*	*shei*	*dai-zhe*	*maozi*	*ma?*
2SG	can	see	who	wear-PROG	hat	Q

'I can see that someone is wearing a hat, can you see who is wearing a hat?'

f)

wo	*neng*	*kanjian*	*yi-ge*	*ren*	*zuo-zhe,*
1SG	can	see	one-CL	person	sit-PROG
ni	*neng*	*kanjian*	*shei*	*zuo-zhe*	*ma?*
2SG	can	see	who	sit-PROG	Q

'I can see that someone is sitting, can you see who is sitting?'

g)

wo	*neng*	*kanjian*	*yi-ge*	*ren*	*zai*	*pao,*
1SG	can	see	one-CL	person	PROG	run
ni	*neng*	*kanjian*	*shei*	*zai*	*pao*	*ma?*
2SG	can	see	who	PROG	run	Q

'I can see that someone is running, can you see who is running?'

h)

wo	*neng*	*kanjian*	*yi-ge*	*ren*	*zhan-zhe,*
1SG	can	see	one-CL	person	stand-PROG
ni	*neng*	*kanjian*	*shi*	*shei*	*ma?*
2SG	can	see	be/FM	who	Q

'I can see that someone is standing, can you see who?'

i) *wo neng kanjian yi-ge ren zai tiao,*

1SG can see one-CL person PROG jump

ni neng kanjian shi shei ma?

2SG can see be/FM who Q

'I can see that someone is running, can you see who?'

Test session

Animate subject S-strings

(1) *wo neng kanjian yi-ge ren zai tui lvse yifu-de nansheng,*

1SG can see one-CL person PROG push green cloth-DE boy

ni neng kanjian shi shei ma?

2SG can see be/FM who Q

'I can see that someone is pushing the boy in green, can you see who?'

(2) *wo neng kanjian yi-ge ren zai zhui zise yifu-de nvsheng,*

ni neng kanjian shi shei ma?

'I can see that someone is chasing the girl in purple, can you see who?'

(3) *wo neng kanjian yi-ge ren ya-zhe lvse yifu-de nansheng,*

ni neng kanjian shi shei ma?

'I can see that someone is on the top of the boy in green, can you see who?'

Animate subject full *wh*-questions

(4) *wo neng kanjian yi-ge ren ya-zhe hongse yifu-de nansheng,*

1SG can see one-CL person be.on.top-PROG red cloth-DE boy

ni neng kanjian shei ya-zhe hongse yifu-de nansheng ma?

2SG can see who be.on.top-PROG red cloth-DE boy Q

'I can see that someone is on the top of the boy in red, can you see who is on the boy in red?'

(5) *wo neng kanjian yi-ge ren zai tui lvse yifu-de nansheng,*

ni neng kanjian shei zai tui lvse yifu-de nansheng ma?

'I can see that someone is pushing the boy in green, can you see who is pushing the boy in green?'

(6) *wo neng kanjian yi-ge ren kao-zhe hongse yifu-de nansheng,*

ni neng kanjian shei kao-zhe hongse yifu-de nansheng ma?

'I can see someone is leaning on the boy in red, can you see who is leaning on the boy in red?'

Animate object S-strings

(7) *wo neng kanjian hongse yifu-de nansheng zai zhui yi-ge ren,*
1SG can see red cloth-DE boy PROG chase one person
ni neng kanjian shi shei ma?
2SG can see be/FM who Q
'I can see that the boy in red is chasing someone, can you see who?'

(8) *wo neng kanjian hongse yifu-de nansheng kao-zhe yi-ge ren,*
ni neng kanjian shi shei ma?
'I can see that the boy in red is leaning on someone, can you see who?'

(9) *wo neng kanjian fense yifu-de nvsheng ya-zhe yi-ge ren,*
ni neng kanjian shi shei ma?
'I can see that the girl in pink is on the top of someone, can you see who?'

Animate object full *wh*-questions

(10) *wo neng kanjian zise yifu-de nvsheng zai zhui yi-ge ren,*
1SG can see purple cloth-DE girl PROG chase one-CL person
ni neng kanjian zise yifu-de nvsheng zai zhui shei ma?
2SG can see purple cloth-DE girl PROG chase who Q
'I can see that the girl in purple is chasing someone, can you see who the girl in purple is chasing?'

(11) *wo neng kanjian hongse yifu-de nansheng ya-zhe yi-ge ren,*
ni neng kanjian hongse yifu-de nansheng ya-zhe shei ma?
'I can see that the boy in red is on the top of someone, can you see who the boy in red is on the top of?'

(12) *wo neng kanjian huangse yifu-de nvsheng zai zhui yi-ge ren,*
ni neng kanjian huangse yifu-de nvsheng zai zhui shei ma?
'I can see that the girl in yellow is chasing someone, can you see who the girl in yellow is chasing?'

Inanimate subject S-strings

(13) *wo neng kanjian yi-ge dongxi zai zhui huangse-de che,*
1SG can see one-CL thing PROG chase yellow-DE car
ni neng kanjian shi shenme ma?
2SG can see be/FM what Q
'I can see that something is chasing the yellow car, can you see what?'

(14) *wo neng kanjian yi-ge dongxi kao-zhe lvse-de saoba,*
ni neng kanjian shi shenme ma?
'I can see that something is leaning on the green broom, can you see what?'

(15) *wo neng kanjian yi-ge dongxi ya-zhe huangse-de che,*
ni neng kanjian shi shenme ma?
'I can see that something is on top of the yellow car, can you see what?'

Inanimate subject full *wh*-questions

(16) *wo neng kanjian yi-ge dongxi kao-zhe baise-de saoba,*
1SG can see one-CL thing lean.on-PROG white-DE broom
ni neng kanjian shenme kao-zhe baise-de saoba ma?
2SG can see what lean.on-PROG white-DE broom Q
'I can see that something is leaning on the white broom, can you see what is leaning on the white broom?'

(17) *wo neng kanjian yi-ge dongxi ya-zhe lvse-de che,*
ni neng kanjian shenme ya-zhe lvse-de che ma?
'I can see that something is on the top of the green car, can you see what is on the top of the green car?'

(18) *wo neng kanjian yi-ge dongxi zai tui huangse-de che,*
ni neng kanjian shenme zai tui huangse-de che ma?
'I can see that something is pushing the yellow car, can you see what is pushing the yellow car?'

Inanimate object S-strings

(19) *wo neng kanjian huangse-de saoba kao-zhe yi-ge dongxi*
1SG can see yellow-DE broom lean.on-PROG one-CL thing
ni neng kanjian shi shenme ma?
2SG can see be/FM what Q
'I can see that the yellow broom is leaning on something, can you see what?'

(20) *wo neng kanjian huangse-de che ya-zhe yi-ge dongxi,*
ni neng kanjian shi shenme ma?
'I can see that the yellow car is on the top of something, can you see what?'

(21) *wo neng kanjian baise-de che zai tui yi-ge dongxi,*
ni neng kanjian shi shenme ma?
'I can see that the white car is pushing something, can you see what?'

Inanimate object full *wh*-questions

(22) *wo neng kanjian lvse-de saoba kao-zhe yi-ge dongxi,*

1SG can see green-DE broom lean.on-PROG one-CL thing

ni neng kanjian lvse-de saoba kao-zhe shenme ma?

2SG can see green-DE broom lean.on-PROG what Q

'I can see that the green broom is leaning on something, can you see what the green broom is leaning on?'

(23) *wo neng kanjian baise-de che zai tui yi-ge dongxi,*

ni neng kanjian baise-de che zai tui shenme ma?

'I can see that the white car is pushing something, can you see what the white car is pushing?'

(24) *wo neng kanjian huangse-de che zai zhui yi-ge dongxi,*

ni neng kanjian huangse-de che zai zhui shenme ma?

'I can see that the yellow car is chasing something, can you see what the yellow car is chasing?'

Notes

1. There are analyses of sluices that involve ellipsis but no movement, including the *wh*-in-situ approach (Kimura 2010 and Abe 2015), as in (i), and the base-generation approach (Chung et al. 1995), as in (ii).

(i) You called someone but I don' t know [$_{CP}$ C$_{[Q]}$ [$_{TP}$ ~~you called~~ who]]

(ii) You called someone but I don' t know [$_{CP}$ who$_i$ [$_{TP}$ ~~you called someone$_i$~~]]

There are also analyses of sluices that involve neither ellipsis nor movement. For example, Culicover & Jackendoff (2005) proposed that the *wh*-phrase is the only daughter node of the S node that is the complement of the matrix verb:

(iii) You called someone but I don' t know [$_S$ who]

2. The use of the terms 'pseudo-sluice/pseudo-sluicing' in previous studies of Mandarin and Japanese is not consistent. In Japanese, a sluice-like construction is argued to be derived from clefts (e.g., Nishiyama et al. 1996; Kizu 1997; Merchant 1998; Saito 2004; Hiraiwa & Ishihara 2012; cf. Takahashi 1994 for a sluicing analysis, and Nishigauchi 1998 for an LF-copying analysis). The main support for this non-movement, pseudo-sluicing analysis comes from the parallels between

Japanese clefts and sluice-like constructions, for example, case-marking and island-sensitivities. Note that the 'pseudo-sluicing analysis' in Japanese usually refers to the reduced cleft analysis. For example:

(i) *John-wa [zibun-ga naze sikarareta ka] wakatteinai ga,*
John-TOP self-NOM why was.scolded Q know.not though
Mary-wa [~~[$_{CP}$ Op$_i$ [$_{TP}$ zibun-ga t_i sikarareta] no] -ga~~ naze$_i$ (da) ka] wakatteiru.
Mary-TOP self-NOM was.scolded that-NOM why be.PRES Q know
'John doesn' t know why he was scolded, but Mary knows why [he/she was scolded].'
(Saito 2004)

However, as we discuss in this paper, the 'pseudo-sluicing analysis' of Mandarin S-strings does not posit any ellipsis in the S-string and proposes that the unspoken information is recovered by a silent subject *pro* in the syntax.

3. Adams & Tomioka (2012) adopt Heim & Kratzer' s (1998) account of E-type pronouns (Evans 1977, 1980) according to which (i) there is an implicit definite determiner, and (ii) it also comes with indexed anaphor of a predicate type, whose semantic content is pragmatically recovered. They thus propose the internal structure of *pro* as [$_{DP}$ [+def] [$_{NP}$ e$_1$]].

4. To be consistent with the previous literature on sluice-like structures in Mandarin, we refer to all S-strings with adjunct *wh*-remnants as '*wh*-adjunct S-strings' . However, when the adjunct *wh*-remnant does not have an overt correlate in the antecedent clause, such as in (8b), the S-string would really be a case of 'sprouting' as opposed to sluicing. A more typical example of adjunct sluicing is the following:

(i) *Lisi zai yi-ge difang jiao-le Mali, wo bu zhidao (shi) zai nali.*
Lisi at one-CL place call-PERF Mali 1SG not know be at where
'Lisi called Mali at a place. I don' t know where.'

5. Wei (2017) treats the *wh*-else S-strings, what he calls '*you*-sluice' , as a variant of pseudo-sluice. In his analysis, *you* 'have' is a possessive verb as opposed to an existential verb, and takes a null subject *pro* (a nominal pronoun or an event pronoun) and the *wh*-phrase as its two arguments. However, *you* cannot be a possessive verb in an S-string. One bit of evidence is that *you* cannot be negated in this case, which is a property of the existential verb *you*, as opposed to the possessive verb *you*.

(i) *Lisi jiao-le yixie ren, wo bu zhidao *mei you shei.*
Lisi called-PERF some people 1SG not know not have who
Intended: 'Lisi called some people. I don' t know who not.'

6. See Huang (1988) for the parallel distribution of *shi* 'be' and *you* 'have' in Mandarin Chinese.

7. But cf. Adams & Tomioka (2012) who propose that *pro* could behave like the so-called 'paycheck' pronoun *it* in English which can have a sloppy interpretation, as illustrated by the following example (Jacobson 2000: 87 (11)):

(i) The woman$_i$ who$_i$ deposited her$_i$ paycheck in the bank is wiser than the woman$_j$ who$_j$ deposited ***it*** in the Brown University Employees' Credit Union.

Adams and Tomioka thus argue that the pseudo-sluice analysis can also derive the sloppy reading of S-strings. Note, however, that their analysis does not provide a clear explanation for the fact that a paraphrased sluiced sentence with an overt pronoun *na* 'that' never produces sloppy interpretations (cf. 19). On the sluice analysis, there is no *pro* in the structure, hence the referential properties of the *na* counterpart are irrelevant.

8. The *wh*-adjuncts are adjoined to the TP, at least at the point the TP-ellipsis happens, regardless of whether they are base-generated as TP-adjuncts or moved from within TP.

9. The existential verb *you* 'have' can also trigger a movement of this sort, which is briefly mentioned in (14) but will not be expanded in details in this paper. That is why the existential verb *you* is also obligatory in the *wh*-else S-strings like (14).

10. If there is an intonational break (i.e., a pause) between the two *wh*-phrases in the multiple S-string, then the second *shi* is also acceptable. Indeed, with intonational breaks between *wh*-phrases, there can be not only two, but also a list of *wh*-phrases in the multiple S-string. But in those cases, the structure is more likely to be a conjunction or a list of two or more clauses, as opposed to one multiple S-string (i.e., one S-string with multiple *wh*-phrases).

11. This accent realization on *shi* might be a case of 'verum focus' (named by Höhle 1992). Verum focus refers to the accent that, instead of focusing the accent-bearing expression, is used to emphasize the truth of the propositional content of a sentence. Although there is a debate on whether verum focus is a focus (e.g., Zimmermann & Hole 2008; Stommel 2012; Gutzmann & Miró 2011; Repp 2013), it does not change our argument here: the (verum) focus accent can only be realized on a copula *shi* but not a FM *shi*.

12. As mentioned in Section 2.1 the overt pronoun *ta* '3SG' or *na* 'that' can alternate with a silent pronoun *pro* due to the *pro*-drop property of Mandarin.

13. Another piece of evidence that *shi* is the copula here is that it can be negated when it is followed by a *wh*-phrase, as in *bu shi shei* 'not be who' . The FM in clefts cannot be negated when followed by a *wh*-pivot, as shown in (i), but there is no such restriction on the copula *shi*, as shown

in (ii).

(i) *(*bu) shi shei jiao-le Mali?*
not FM who call-PERF Mali
'Who was (*not) it that called Mali?'

(ii) *jiao-le Mali de (ren) (bu) shi shei?*
call-PERF Mali C person not be who
'Who isn' t the person that called Mali?'

When the pivot is not a *wh*-phrase, negative clefts are acceptable, as below:

(iii) *bu shi Lisi jiao-le Mali.*
not FM Lisi call-PERF Mali
'It is not Lisi who called Mali.

14. Theoretically speaking, there can be two alternative analyses, which are not proposed in previous studies on the derivation of Mandarin S-strings. We will call them the 'reduced cleft' and the 'reduced pseudo-cleft' analyses. The following table lays out the differences among the four analyses:

	structure of S-string	*shi*	ellipsis	movement
a. pseudo-sluicing	[*pro* be *wh*-phrase]	copula	no ellipsis	no movement
b. movement + ellipsis	[FM *wh*-phrase$_i$ ~~[$_{TP}$…t$_i$…]~~]	FM	TP ellipsis	*wh*-focus movement
c. reduced cleft	[FM *wh*-phrase ~~[$_{XP}$ OP$_i$ …[$_{TP}$…t$_i$…]]~~]]	FM	XP ellipsis	covert OP movement
d. reduced pseudo-cleft	[~~[$_{CP}$ [[$_{TP}$…t$_i$…] C] OP$_i$]~~ be *wh*-phrase]	copula	CP ellipsis	covert OP movement

The reduced cleft analysis proposes that the S-strings derive from clefts. It is similar to the movement + ellipsis analysis, except that the *wh*-phrase is an in-situ focus in the cleft, as opposed to a focus moved from within the elided TP. The reduced pseudo-cleft analysis suggests that S-strings derive from pseudo-clefts with the ellipsis of the relativized CP, a free relative clause that is the subject of the copula *shi*. For reasons of space, we will not discuss these alternative approaches. (To anticipate our discussion on the acquisition of S-strings in Mandarin, these two analyses would make the same predictions as the movement + ellipsis analysis since they both posit OP movement in the derivation, parallel to the focus movement in the movement + ellipsis analysis.)

15. The effects of intervention are also observed in other constructions that derive from A'-movement of an object. For example, children up to the age of six experience difficulties with object relative clauses (Friedmann et al. 2009; Friedmann & Novogrodsky 2004; McKee et al. 1998), object *wh*-questions (de Vincenzi et al. 1999; Friedmann et al. 2009), object topicalization

(Friedmann & Lavi 2006), as well as A-dependencies such as passives and raising (Hyams & Snyder 2005; Snyder & Hyams 2015), etc.

16. Studies of adult English speakers' on-line comprehension of sluices find an asymmetry in the opposite direction: When both the subject and object in the antecedent clause of the sluice are potential correlates (i.e., indefinite DPs) for the *wh*-remnant, participants prefer to associate the *wh*-remnant with the object (arguably due to the default focus alignment, see Carlson et al. 2009). An eye-tracking experiment also found greater interference effects from a distractor (underlined) in object position, as in (b), than in subject position, as in (a) (potentially due to Locality Bias, see Harris, 2015).

(a) The tourists sampled some wine(s), but I don' t know which {wines/ones}.

(b) Some tourist(s) sampled the wines, but I don' t know which {tourists/ones}.

These results seem to contradict those found in English-speaking children' s comprehension of sluicing. However, we believe that the intervention effects triggered by the A' -movement from an object position are robust enough that they mask any effects of default focus assignment or Locality Bias in processing. We suspect that the object advantage observed for adults would be apparent in older children, once they fully master whatever syntactic operation (e.g., smuggling) allows them to circumvent intervention.

17. In total, there were nine 3-year-olds, four 4-year-olds, and one 5-year-old were excluded for this reason.

18. In our experiment, there were no animacy mismatch trials – either both subject and object were animate or both inanimate. Some previous studies showed that the intervention effects are stronger when the moved element shares the same feature as the intervening element (see Friedmann et al. 2009; Belletti et al. 2012; a. o. for the effects of mismatched features in A' - movement constructions and especially Mateu & Hyams 2018 for animacy mismatch effects in English sluice acquisition).

19. During the tests, most children tended to point to the characters/items as opposed to verbally responding to the questions.

20. The partially hidden character/item was either the leftmost or the rightmost one of the three, but not necessarily the correct answer and the *yes/no* answers were equally divided into the images with hidden characters/items.

21. The boy in the middle is wearing a red T-shirt, and the girl behind him is wearing a purple T-shirt.

22. The color of the three jeeps from left to right is green, yellow, and red respectively.

23. When a child responded ‘yes’ , s/he was asked to point out which. When a child responded ‘no’ , s/he was asked to explain why.

24. Since there were three characters/items in each image for a child to choose from, chance performance would be 33% correct and a response of 23%–43% correct would be non-significant from chance performance.

25. However, see Yoshinaga (1996) who found in an elicited production task that 2- to 3-year-old English-speaking children show a very strong subject bias in *wh*-questions (subject *who*-questions: 100% and 97. 2% correct, respectively; object *who*-questions: 8. 3% and 41. 7% correct, respectively). By age 4, the correct production of object *who*-questions (79. 6%) almost equals that of subject *who*-questions (88. 6%). The discrepancy between Yoshinaga’s results and Mateu’s may be due to the fact that the former was a production study and the latter a comprehension study.

26. The corpora we searched were Chang1 (*N* = 24; ages 3–6), Chang2 (*N* = 16; ages 3–4), Context (*N* = 25; age 2), LiZhou (*N* = 80; ages 3–6), Tong (*N* = 1; ages 1; 7–3; 4), Zhou1 (*N* = 15; ages 3–6), Zhou2 (*N* = 15; ages 3–6), Zhou3 (*N* = 1; ages 0; 8–4; 5), ZhouDinner (*N* = 80; ages 3–6), and ZhouNarratives (*N* = 200; ages 3–6).

27. In this corpus study, we investigated only the sentence-initial FM *shi* but not vP/VP peripheral *shi*, such as in (i). The reasons are two-fold: First, the movement + ellipsis derivation suggests that the FM in S-strings is at the CP periphery, which is higher than the *shi* in (i) but might be the same element as the sentence-initial FM *shi* in clefts, which we take to be the trigger for FM development in children. Additionally, the readings in (i), shown in (a)–(d), heavily rely on contextual or prosodic information and it is not straightforward whether *shi* is a FM or not in readings like (a) and (d).

(i) *Lisi shi tui-le Mali.*

Lisi SHI push-PERF Mali

a) Accenting *shi*: ‘Lisi INDEED pushed Mali. ’

b) Accenting the verb: ‘Lisi PUSHed Mali (not kicked, pulled, beat, etc...)’

c) Accenting the object: ‘Lisi pushed MALI (not others). ’

d) No accenting: ‘What Lisi did was to push Mali. ’

28. To decide whether the single token found in age 3 is an “isolate” (due to transcription error or the child’ s use of a memorized routine) or rather evidence that children have acquired clefts by this age, we borrowed the criterion for acquisition of a construction used in longitudinal studies: “First clear use, followed soon after by Repeated Use” (FRU, Snyder 2007: 77). More specifically, if a potential first use of a construction is not followed soon afterwards (the criterion of Snyder

is within one month) by repeated use, then we cannot rely on it and it needs to be excluded as an 'isolate'. By this criterion, the one occurrence of clefts at age 3 should be an isolated production. However, it is not clear to what extent a criterion used in longitudinal studies can apply to the current corpus study, which contains data from both longitudinal studies and cross-sectional ones.

29. By contrast, English argument sluices appear quite early in children's speech (Mateu et al. 2017):

(i) a) MOT: *I don't know what happened.* b) MOT: *Tell daddy what you did in school today.*
CHI: *You never know what.* (2; 04) CHI: *Do you know what?* (2; 08)

In total, Mateu et al. (2017) found 24 argument sluices in the production of English-speaking children aged 0; 10–10; 2, as well as 99 adjunct sluices. As for Mandarin, the results of a search for *shi* does not necessarily include adjunct S-strings because the presence of *shi* is not required in those cases. Future study is needed to decide whether there is spontaneous production of adjunct S-strings in this age range.

As for the age difference in sluice production in English- vs. Mandarin-speaking children, English sluices require *wh*-movement, a very early acquisition (Klima & Bellugi 1966 a.o.) while Mandarin sluices require focus movement, a later acquisition, as evidenced by the cleft data. However, the question remains as to why Mandarin-speaking children do not produce pseudo-sluices (with copula *shi*) early on. At present we have no proper explanation for this.

30. We might refer to this as the 'captive audience effect'. In experimental settings (as in natural language contexts) if children are presented with structures beyond their grammatical capacity, they will assign some interpretation consistent with their grammar. Sometimes this involves a non-target-like reanalysis of the input (see the *think/be* strategies used by children in raising *seem* experiments, e.g., Hirsch et al. 2007). In the case at hand, there is a derivation fully compatible with the input string accessible to children that happens to be part of the adult grammar of Mandarin.

References

Abe, J. 2015. *The in-situ approach to sluicing*. Amsterdam/Philadelphia: John Benjamins.

Adams, W. 2004. The structure of sluicing in Mandarin Chinese. In *Penn Working Papers in Linguistics,* University of Pennsylvania. 10. 1: 1–16.

Adams, W. & Tomioka, S. 2012. Sluicing in Mandarin Chinese: An instance of pseudo-sluicing. *Sluicing: Cross-linguistic perspectives*. 219–247.

Bates, D. & Maechler, M. 2009. *Ime4: Linear mixed-effects models using S4 classes. R package version 0. 999375–999331.*

Belletti, A., Friedmann, N., Brunato, D. & Rizzi, L. 2012. Does gender make a difference? Comparing the effect of gender on children' s comprehension of relative clauses in Hebrew and Italian. *Lingua,* 122: 1053–1069.

Cao, X., Goodluck, H., Shan, Y. & Otsu, Y. 2005. Double-gapped relative clauses in Chinese: grammar and processing. In *The proceedings of the Sixth Tokyo conference on psycholinguistics*. 53–68.

Carlson, K., Dickey, W., Frazier, L. & Clifton Jr, C. 2009. Information structure expectations in sentence comprehension. *The Quarterly Journal of Experimental Psychology*, 62(1): 114–139.

Chang, W. 1984. The comprehension of complex Chinese sentences by children-relative clause. *Chinese Journal of Psychology*, 26(1): 57–66.

Chen, L. 2004. On argument-adjunct asymmetry of sluicing in Mandarin Chinese. In *Proceedings of the 18th Pacific Asia conference on language, information and computation*. 227–234.

Chiu, B. 1996. *The nature of relative clauses in Chinese-speaking children.* NSC research report, National Taiwan Normal University.

Chiu, L. 2007. A focus-movement account on Chinese multiple sluicing. *Nanzan Linguistics: Special Issue*, 1: 23–31.

Chomsky, N. 1972. Some empirical issues in the theory of transformational grammar.

Chung, S., Ladusaw, W. & McCloskey, J. 1995. Sluicing and logical form. *Natural Language Semantics*, 3(3): 239–282.

Culicover, P. & Jackendoff, R. 2005. *Simpler syntax*. Oxford: Oxford University Press.

Dahl, O. 2000. Animacy and the notion of semantic gender. *Trends in Linguistics Studies and Monographs*, 124: 99–116.

de Vincenzi, M., Arduino, L., Ciccarelli, L. & Job, R. 1999. Parsing strategies in children comprehension of interrogative sentences. In *Proceedings of European conference on cognitive science.* Rome: Istituto di Psicologia del CNR. 301–308.

Erteschik-Shir, N. 1977. *On the nature of island constraints*. Indiana University Linguistics Club.

Evans, G. 1977. Pronouns, quantifiers, and relative clauses (I). *Canadian Journal of Philosophy*, 7(3): 467–536.

Evans, G. 1980. Pronouns. *Linguistic Inquiry*, 11(2): 337–362.

Fox, D. & Lasnik, H. 2003. Successive-cyclic movement and island repair: The difference between sluicing and VP-ellipsis. *Linguistic Inquiry*, 34(1): 143–154.

Fox, D. & Pesetsky, D. 2005. Cyclic linearization of syntactic structure. *Theoretical Linguistics*,

31(1–2): 1–45.

Frazier, L. & Clifton, C. 1998. Comprehension of sluiced sentences. *Language and Cognitive Processes*, 13(4): 499–520.

Friedmann, N., Belletti, A. & Rizzi, L. 2009. Relativized relatives: Types of intervention in the acquisition of A-bar dependencies. *Lingua*, 119: 67–88.

Friedmann, N. & Lavi, H. 2006. On the order of acquisition of A-movement, *wh*-movement and V-C movement. *Language Acquisition and Development*, 211–217.

Friedmann, N. & Novogrodsky, R. 2004. The acquisition of relative clause comprehension in Hebrew: A study of SLI and normal development. *Journal of Child Language*, 31(3): 661–681.

Gutzmann, D. & Miró, C. 2011. The dimensions of verum. *Empirical issues in syntax and semantics*, 8: 143–165.

Harris, A. 2015. Structure modulates similarity-based interference in sluicing: An eye tracking study. *Frontiers in Psychology*, 6.

Hiraiwa, K. & Ishihara, S. 2012. Syntactic metamorphosis: Clefts, sluicing, and in-situ focus in Japanese. *Syntax*, 15(2): 142–180.

Hirsch, C., Orfitelli, R. & Wexler, K. 2007. When seem means think: The role of the experiencer-phrase in children' s comprehension of raising. In *Proceedings of the 2nd conference on generative approaches to language acquisition North America (GALANA)*. Somerville, MA: Cascadilla Press. 135–146.

Höhle, N. 1992. Über Verum-Fokus im Deutschen. In Jacobs, J. (Ed.), *Informationsstruktur und Grammatik*. Opladen: Westdeutscher Verlag. 112–141.

Hsu, N., Hermon, G. & Zukowski, A. 2009. Young children' s production of head-final relative clauses: Elicited production data from Chinese children. *Journal of East Asian Linguistics*, 18(4): 323–360.

Hu, S., Gavarró, A., Vernice, M. & Guasti, T. 2016. The acquisition of Chinese relative clauses: contrasting two theoretical approaches. *Journal of Child Language*, 43(1): 1–21.

Huang, J. 1988. Shuo '*shi*' he '*you*' [On 'be' and 'have' in Chinese]. *The bulletin of the institute of history and philology, Academia Sinica*, 59(1). 43–64. In Peters, S. (Ed.), *The goals of linguistic theory*, Englewood Cliffs, NJ: Prentice-Hall. 63–130.

Hyams, N. & Snyder, W. 2005. Young children never smuggle: Reflexive clitics and the Universal Freezing Hypothesis. Paper presented at the *30th Boston University Conference on Language Development* [BUCLD 30]. Boston, MA.

Jacobson, P. 2000. Paycheck pronouns, Bach-Peters sentences, and variable-free semantics. *Natural*

Language Semantics, 8(2): 77–155.

Kimura, H. 2010. A *wh*-in-situ strategy for sluicing. *English Linguistics*, 27(1): 43–59.

Kizu, M. 1997. A note on sluicing in *wh*-in-situ languages. Ms., McGill. To appear in *Proceedings of SCIL*, MIT Working Papers in Linguistics.

Klima, E. & Bellugi, U. 1966. Syntactic regularities in the speech of children. In Lyons, J. & Wales, R. (Eds.), *Psycholinguistic Papers*.

Kratzer, A. & Heim, I. 1998. *Semantics in generative grammar, vol. 1185*. Oxford: Blackwell.

Lasnik, H. 2001. When can you save a structure by destroying it? In Kim, M.-J. & Strauss, U. (Eds.), *Proceedings of the 31st North East Linguistic Society [NELS 31]*. Amherst, MA: University of Massachusetts, Graduate Linguistic Student Association. 301–320.

Lawn, R. & Harris, A. 2017. Structural bias, cue-relevancy and similarity-based interference in Spanish sluiced sentences. Talk presented at the *1st California Annual Meeting on Psycholinguistics*. University of California, Los Angeles. December 2–3, 2017.

Lawn, R. & Harris, A. 2019. Similarity-based interference and morphological retrieval in Portuguese sluiced sentences. Poster presented at the *32nd annual CUNY conference on human sentence processing (CUNY)*. University of Colorado, Boulder, March 29–31, 2019.

Li, A. & Wei, C. 2014. Ellipsis. In Huang, C.-T. J., Li, Y.-H. A. & Simpson (Eds.), *The handbook of Chinese linguistics*. Malden, Mass: Wiley-Blackwell Publishers. 275–310.

Li, A. & Wei, C. 2017. Sluicing, sprouting and missing objects. *Studies in Chinese Linguistics*, 38(2): 63–92.

MacWhinney, B. 2000. *The CHILDES project: Tools for analyzing talk.* Third Edition. Mahwah, NJ: Lawrence Erlbaum Associates.

Mateu, V. & Hyams, N. 2018. Intervention and animacy effects in the acquisition of sluicing. Talk presented at the *43rd Boston University conference on language development* [BUCLD 43]. Boston, MA.

Mateu, V., Hyams, N. & Winans, L. 2017. Intervention effects in early grammar: Evidence from sluicing. Talk presented at the *42nd Boston University conference on language development* [BUCLD 42]. Boston, MA.

McKee, C., McDaniel, D. & Snedeker, J. 1998. Relatives children say. *Journal of Psycholinguistic Research*, 27(5): 573–596.

Merchant, J. 1998. ‘Pseudosluicing’ : elliptical clefts in Japanese and English. *ZAS working papers in linguistics*, 10: 88–112.

Merchant, J. 2001. *The syntax of silence: Sluicing, islands, and the theory of ellipsis*. Oxford:

Oxford University Press on Demand.

Merchant, J. 2013. Voice and ellipsis. *Linguistic Inquiry*, 44(1): 77–108.

Nishigauchi, T. 1998. 'Multiple Sluicing' in Japanese and the functional nature of *wh*-phrases. *Journal of East Asian Linguistics*, 7(2): 121–152.

Nishiyama, K., Whitman, J. & Yi, Y. 1996. Syntactic movement of overt *wh*-phrases in Japanese and Korean. *Japanese/Korean Linguistics*, 5: 337–351.

Øvrelid, L. 2004. Disambiguation of syntactic functions in Norwegian: modeling variation in word order interpretations conditioned by animacy and definiteness. In *Proceedings of the 20th Scandinavian conference of linguistics*. Helsinki: University of Helsinki. 1–17.

Pollmann, T. 1975. Een regel die subject en copula deleert. *Spektator*, 5: 282–292.

R Development Core Team. 2014. *R: A language and environment for statistical computing*. Vienna: R Foundation for Statistical Computing.

Repp, S. 2013. Common ground management: Modal particles, illocutionary negation and VERUM. In *Beyond Expressive: Explorations in use-conditional meaning*. BRILL. 231–274.

Ross, R. 1969. Guess who? In Binnick, R., Davison, A. Green, G. & Morgan, J. (Eds.), *Proceedings of the fifth regional meeting of the Chicago linguistic society*. Chicago, IL: University of Chicago. 252–286.

Saito, M. 2004. Ellipsis and pronominal reference in Japanese clefts. *Nanzan Linguistics* 1: 21–50.

Scott, M. & Fisher, C. 2009. Two-year-olds use distributional cues to interpret transitivity-alternating verbs. *Language and Cognitive Processes*, 24(6): 777–803.

Snyder, W. 2007. *Child language: The parametric approach*. Oxford: Oxford University Press.

Snyder, W. & Hyams, N. 2015. Minimality effects in children' s passives. In Domenico, E., Cornelia, H. & Matteini, S. (Eds.), *Structures, strategies and beyond: Studies in honor of Adriana Belletti*. Amsterdam/Philadelphia: John Benjamins. 343–368.

Song, W. & Yoshida, M. 2017. Ellipsis or Pro-Form: Reconstruction effects of sluicing in Mandarin Chinese. In *34th west coast conference on formal linguistics*. Cascadilla Proceedings Project. 481–489.

Stommel, H. 2012. Verum-Fokus als Kontrast-Fokus. *Wahrheit-Fokus-Negation*, 15.

Su, Y.-C. 2006. Word order effect in children' s garden path of relative clauses. *Concentric*, 32 (2): 33–57.

Takahashi, D. 1994. Sluicing in Japanese. *Journal of East Asian Linguistics*, 3(3): 265–300.

Tsai, D. 2008. Left periphery and how-why alternations. *Journal of East Asian Linguistics*, 17(2): 83–115.

Wang, A. & Wu, I. 2006. Sluicing and focus movement in *wh*-in-situ languages. *University of Pennsylvania Working Papers in Linguistics*, 12(1): 375–387.

Wang, Q., Lillo-Martin, D., Best, T. & Levitt, A. 1992. Null subject versus null object: Some evidence from the acquisition of Chinese and English. *Language acquisition*, 2(3): 221–254.

Wei, C. 2009. Some notes on sloppy identity in Mandarin sluicing. *Concentric: Studies in Linguistics*, 35(2): 269–306.

Wei, C. 2011. Island repair effects of the left branch condition in Mandarin Chinese. *Journal of East Asian Linguistics*, 20(3): 255–289.

Wei, C. 2017. *You* sluice and *hai* modification in Chinese. *Studies in Chinese Linguistics*, 38(1): 1–17.

Yoshinaga, N. 1996. *Wh*-questions: A comparative study of their form and acquisition in English and Japanese. Ph. D. dissertation, University of Hawaii at Manoa.

Zimmermann, M. & Hole, D. 2008. Predicate focus, verum focus, verb focus: Similarities and difference. Talk at the *Potsdam-London IS Meeting*. December 12, 2008.

Author work unit: Department of Linguistics, University of California, Los Angeles

Author email: Nina Hyams: hyams@humnet.ucla.edu;

Minqi Liu: liuminqi@ucla.edu

现代汉语类截流式省略结构的句法与习得研究

Minqi Liu, Nina Hyams, Victoria Mateu

摘要：截流式省略（sluicing）是一种特殊的省略结构，在该结构里，一个标句词词组（CP）除了保留一个显性的疑问词组（wh-phrase）外，其余的部分全部被截断省略了，如 Someone left. I don't know who。在现代汉语里，类似于英语截流式省略结构的片段，如果保留的疑问词是论元成分，该成分前需要出现"是"，一个既可做系词又可做焦点标记的成分。本文认为现代汉语类似于英语截流式省略结构的片段有两种可能的生成分析，一种是真截流式省略分析，一种是准截流式省略分析。除非有独立的因素决定取一种分析，否则两种可能都存在。当相关片段里的"是"为系词时，片段应分析为准截流式省略，即［pro 系词 疑问词］，此种情况下既无移位亦无省略。当相关片段里的"是"为焦点标记时，片段应分析为真截流式省略，此种情况下有焦点移位及紧随其后的 TP 省略。本文以 59 名汉语母语儿童为被试进行理解实验，结果表明：3—4 岁的儿童对相关的汉语片段只能得到准截流式理解，直到大约 5 岁时才能得到截流式理解，而此时正是小孩展现出一般与非论元词组移位相联系的"主语优势效应"的时间节点。

关键词：省略习得，阻隔效应，非论元词组移位，现代汉语截流式省略，准截流式省略

作者单位：加州大学洛杉矶分校语言学系

作者邮箱：Nina Hyams: hyams@humnet.ucla.edu;

Minqi Liu: liuminqi@ucla.edu

跨语言语义研究的方法问题

沈　园

摘要： 本文探讨跨语言语义研究中的一些方法论问题。文章首先简要论述了跨语言研究采用普遍性假设这一做法的优势，然后以时态为例，探讨如何进行跨语言研究，并重点讨论了在跨语言研究中设立零形式的问题。文章接着探讨了微观语义差异和宏观语义差异，并讨论了跨语言研究中欧洲语言中心论的影响及其消解途径。

关键词： 跨语言语义研究，时态研究，零形式，语义差异

1. 引言

跨语言研究的目标是揭示语言的共性和个性，其中也包括跨语言语义变异和一致性问题（von Fintel & Matthewson，2008）。语义是否具有普遍性？是否存在跨语言差异？语言之间句法语素差异和语义差异是怎样的关系？句法语素差异是反映相应的语义差异，还是说表面句法语素差异背后隐藏着相同的语义属性或机制？从语义组合方式来看，又有哪些可能的跨语言变异？在方法方面，应该如何着手开展跨语言语义研究？如何避免欧洲语言中心论问题？如何建立比较的基础？这些都是近年来语义学家在跨语言研究中聚焦的问题，值得我们关注。本文主要讨论跨语言语义研究的方法问题。

2. 从普遍性假设出发

跨语言语义研究的首要问题是如何“跨”。提出假设、验证假设的假设演绎法是形式语言学研究的基本方法，形式语义学也不例外。

形式语义学跨语言研究主要基于普遍性假设：虽然语言之间有句法语素差异，但假设语义上并不存在差异（Matthewson，2001）。

假设演绎法的优势在于假设具有可预测性、可检验性。之所以特别选择普

遍性假设为出发点，是因为相对差异假设来说普遍性假设有以下优势。当我们假设两种语言相同，基于对 A 语言的已有研究，从普遍性假设出发，可以就 B 语言生成明确的预测。有差异的情形可以有很多种，而相同的情形只可能有一种。普遍性假设也使得分析更加有章可循。先看相关预测是否可以在 B 语言内部找到证据，如果普遍性假设被推翻，从这一假设出发也更容易发现差异所在。另外，普遍性假设引领我们去寻找两种语言可能存在的相似之处（普遍性），这是差异假设无法做到的。差异假设一开始就没有将普遍性作为可能性来进行探索，不具有普遍性假设在探索普遍性方面的先天优势。

另外，要特别强调的是，假设不等于结论。假设两种语言相似，最终得出的结论不一定就是两种语言相似，普遍性假设并没有排除探索差异性的可能。并且因为普遍性是最容易被证伪的，结果反倒可能是不相似。形式语义学近年来的跨语言研究成果也表明，借助普遍性假设可以找到语言之间在语义上的普遍性，也可以找到差异。形式语义学家并没有像 Evans & Levinson（2009：430，432）认为的那样，试图通过假定一个抽象层面来消解具体语言的差异，差异性没有被排除在跨语言语义研究议程之外。

3. 比较的基础

跨语言语义研究的一个重要方面是语义的编码。不同语言句法语素库藏不同，无论是功能范畴还是词汇范畴都有差异。语义编码基于哪些句法语素形式？语言之间有何差异？语境因素在不同语言中对语义解读有何影响？以“时”的编码为例，从跨语言的角度来看，可能会受到时标记、体标记、时间状语、小句地位（主句和从句）、语境等各种因素的影响。研究语义编码的跨语言影响因素，既要区分不同语言的句法语素库藏，又要梳理句法、语义、语用的关系，是一个就语义解读追根溯源的过程。

研究语义编码，首先的问题是对语义对象有一个明确的定义。由于语义在不同语言中呈现不同的编码形式，因此作为研究的起点，这个定义应当尽量避开句法语素的语言特殊性。形式语义学从真值语义的角度来定义，既能避免模糊性，又能避开句法语素的干扰。

对于常和功能语类联系的语义，可以先对功能语类的语义进行定义，作为工作定义。如“时”“体”的定义，通常研究采用的是新莱辛巴赫（Neo-Reichenbachian）系统（Reichenbach，1947；Hornstein，1990；Kamp & Reyle，1993；Klein，1994）。新莱辛巴赫系统是个三分系统，包括言说时间（UT）、事件时间（ET）和参照时间（RT，也叫话题时间）。言说时间是指句子被言说的时间，事件时间指事件发生的时间或者是状态持续的时间，参照时间是指句子所“讨论”的时间。“时”“体”基于言说时间、事件时间和参照时间来定义。“时”是关于参照时间和言说时间的关系。“体”是关于事件时间和参照时间的关系。所谓过去、现在、将来的时间解读在这个形式系统里的定义就分别是参照时间先于言说时间（RT < UT）、参照时间包含言说时间（UT ⊆ RT），参照时间晚于言说时间（UT < RT）。未完成体（imperfective）和完成体（perfective）的定义则分别是事件时间包含参照时间（RT ⊆ ET）和参照时间包含事件时间（ET ⊆ RT）。

虽然时间编码在一些语言中和特定的时体标记密切联系，但不能将两者等同起来。“过去”“现在”“将来”的时间解读和有标记“过去时”“现在时”“将来时”的功能语素并不是一回事。不同语言的句子都可以有过去、现在、将来的时间解读，但这些语言未必有“过去时”“现在时”“将来时”这样的时标记。“过去”“现在”“将来”的时间解读虽然在一些语言中可以归因于标记“时”的功能语素，但在另一些语言中也可能是其他因素互相作用的结果。这也是绝对意义上的可译性（例如功能词类的对等）不是总能做到的原因。

只有避开句法语素的影响，给出独立于具体时体标记的纯语义定义（例如上文所提到的，将“时”“体”分别定义为参照时间和言说时间的关系、事件时间和参照时间的关系），我们才有可能开展有关时间编码的跨语言语义研究，即研究事件时间、参照时间、言说时间的关系在具体语言中是通过怎样的手段来表现的，又是如何得到限制的。

4. 零形式

在跨语言研究中，一种语言通过功能语类表现某个语义范畴，而另一种语言没有对应的句法语素表现的情况十分普遍。每种语言从另一种语言的角度来看似乎都充满了孔洞。从有“时”标记语言的角度看表面无“时”标记的语言，从有限定词语言的角度看表面无限定词的语言，似乎后者都充满了这样的孔洞。

假设有看不见的成分存在（即存在没有音系表现的零形式），这是形式语言学研究的经常性做法。仅从普遍性假设出发，形式语义学的跨语言研究也需要这样的操作。

但看不见的成分是否真的存在，就需要语言事实来证明。要证明表面不可见的成分真实存在并不容易，但仍有可能在语言中找到线索。例如，句法学研究利用 wanna 这一缩略形式，证明没有音韵表现的“语迹”真实存在。

语义研究中一个有争议的现象是所谓“无时态”语言。近年来对表面无“时”语言的深入研究无论在研究思路还是方法上都对跨语言语义研究的“孔洞”问题颇有启发。是应该认为表面无“时”语言事实上都存在零形式的“时”标记，还是应该认为的确存在没有“时”的语言，无论要得到哪种结论，都需要语言内部证据。

从近年的研究来看，“无时态”主要有两类分析：一类是分析为零形式的“时”标记［如 Matthewson（2006）对 St’át’imcets 语的研究，Jóhannsdóttir & Matthewson（2008）对 Gitxsan 语的研究］；另一类是将它们看作没有“时”的语言［例如 Bohnemeyer（2009）对 Yukatek Maya 语的研究，Bittner（2005）对 Kalaallisut 语的研究，Lin（2006）对汉语的研究］。

Matthewson（2006）为没有显性时标记的语言做“有时”（tensed）分析提供了研究思路和证据。Matthewson 对 St’át’imcets 语的分析结果是这种语言的确存在隐性的时标记。假设 St’át’imcets 语和英语有同样的时标记（只不过是隐性的，是零形式），由于我们对于有显性时标记语言的句法语义特点已经有一定了解（例如时标记和时间状语的匹配），从这一假设出发可以生成清晰的预测供我们检验。

St’át’imcets 语的限定小句（finite clause）没有显性的时标记，如（1）所示，只有动词原形和主语。（1）可以做过去时也可以做现在时解读，但不能做将来时解读。

（1）k’ác-an’ -lhkan

dry-DIR-1SG. SUBJ

（我把它弄干了；我正在弄干它。）

一般来说，时间副词可以消除句子的歧义。在（1）的基础上加上表示过去时间的状语“昨天”，时间指称就限制到了过去。但同样是加时间状语，St’át’imcets语加上表示未来时间的时间状语，不仅不能得到将来时解读，反而会让句子不合语法。这种使用上的严格限制从语用层面无法得到解释。因为存在语义冲突，加上表示将来的时间状语不应该得到不合法的句子，结论只能是St’át’imcets语存在一个表示非未来时的零形式时标记。

随着近年来对时、体、语气等关系研究的深入，我们对“无时”分析也可以形成一些预测。Tonhauser（2011）对Guaraní语的研究就是比较“有时”分析和“无时”分析的预测。根据“有时”分析，Guaraní语中“非将来”的意义被认为是来自一个零形式的非将来时语素，这个零形式非将来时语素虽然和英语的显性时标记相比无音韵表现，但语义是一样的，都要求RT ≤ UT（即言说时间和参照时间相同或在参照时间之后）。根据“无时”分析，Guaraní语没有来自语法上的时标记（无论显性、隐性）的贡献，时间指称来自语境和时间状语的贡献。Tonhauser比较了“有时”分析和“无时”分析形成的不同预测，得出“无时”分析比“有时”分析从预测来看更符合Guaraní语时间指称情况的结论。

跨语言语义研究关于“零形式”研究的另一个亮点，在于进一步思考如果有“零形式”的话，是同形异义还是标示不足。例如，在证明St’át’imcets语存在零形式时标记之后，Matthewson进一步探究St’át’imcets语是否和英语一样也有两个时标记，一个是过去时零形式，一个是现在时零形式。

检验St’át’imcets语是否和英语一样有两个时标记，还是用普遍性假设。Matthewson证明这个假设并不成立。设想你的朋友Theresa、Charlie和Marie想要每人建一个狗屋。Theresa已经建好了，Charlie正在建，Marie还没开始建。这时另一个朋友打电话来问你Theresa、Charlie和Marie三人建了或在建什么。（2a）是问题，（2b）是对这一问题的回答。

（2）a. stam’ ku máys-en-as i snek’wnuk’wa7-lhkálh-a
what DET build-TR-3ERG DET. PL friend(PL)-1PL.POSS-DET
（我们的朋友建了/在建什么？）

b. mays-en-ítas kw-s Theresa múta7 s-Charlie
build-TR-3PL.ERG DET-NOM Theresa and NOM-Charlie

i　　　　sqax7-álhcw-a
DET.PL　　dog-house-DET
（特蕾莎和查理建了 / 在建狗屋。）

如果说 St'át'imcets 语和英语一样有两个时标记，一个是过去时零形式，一个是现在时零形式，那么（2）的解读只能选择零形式中的一种，也就是要么作过去时解读，要么作现在时解读。而（2）呈现的事实并非如此。根据情境的设定，和特蕾莎相关的时间是“过去”，和查理相关的时间是“现在”，既然（2）是可以说的句子，就表明 St'át'imcets 语的零形式应该能够同时覆盖过去和现在两种时间。忽略显性和隐性的差别，St'át'imcets 语和英语的时标记在形义对应方面并不相同，St'át'imcets 语是同一形式对应不同意义，而非不同形式分别对应不同意义。用普遍性假设来检验，结论并不支持 St'át'imcets 语零形式时标记同形异义的假设。通过两次使用普遍性假设，既证明了 St'át'imcets 语和英语一样有时标记，又证明了它不像英语那样在时标记上区分过去和现在，即 St'át'imcets 语和英语的时标记在相似的同时又有差异。

St'át'imcets 语和英语的比较研究也进一步表明，同样用普遍性假设，得出的结论可能支持也可能不支持假设。St'át'imcets 语和英语从句法语素层面上看都有时标记，但是从句法语素–语义关系来看，前者时标记对过去时和现在时做了区分，后者的时标记对过去和现在的语义区分标示不足。假设推理方法不仅可以揭示跨语言的相似和差异之处，还使得对语言普遍性和多样性的研究精细化。这样的探索也适用于“零形式”。

5. 从微观语义差异到宏观语义差异

如果一种语言中没有相应的功能词类出现，该如何进行相应的跨语言研究？应该如何探索该功能语类表达的语义范畴在该语言中的表现？我们认为至少应该思考以下问题：首先，是否存在音韵上为空的功能词类？它们的语义是什么？其次，如果证明该语言没有通过功能词类对相关语义范畴进行编码，那么是否会在其他方面标记？有怎样的可能性？最终目标是弄清是否所有语言都有标记相关语义范畴的句法语素手段（如果不是，有其他哪些相关表现手段）。

从研究方法来看，假设功能语类存在的普遍性假设不仅允许我们去发现差异，而且能够帮助我们更系统地去寻找差异，从是否有语义完全对应的功能语类，到语义上有所差异的功能语类，到如果功能语类的假设被证伪，相应的语义又是通过怎样的途径来表现等，普遍性假设让我们这种对差异性的探索过程有章可循。

从探索的结果来看，普遍性假设不仅能够帮助我们找出差异，而且能找出不同程度不同层面的差异。差异如果在功能语类的特征，那么至少是都有相关功能语类（参看 Fukui，1988），这是微观差异。如英语和 St'át'imcets 语的时标记就是属于这种差异。英语和 St'át'imcets 语都有时标记，两种语言时标记在语义上的区别主要是前者表达过去时和现在时有不同的标记，而后者只有一个语义上对过去时 / 现在时区分标示不足的时标记，两种语言的差异主要在功能语类的内容方面，是微观层面的差异。如果不存在相应功能语类（包括显性、隐性），如汉语（Lin，2006）和 Navajo 语（Smith et al.，2003，2007），在句法结构表征上没有时间投射，时间指称依靠其他途径得到，在时间指称方面与英语的差异因此就比英语和 St'át'imcets 语之间的差异大，属于宏观差异。Lin（2006）提出汉语时间解读主要是由体特征来驱动。一类是缺省视点体（default viewpoint aspect），没有时间副词和显性体标记句子的时间解读由缺省视点体决定。另一类是"过""了"这样的显性体标记提供的体特征。根据 Klein（1994），"体"是关于事件时间和参考时间的关系，和表示参照时间和言说时间的"时"并不是一回事，但是汉语语言事实表明，汉语体特征综合其他因素可以推知时间指称。汉语虽然有"过去时""现在时"的解读，但是这样的时间解读主要是体特征、语用推理等因素综合作用的结果，并不等于说汉语就有过去和现在时。

6. 欧洲语言中心论的疑虑

在跨语言研究中，以英语和其他欧洲语言为中心是经常受到诟病的一种现象（参看 Gil，2001）。

语言学（包括语义学）研究很大程度上建立在英语或其他欧洲语言的基础上。使用普遍性假设作为跨语言语义研究的一种重要方法，意味着在研究其他语言时，从英语或其他欧洲语言提出的分析理论出发，这是否会从方法论角度加剧欧洲语言中心主义问题？

以形式语义学最重要的理论之一广义量词理论为例。广义量词理论是基于英语的研究提出的，认为限定词和类型 <e,t> 的普通名词短语组成类型为 <<e,t>,t> 的广义量词。Barwise & Cooper（1981）认为广义量词是自然语言中的普遍现象。

英语量化名词短语句法上是由限定词（D）和普通名词短语（NP）组合得到 DP，如 all women 是由限定词 all 和普通名词短语 women 组合得到的。Matthewson（2001）发现，St’át’imcets 语中量词是和 DP 而不是 NP 进行组合。St’át’imcets 语中限定词先和普通名词短语组合得到 DP，然后量词和 DP 组合得到 QP。St’át’imcets 语和英语这种表面的句法差异是否意味着语义的差异？广义量词作为语言普遍现象是否还能得到维护？

从普遍性假设出发，St’át’imcets 的量化名词短语应当和英语一样，量词和普通名词短语（类型为 <e,t>）组合，但事实是 St’át’imcets 语中和量词组合的只能是限定词短语。St’át’imcets 语中的限定词短语和指称性名词短语一样，类型为 <e>，限定词是一个从普通名词短语指谓到实体的函数，类型为 <<e,t>,e>。St’át’imcets 语中和量词组合的全都不能是类型为 <e,t> 的普通名词短语，这就违反了广义量词理论的分析。广义量词是自然语言普遍现象的论断因此也受到挑战。

在 St’át’imcets 语不符合普遍性假设预测的情况下，可以完全放弃原有假设，也可以换一种思路来坚持普遍性假设，即检验英语是否有可能和 St’át’imcets 语量化名词短语做同样的分析，即类型为 <e,<<e,t>,t>> 的量词和类型为 <e> 的限定词短语（而非类型为 <e,t> 的名词短语）组合。

Matthewson 采用的正是这一思路，她修正了对英语量词的分析，认为英语量词的第一个论元和 St’át’imcets 语一样类型也是 <e>。量词的类型都为 <e,<<e,t>,t>>。Matthewson 认为量化名词短语的语义组合有两个步骤，首先是限定词（类型为 <<e,t>,e>）与普通名词短语（类型为 <e,t>）组合，得到限定词短语（类型为 <e>），然后量词再与限定词短语组合，得到量化名词短语（类型为 <<e,t>,t>）。英语和 St’át’imcets 语在组合步骤和语义类型方面都一样。von Fintel（1994）提出，量词的论元中有一个语境变量，量词以该语境变量 C 引出的集合和名词短语指谓的集合形成的交集为定义域，该定义域因此是一个受语境限制的定义域。这个 C 变量在语言中通常是隐性的。Matthewson（2001）认为 St’át’imcets 语和英语的区别就在于前者将这个语境变量显性化了。

Cooper（1996）、Matthewson（2001）都提出，英语中一些量化结构不允许作量词定义域受限的解读。例（3）中 all/most 后接的名词短语 linguists 都不能表示是上一句提到的 party 上的 linguists，也就是不能接受语境的限制。

（3） Last night I threw a party and a bunch of linguists and philosophers came.
（昨晚我开派对，来了一帮语言学家和哲学家。）
#All/most linguists got drunk.
（几乎所有 / 大多数语言学家都喝醉了。）

因为 all、most 引出的量化名词短语中的名词不可以是单数名词，只能是复数光杆名词和不可数名词，这一点和新卡尔森主义理论认为英语的论元只能是复数光杆名词和不可数名词吻合。新卡尔森主义认为英语复数光杆名词和不可数名词的指谓是类（类型为 <e>）。在这样的分析下，英语 all、most 引出的量化名词短语就可以和 St’át’imcets 语中的量化名词短语做同样的语义分析。

在一定情况下 all、most 引出的量化名词短语也的确可以有语境限制解读，但仅限于 Condoravdi（1994）提出的“功能”解读的情况。例（4a）students 的解读和（4b）中有定名词短语 the students 相同（上文校园里的所有学生），和（4c）中作存在解读的 students 不同。

（4） In 1985 there was a ghost haunting the campus…
（1985 年这个校园闹鬼……）
a. Students were aware of the danger.
（学生都意识到了危险。）
b. The students were aware of the danger.
（学生都意识到了危险。）
c. There were students who were aware of the danger.
（有学生意识到了危险。）

英语中允许“功能”解读的情况也恰恰是可以用 all、most 引出量化名词短语的情况。

综上所述，英语中量词 all、most 直接和普通名词短语组合的情况涉及的复数光杆名词和不可数名词的解读要么是类指解读要么是“功能”解读，两种情况下名词短语的指谓类型都是 <e>。也就是说，基于 St’át’imcets 语所做的量化名词短语分析对英语也同样适用。

英语中“所有女人”可以说 all women，而法语中必须说 tous les femmes，不能说 tous femmes，必须加限定词 les。法语属于 Chierchia（1998）所说的光杆名词类型为表语型的语言，也就是说法语光杆名词短语不能直接出现在论元位置，必须加限定词，变为限定词短语才能出现在论元位置。这点和 Matthewson 讨论的 St’át’imcets 语名词短语句法表现完全相同。这样看来，法语和 St’át’imcets 语都要求量化名词短语中限定词的出现这一句法限制，跟两种语言普通名词短语指谓类型（类型均为 <e,t>）不无关联。其中的联系并非偶然：法语和 St’át’imcets 语中量化名词短语中要求限定词出现是因为 Q 要求和类型为 <e> 的 DP 组合，法语和 St’át’imcets 语普通名词短语都是 <e,t> 类型，不能是 <e> 类型。法语和 St’át’imcets 语中量化名词短语中要求限定词出现并不说明这两种语言的量化名词短语的语义分析和英语不同，只是说明有另外一个语义参数在起作用，这个语义参数决定法语和 St’át’imcets 语中只有限定词短语的指谓类型才是 <e>。

所以普遍性假设并不会导致或强化欧洲语言中心主义或英语中心主义。对其他语言的研究使得我们发现新的语料，提出新的分析。当我们无法将新语料纳入原有的理论分析中，仍可以坚持普遍性假设，只是考虑另一种可能性，即原有语料（往往来自英语或其他欧洲语言）能否在新的分析框架中得到解释。这使得原有语料和分析有可能得到新的审视。普遍性假设有利于这一目标的实现。欧洲语言的研究从时间上可能在先，但是当我们进行其他语言的研究之后，普遍性假设对于两种语言来说是机会均等的。普遍性假设本身并不会导致欧洲语言或英语中心主义。从普遍性假设出发开展的对 St’át’imcets 语和英语量化名词短语的语义研究以及对原有分析的修正就很好地说明了这一点。

Bittner（2007）从对 Kalaallisut 这种无时标记语言的研究和跨语言研究中得到启发，写道：“与其试图将一种基于英语的理论扩展到类型学上关系遥远的语言，不如从相反的方向来进行——将基于 Kalaallisut 语的理论推广到英语。

从理论的观点来看，所有语言的地位都是平等的，因此无论哪种角度都可以用来寻找跨语言研究的灵感。然而，由于形式语义学最近才开始跨出英语和类似语言的研究，我认为迫切需要以真正不同的语言作为出发点开展研究，以揭示和纠正当前语义理论中盎格鲁为中心的偏见。”（Bittner，2007：383）这一段话虽然没有提到普遍性假设，但是我们看到其研究宗旨和普遍性假设旨趣相同。同样是在跨语言研究中坚持普遍性假设，但是可以从不同角度来进行。将基于其他语言的理论分析扩展到英语，这是个之前被忽略的角度，特别值得关注。普遍性假设和英语或欧洲语言中心论并没有必然联系，如果能从其他语言的分析出发反观英语，还有可能纠正英语或欧洲语言中心论所带来的后果。

参考文献

Barwise, J. & Cooper, R. 1981. Generalized quantifiers and natural language. *Linguistics and Philosophy*, 4: 159–219.

Bittner, M. 2005. Future discourse in a tenseless language. *Journal of Semantics*, 22: 339–387.

Bittner, M. 2007. Aspectual universals of temporal anaphora. In Rothstein, S. (Ed.), *Theoretical and crosslinguistic approaches to the semantics of aspect*. Amsterdam: John Benjamins. 349–385.

Bohnemeyer, J. 2009. Temporal anaphora in a tenseless language: The case of Yucatec. In Klein, W. & Li, P. (Eds.), *The expression of time*. Berlin: Mouton de Gruyter. 83–128.

Chierchia, G. 1998. Reference to kinds across languages. *Natural Language Semantics*, 6: 339–405.

Condoravdi, C. 1994. Descriptions in context. Ph. D. dissertation, Yale University.

Cooper, R. 1996. The role of situations in generalized quantifiers. In Lappin, S. (Ed.), *The handbook of contemporary semantic theory*. Oxford: Blackwell. 65–86.

Evans, N. & Levinson, C. 2009. The myth of language universals: Language diversity and its importance for cognitive science. *Behavioral and Brain Sciences*, 32: 429–492.

Fukui, N. 1988. Deriving the differences between English and Japanese: A case study in parametric syntax. *English Linguistics*, 5: 249–270.

Gil, D. 2001. Escaping eurocentrism: Fieldwork as a process of unlearning. In Newman, P. & Ratliff, M. (Eds.), *Linguistic fieldwork*. Cambridge: Cambridge University Press. 102–132.

Hornstein, N. 1990. *As time goes by: Tense and universal grammar*. Cambridge, MA: MIT Press.

Kamp, H. & Reyle, U. 1993. *From discourse to logic: Introduction to model-theoretic semantics of natural language, formal logic, and discourse representation theory*. Kluwer: Dordrecht.

Jóhannsdóttir, M. & Matthewson, L. 2008. Zero-marked tense: The case of Gitxsan. In Elfner, E. & Walkow, M. (Eds.), *Proceedings of NELS 37*. Amherst, MA: GLSA. 299–310.

Klein, W. 1994. *Time in language*. London: Routledge.

Lin, W. 2006. Time in a language without tense: The case of Chinese. *Journal of Semantics*, 23: 1–53.

Matthewson, L. 2001. Quantification and the nature of cross-linguistic variation. *Natural Language Semantics*, 9: 145–189.

Matthewson, L. 2006. Temporal semantics in a superficially tenseless language. *Linguistics and Philosophy*, 29: 673–713.

Reichenbach, H. 1947. *Elements of symbolic logic*. Berkeley, CA: University of California Press.

Smith, S., Perkins, E. & Fernald, T. 2003. Temporal interpretation in Navajo. In Anderssen, J. & Menéndez-Benito, P. (Eds.), *Proceedings of SULA 2*. Amherst, MA: GLSA. 175–192,

Smith, S., Perkins, E. & Fernald, T. 2007. Time in Navajo: Direct and indirect interpretation. *International Journal of American Linguistics*, 73: 40–71.

Tonhauser, J. 2011. Temporal reference in Paraguayan Guaraní. *Linguistics and Philosophy*, 34: 257–303.

von Fintel, K. 1994. Restrictions on quantifier domains. Ph. D. dissertation, University of Massachusetts at Amherst.

von Fintel, K. & Matthewson, L. 2008. Universals in semantics. *The Linguistic Review*, 25(1-2): 139–201.

作者单位：复旦大学外国语言文学学院

作者邮箱：yshen8@fudan.edu.cn

On the methodology of cross-linguistic semantic research

Yuan Shen

Abstract: This paper discusses the methodology of cross-linguistic semantic research. The advantages of using generalizations made based on some languages as universals to guide the study of other languages are first made clear. Then using tense as an example, I illustrate how to do cross-linguistic semantic research, and elaborate on whether or not to postulate null forms in tense studies. Next, I discuss how to deal with micro and macro semantic variations across languages. Lastly, the influence of a Euro-centric perspective on cross-linguistic semantic research is touched upon and a few suggestions on how to avoid it are made.

Keywords: cross-linguistic semantic research, tense, null form, semantic differences

Author work unit: College of Foreign Languages and Literature, Fudan University

Author email: yshen8@fudan.edu.cn

《清华语言学》稿约

《清华语言学》是由清华大学语言学研究中心主办的专业性学术刊物，刊登以自然语言尤其是中国境内语言为研究对象的语言学学术论文、学术译作和严肃的学术评论。交叉与融合是语言学研究的一大走向，因此本刊大力提倡定性分析与定量研究的融合、理论探讨与实证研究的融合、中西范式与文理取向的融合，希望能够推动中国语言学往纵深方向发展，走出一条立足本土、面向世界、融会贯通的道路。

本刊恪守求真、务实、平等、自由的原则，积极鼓励学术创新与学术争鸣，接受中、英文两种语言的稿件，篇幅较为自由，深度长文或精练短文均可。每年出版一期，欢迎国内外专家学者赐稿。

本刊实行编辑委员会指导下的主编责任制，下设编辑部处理日常事务，实行双向匿名审稿制度。来稿请注意以下事项：

1. 实行通信作者制度，编辑部只接受文章通信作者的来稿。

2. 来稿请提供 word 和 pdf 格式的电子文本各一份，为方便匿名评审，文中应避免出现作者相关信息。作者信息（包括姓名、工作单位、研究方向、通信地址、电子邮箱、电话号码）另页给出。冷僻字、特殊符号、需要制版的图表请另设一个新的文本并用较大字号列出，并注明在稿件中的位置。中文稿件除有必要使用繁体字、异体字（请圈明）外，一律使用简体字。来稿体例格式参照本辑论文。

3. 来稿请发至编辑部电子邮箱。编辑部收到来稿后会确认收稿，并会在三个月内将评审结果通知作者本人。三个月后如未接到编辑部通知，作者可自行处理。审稿期内请勿另投他处，如需撤稿，请告知编辑部。稿件一经刊用，作者将获赠刊 2 本。

4. 凡向本刊投稿，默认同时授予本刊稿件的信息网络传播权。

编辑部通信地址：中国北京海淀区清华大学蒙民伟人文楼（人文学院）301 室，
邮编 100084

电子邮件地址：tel@tsinghua.edu.cn